Bob, the Other Builder

DEDICATION

To Absent Friends

Bob is a man of great, great stature;
a selfless man who thinks of other people before he thinks of himself.
He has raised millions to help others.
I have never seen the like of him.

Professor Neville Butler, CLIC's first Chair and former Head of the
Institute of Child Health at the University of Bristol.

Bob, the Other Builder

The Remarkable Life of Bob Woodward:
Property Developer, Mosaicist,
and Founder of CLIC

Pamela Linham and
Simon Siddall

MERTON

First published 2006

Published by
Merton Priory Press Ltd
5 Oliver House, Wain Avenue
Chesterfield S41 0FE

© Pamela Linham and Simon Siddall 2006

ISBN 1 898937 69 9

Printed by
Dinefwr Press
Rawlings Road, Llandybie
Carmarthenshire SA18 3YD

Contents

List of illustrations   7

Acknowledgements   9

Foreword   10

1   Turning Point   11

Part 1: Building, 1933–1995

2   The Boy with No Name   15
3   Pied Piper   25
4   Boys Will Be Boys   29
5   Out of Pie Tins and into Glue Pots   34
6   Young Love   37
7   The Gospel According to Billy Graham   40
8   The House that Bob Built   46
9   To Judy and Bob, a Daughter, Rachel   49
10   The Houses that Bob and John Built   54
11   To Judy and Bob, a Son, Robert   59
12   Brazil 1 England 0   63
13   To Judy and Bob, a Second Son, James Sigmund   68
14   The Street That Bob and John Rebuilt   70
15   The Mosaic That Bob and John Built   78
16   Robert, a Most Promising Footballer   89
17   Infinity Times Infinity   99
18   Something will Click   101
19   My Name is Woodward, Bob Woodward   108
20   Thinking of Heaven   115
21   To Bob and Judy, a Third Son, Hugh   121
22   Top Hat and Skateboard   124
23   Being Brave for Each Other   128
24   Tulip Trees   132
25   Pedro Gabriel   134
26   Mentors, Counsellors and Friends   136
27   What On Earth Is It All About?   139

28   Degree of Doctor of Laws, Honoris Causa   142
29   King of the Jumble   147
30   Money Raised for Charity is on a Different Level 150
31   Beyond the South West   156
32   The Hole in the Wall Gang Camp   165
33   Lesley and Kate   169
34   Chernobyl: Nuclear Energy, Out of Control   173
35   The $1 million Brick   179
36   The Gorbachev Lectures   189
37   Budapest   191
38   Le Walk   195
39   Unrest Within   199

Part 2: Demolition, 1995–2006

40   Million Dollar Smile   207
41   Kangaroo Court   209
42   Political Manoeuvrings   214
43   Charity Commission Suspension Orders   216
44   The New Broom   220
45   Follow the Trail of the Yellow Balloons   225
46   Building Bridges to Nowhere   228
47   'No, never alone, he promised never to leave me,
     never to leave me alone.'   232

Part 3: Rebuilding, 1996–2006

48   Moving on   239
49   The Starfish Trust   242
50   'How often do you get a great big hug
     from a former world leader?'   249
51   Below us, the Sea of Galilee   253
52   From John O'Groats to Land's End   258
53   Would it Work?   261
54   CLIC Sargent   264
55   Budapest Revisited   266
56   Epilogue   268

List of Illustrations

Between pages 48 and 49.

1. Bob in 1937 aged four.
2. Bob and Judy on a day trip to Brighton.
3. Bob and Judy leave Eastville Park Methodist church in Bristol after their wedding in 1958 *(Western Daily Press)*.
4. Judy with Robert aged six months *(J.L. Matthews)*.
5. Hugh aged three months.
6. Rachel aged three months *(Navana Photos)*.
7. James aged three months.
8. Market Street, Wotton-under-Edge, in decay *(David Iddles)*.
9. Bob with his demolition gang *(David Iddles)*.
10. The first two phases of the Parklands development at Wotton-under-Edge *(David Iddles)*.
11. Bob surveys the start of demolition at Market Street in Wotton *(David Iddles)*.
12. Market Street rebuilt, for which Bob and John received a European Architectural Heritage Year award in 1975 *(David Iddles)*.
13. Judy, Bob, Rachel, Robert and James in the Tabernacle at the beginning of the mosaic project in 1974 *(David Iddles)*.
14. The central section of the mosaic with an overhead drawing of the original *(David Iddles)*.
15. The Great Orpheus Pavement in its new home at Prinknash Abbey. *(Gloucestershire Gazette Series)*.
16. Robert aged six and in his Wolves football kit.
17. Sister Frances Dominica, the founder of Helen House in Oxford, the world's first children's hospice.
18. Professor David Baum, Head of Child Health at the University of Bristol and president of the Royal College of Paediatrics and Child Health.
19. The Duchess of Kent, patron of CLIC, with Bob at the opening of the CLIC Annexe *(Malcolm Simmonds)*.
20. CLIC House, Fremantle Street, Cotham, Bristol *(Malcolm Simmonds)*.
21. Judy and James with Bob after he received an honorary degree from the University of Bristol *(Malcolm Simmonds)*.

22   John Nickolls is crowned 'King of the Jumble' at the CLIC Shops Conference at Bristol Grammar School *(Malcolm Simmonds)*.

23   HTV news presenter Bruce Hockin opening the CLIC shop at Downend with Bob, John Nickolls and the manager, Hazel Wilson *(Malcolm Simmonds)*.

24   Jane Seymour, Father Christmas and Bob with children at a Christmas party held at her home, St Catherine's Court *(Malcom Simmonds)*.

25   Paul Newman greets Bob at the Hole in the Wall Gang Camp in Connecticut.

26   Lesley Gesa, her mother Margaret and Bob after Lesley's sponsored walk.

27   Mikhail Gorbachev greets David Baum and Bob at the Gorbachev Foundation in Moscow.

28   Mikhail Gorbachev signing the documents to become president of CLIC International.

29   Milhail Gorbachev and Bob in a bear-hug embrace.

30   The 1994 Channel Tunnel charity walk.

31   Bob carries three polystyrene children around the London Marathon course in 1995.

32   Kate Jeffery with her brother Eddie and Bob.

33   Bob with the ageing owner of the dacha shown below.

34   The timber dacha in Minsk which Bob visited.

35   Daniel Palumbo enjoying his yellow balloon *(Palumbo Family)*.

36   Bob, Charlie Dobson and Mary Dobson with the Jack and Jill Appeal chairman David Giles at the presentation of £1 million from the Starfish Trust to the new children's unit at Frenchay Hospital *(Gloucestershire Gazette Series)*.

37   Bob has lots of help laying the foundation stone for the Barbara Russell Children's Unit at Frenchay Hospital *(Western Daily Press)*.

38   Bob receiving the Freedom of the City of Bristol from the Lady Mayor and Lady Mayoress *(Paul Gillis)*.

39   Outside the CLIC flats in Budapest the head of the children's unit, Professor Gyorgy Fekete, presents Bob with a medal of appreciation, accompanied by Professor Dezslo Schuler *(Warren Linham)*.

Acknowledgements

When we approached Bob to write his biography, we were amazed to find that no one else had written it. Our ideas were clear about the way it would be: about a sincere man who had done so much for so many, especially children with cancer. We felt that it would be uplifting for others to read how this man coped with his tragedies and then went on to achieve so much.

It came as a surprise when, after a year or so of research, we discovered some disturbing information. This book was never meant to be an exposé or investigative journalism but we felt we would be telling only half the story if we were to leave all the troubles out.

We would like to express our thanks to everyone who helped in the research of this book but in particular to Dr Robert N. Woodward for his generosity. The stories from contributors were overwhelming and we had to make some tough decisions about which ones we could include. Throughout, Bob has wanted to name everyone he met who helped him along the way but, with respect, we could not mention them all.

The following publications were of great help as sources of information:

James Belsey, *A Model of Care* (CLIC Publications, 1990).
Don Carleton, *The CLIC Story* (CLIC Publications, 1990).
CLIC News
Association for Charities, *Power Without Accountability* (2004).
Robert N. Woodward and John Cull, *The Wotton Mosaic* (1980).
Gloucestershire Gazette
Bristol Evening Post

We would also like to thank Frenchay Village Museum, Catherine Mason and Philip Riden.

Pamela Linham
Simon Siddall   *June 2006*

9

Foreword

There is a Chinese proverb, which says: It is better to light a candle than to curse the darkness. Bob Woodward has known much darkness in his life, not least the death of his sons, Robert and Hugh. For a less courageous person the darkness would surely have been overwhelming. But Bob was determined that somehow good would come out of this indescribable tragedy and he set about finding a way to ease the distress of other families in similar situations. And so CLIC was born and quickly gained the respect and loyalty of countless supporters who came alongside Bob in his mission. The work of CLIC spread rapidly and the families themselves bear testament to its success.

But Bob was to experience yet more desolation. Some years after it was founded, events led to his separation from CLIC. He cared so passionately about the work of CLIC that this was like yet another major bereavement.

Anyone who does not know Bob might be excused for imagining that he would have withdrawn from public life at this stage. But to know him is to know that this bitter blow spurred him on to channel his immense energy in different directions, still to the benefit of children and families in distress.

CLIC, more than thirty years on, is evidence of Bob's astonishing success in realising his original vision. Countless candles have been lit; the long, lonely journey of families without number has been made a little easier.

It is my hope that in telling the true story this book will not only give praise where praise is so rightly due, but will inspire others to light candles in the darkness.

Sister Frances Dominica
Founder of Helen House and Douglas House, Oxford

1

Turning Point, January 1974

An immense rock, the Peñón de Ifach, towers 1,000 feet into the cloudless skies of Calpe, on the Costa Blanca, a Mediterranean region of Spain recognised for its outstanding natural beauty where fragrant citrus groves, vineyards and olive trees stretch as far as the eye can see. Calpe is protected from the winds by mountains on all sides; it is an area of contrasts where modern construction and narrow streets harmonise with the charms of an ancient fishing village. The Costa Blanca enjoys an exceptional climate of long hot summers and moderate winters; it is an ideal location for a successful businessman to make a second home for his family.

On a not-too-distant beach, a man races his young son across the sands. They laugh and play ball together in the winter sunshine. Suddenly, the boy slows. The man senses something is amiss, takes the boy's hand into his and they continue to run together side by side.

That night, the boy wakes in distress. His parents speak of growing pains and take turns to rub embrocation into his aching limbs to relieve his discomfort.

On the journey home to Bristol the boy develops a sore throat and feels unwell.

Concern subsides when he seems to get better but reappears when he shows a reluctance to return to school. This is most unlike him: he loves school. He scored 22 goals for the school team in the previous term. He is a promising sportsman. The boy takes part in a cross-country race of 33 runners; his hip locks and he accepts help from his friends who carry him some of the way. He finishes last.

Parents know instinctively when there is something seriously wrong and the mother and father are deeply concerned. Within days, the boy's colour changes and he becomes desperately ill.

The boy is admitted to the Bristol Royal Hospital for Sick Children for four days of tests. The father is summoned to the hospital where the mother waits anxiously at the boy's bedside.

At 2.10 p.m. on Thursday, 21 February 1974, the doctor delivers the grim news to the fearful parents.

Robert has cancer: stage 4 neuroblastoma.

Part 1

Building

1933–1995

'Where your talents and the needs of the world cross, lies your calling.'
Aristotle

2

The Boy with No Name

Tuesday, 28 February 1933 saw the birth of a third son to Cyril and Beatrice Woodward who rented a couple of rooms in a modest bungalow situated behind the village garage in Cleeve, Somerset, halfway between Weston-super-Mare and Bristol.

When Beatrice, drained of all energy from childbirth and a life in near poverty, developed septicaemia, baby Woodward was cared for by two aunts, one of whom, Joyce, still only a child herself, was sent from her home in Wotton-under-Edge to Cleeve to look after the two older boys. Although this was a great help, after several weeks both aunts returned to Wotton, taking the baby boy with them to give Beatrice some time to recover. Her debilitating illness resulted in the baby's birth not being registered until 4 May and even then no name was given to the child. Indeed, baby Woodward remained 'the boy with no name' for four months until his parents finally decided on Robert Norman, a new brother for John and David.

Aunt Joyce remembered Robert as an angelic child, sitting in a high chair, a long blonde curl caressing his cheek, stretching his arms towards her, begging to be picked up.

'I thought, no, I don't want to. I'm going out to play,' Joyce said. 'After all, I was only about twelve years old but to this day I can still see his eyes pleading with me. I wish I had lifted him out of that high-chair and cuddled him.'

Just staying alive in the 1930s was a challenge for the poor, as tuberculosis, scarlet fever, measles, diphtheria, rickets and whooping cough constantly threatened young lives. Bob, as baby Woodward became known, was a sickly child and suffered several bouts of pneumonia before he was five. Following the last one, the doctor warned Cyril and Beatrice that another would probably prove fatal: their boy was a weakling who was not going to last. Slowly, however, his health improved and he grew strong. It was not the only time Bob would confound his critics.

Money was always tight because Cyril, an AA patrolman, was in poor health: he was a chronic TB sufferer, a disease that was to claim him some years later. Cyril also smoked and drank heavily and, because of it, rarely completed a full working week.

As a small child, Bob often spent Saturday afternoons with his mother, travelling by bus from Fishponds, where the family now lived, to the centre of Bristol where they took a connecting green single-decker country bus to see his father in the Winsley Sanatorium—a bleak place for a child to visit. The boys usually took it in turns to accompany their mother, but Bob was always ready to take the place of one of the others if they could not or would not go with her. When Cyril became a regular in-patient at both Southmead and Ham Green hospitals, his constant ill-health put further pressure on the family finances.

At home, life with Cyril was not easy as he could be so changeable and, although he fathered five children, he found it difficult to show loving paternal feelings; nevertheless, he possessed some caring qualities. The children knew what it was like to be hungry and to feel the cold and, when they were shivering in their beds on bitter winter nights, they longed to hear their father come home. Cyril would climb the stairs and place his heavy army greatcoat over his children to lend any extra warmth that it might provide.

There were other times when he was less thoughtful. After work, at whatever time of day, Cyril always headed straight for the Downend Tavern and the boys often had to go over to the pub to remind him to come home. Kneeling on the pub window ledge, necks straining, they peered through the clear top of the half-frosted window hoping to catch their father's eye. They never dared to wave, shout or tap on the windowpane because they knew their efforts would be rewarded with a clip around the ear for embarrassing their father in front of his cronies.

In spite of his regular spending in the Downend Tavern and his irregular earnings, Cyril managed to scrape enough money together to rent a larger, end-of-terrace Victorian house in Overndale Road. It was a poor deal: although the landlord was happy to collect the rent, he rarely did any maintenance. One night, when one of Bob's brothers was fast asleep in bed, part of the bedroom ceiling collapsed on top of him. Luckily, he escaped unhurt but the landlord merely undertook to repair the fallen section and chose to ignore the rest, even though the ceiling was still unsound.

But things were not all bad: there were times in Bob's young life that he recalls with great warmth and he remembers their family Christmases with unclouded joy. It was only at this time of year that their dusty, cold and damp front room was used. Beatrice diligently cleaned and spruced the unlived-in room until it shone, and, when the open fire had been burning for some hours, its cosy welcome made their Christmas Day extra special.

'Mum kept a large box of colourful Christmas trimmings which came from her father's pub—The Black Swan in Eastville,' said Bob. 'When we watched her drag them down from the airing cupboard, we got so excited we could hardly wait for Father to come home to hang them from the ceiling with drawing pins.'

On Christmas morning the children woke up around five o'clock, feeling the heavy weight of presents at their feet. Their better-off relatives did their best to ensure that the Woodward children received a fair share of Yuletide enjoyment but one year in particular the children received rather more than usual. Cyril had taken a new job in the metal department of the local aircraft factory, the Bristol Aeroplane Company. An innovative man with some expertise in technical drawing, he secretly made toy battleships for all of his boys, smuggling them out of the factory under his army greatcoat just in time for Christmas. On that special day Cyril did his best to make sure that his children never went without.

Over the years Cyril conjured up a host of toys including four-wheeled carts that both thrilled and amazed his children. Sometimes they were used to carry treasured possessions; at other times the youngsters climbed aboard and careered down steep hills without steering or brakes, showing a complete disregard for any oncoming traffic — infrequent though it was.

Without fail, Sid Young, landlord of the Downend Tavern, would also give the Woodward children Christmas presents. All year he saved the shiny, newly minted copper pennies from his takings until he had enough to fill small, gold-coloured net pouches; it was his way of showing his appreciation to one of his best customers. But while the boys looked forward to Sid's contribution to their seasonal enjoyment, they all experienced pangs of guilt.

In one unlit corner of the yard behind the Downend Tavern lay a large pile of empty Tizer bottles — calling out to be pinched. And, after dark, they were. Joined by several of their friends, the Woodward boys took it in turns to clamber over the wall and pass as many empty bottles as they could to the others waiting furtively on the other side; then, bold as brass, they all marched into the 'bottle and jug' to collect a penny on each of the Tizer empties.

'Then we used to watch Sid Young replace the empty bottles back on the same pile that we just got them from,' said Bob. 'Dreadful, really.'

The boys' guilt was short-lived: as soon as the Christmas celebrations were over, they were back in business once more.

Bob's Uncle Wally, who ran his own butcher's shop, always supplied a large succulent chicken and a breast of lamb for the family's Christmas dinner: it was a veritable feast. Beatrice would spend the whole of her Christmas morning preparing this tasty fare but before she could serve the mouth-watering meal they always had to wait for Cyril to come home from the pub. Only when he eventually joined them—accompanied by several well-imbibed friends—were they able to sit down together to eat.

It seemed no time at all before Cyril left his family again to spend his Christmas evening in the tavern—not to be seen till after closing, when he suddenly reappeared with several more of his pals in tow. The remaining hours of Christmas day were filled with tremendous pleasure when Cyril, freed from inhibitions, led his family and friends in a hearty singsong. With their stomachs full, warm and happy, they sang the old favourites at the top of their voices: 'Down at the Old Bull and Bush', 'You are my Sunshine' and 'Roll out the Barrel' rang out late into the night. It was one of the few times when the family was united in happiness.

'Christmas was always a magical time. It was wonderful.'

Although the house had three large reception rooms on the ground floor, for most of the year (except for Christmas) the family only ever used the one at the end of the passage, next to the kitchen. One day, an unusual delivery arrived consisting of sections of fairground hoop-la sideshows to be stored in their middle room. It appeared that during one of Cyril's drinking sessions a business deal had been struck.

In another attempt to make ends meet, Cyril sub-let their shabby front room to a Miss Kershaw. Living in the Woodward house, sharing space with three noisy, energetic boys and an often heavily inebriated landlord could not have been easy for this elderly spinster. The only compromise offered to their lodger was that the boys were forbidden to use the bathroom upstairs; they had to troop into the back garden to use the outside lavatory instead. Miss Kershaw did not stay too long so the front room was re-let to Mrs Wyatt, a widow, who managed to stay the course a while longer.

The family increased in 1936 with the addition of another son, Alan, and then again in 1942, with a daughter Diane.

'I was always jealous of my sister,' joked Bob, 'because she had four brothers and I had only three. Mind you, she was probably jealous of me because I had a sister and she had none.'

Of the numerous disappointments in Bob's early life, one of the biggest should have been a most happy event—when his mother gave birth, at home, to his sister Diane. So enthralled was he by the marvel of his sister's birth that, in his naivety, he ran to the bus stop to wait for his father to break the wonderful news that there was a baby girl at home. A daughter! A sister! The boys had no idea their mother had been pregnant. No reference had been made of it and, as was so often the case in those days, children had little idea about sex or childbirth—Diane could have been discovered under a gooseberry bush for all they knew. Little Bob waited at the bus stop for ages and ages, bursting with this vital information. Finally, his father arrived—and walked straight past him into the pub without even stopping to hear what the young lad had waited so long to tell him.

The walls of the house in Overndale Road frequently reverberated to the sounds of quarrelling well into the night. At such times, the boys awoke from their sleep with a start: always scared, they whispered together for a moment before quietly creeping halfway down the stairs to listen to what the argument was about that night. If they did not take the greatest of care, their father would hear them and mete out his usual brand of punishment. These scenes were dramatic and traumatic, as Beatrice, through her tears, pleaded with her husband to stop the children's hidings. At other times, the tables turned and the boys, united in their misery, ran all the way downstairs to beg their father to be gentle and to stop shouting at their mother.

Cyril was particularly hard on David and Alan: when Alan refused to clean his teeth, Cyril warned, 'Do as you're told or I'll clean them for you.'

'I was very bad at cleaning my teeth,' said Alan, 'and he was always collaring me.'

Two days later, Cyril deemed that his son had ignored his warning so he held Alan down and scrubbed the boy's teeth with Vim.

'I remember another incident,' said Alan. 'I was 7 or 8 at the time, when I accidentally walked into a lamp post. Dad came straight over and clouted me round the ear for not looking where I was going.'

Cyril also appeared jealous when Beatrice was finally blessed with the girl that she yearned for but even Diane, his only daughter, was not spared his frequent angry outbursts.

Recalling these painful incidents for the first time in decades, Bob realised how dearly he loved his mother but sadly admitted that he had never really known how he felt about his father. Perhaps in an effort to understand Cyril's behaviour and in some ways to justify it, Bob said, 'I have always felt so sorry for my father because he endured a hard upbringing including being starved as a child in absolute poverty. And he was continually in such poor health; there were so many visits to the sanatorium even when he was a boy.'

Was it because Cyril was so embittered by his gruelling childhood that he frequently took his lifelong frustrations out on his own family?

One possibility Bob considered was that his father carried a lot of guilt and a ghastly incident that occurred during Cyril's early years may have contributed to his behaviour. When he was eighteen months old, while sitting on his brother Harold's lap, young Cyril lifted a fork from the table and swung it playfully into the air; it caught in his brother's eye and pulled it out. Harold later developed a brain tumour and died. Any connection between this incident and Harold's ultimate death is unknown but growing up and living with this traumatic memory must have been a terrible burden for the younger brother.

Young Bob was an emotional child who often cried for hours throughout the night, dwelling on his father's suffering. Ironically, this led to another rebuke from his father that Bob was too sensitive and should have been born a girl. 'That boy cries more than he pees,' Cyril was heard to say.

'There is probably a lot of stifled grief left inside me and I would be too frightened to try to release it in case I went out of control,' said Bob. 'Even today, men still feel that they shouldn't cry … we are not expected to cry.'

Happier times were spent on rare days out when Bob accompanied his father fishing. 'I so wanted to be his friend and sometimes it seemed as if he wanted to be nice to me but this made him feel awkward and he just couldn't bring himself to do it.'

Again, the ever-changeable Cyril could turn even these happy occasions into a cause for worry and upset. The lure of the local hostelry always proved too strong to resist and the wonderful fishing trip would come to an abrupt end. Bob would be left outside the pub sometimes for several hours with a packet of crisps in hand, his insecurities rushing to the surface, convinced that either his father had gone home without him or, even worse, had dropped dead inside the pub. Bob's childish fears caused Cyril to lose his temper and he dealt with his son in the usual fashion for causing a scene.

Aunt Joyce recalled how Cyril ruled the roost and the numerous occasions he admonished Beatrice for not cutting the salad to exactly the right size; he always insisted that each ingredient should be cut into small pieces. However much Cyril enjoyed his meal, he never cleared his plate; he always left something but, conversely, expected his children to eat every morsel. The rule never applied to him. This rankled with Bob as he considered the effort that his mother always made to cook for them all. Even now, he thinks it is one of the greatest signs of appreciation to say how much you have enjoyed a meal. Throughout his married life Bob has made it his policy to always say thank you.

Bob lived in a household where there was little communication and physical affection, where his father only spoke to the children when he had to, and this led to a significant level of insecurity. Unsurprisingly, this distancing affected them all: the Woodward males became insular and when they met outside in the street they passed like strangers without speaking.

As a child Bob feared death and the thought of not waking often prevented him from sleeping. He asked questions. Where was I before I was born? What was I thinking of before I was born? Where will I go when I die? What will it be like there? His fears grew when no one attempted to answer him and no measure of comfort was ever offered to him. Things got worse when, on an errand, he was unable to open the back door of a neighbour's house. He pushed, shoved, and eventually forced his way in. The neighbour's dead body had been in the way.

'I was stunned. I couldn't take my eyes off him. His entire colour had drained away; he looked just like a waxwork dummy. I rushed back to our house to tell mum what had happened to Mr Ryman and she took John round to sort it out. I didn't get over that for some time.'

Meanwhile Beatrice Woodward led a life of domestic drudgery. There was an occasion when she visited the dentist to have thirteen teeth extracted. In spite of her grogginess from the ordeal and a walk of over a mile to get home, she stoically refused gas to lessen the pain because she had to get back to prepare the boys' tea.

As was common in many households, Monday was forever washday. First, the enormous galvanised bath was carried in from the yard to be filled with cold water in which to soak the soiled linen before lighting the fire under the old copper to bring the water up to the boil.

'Mother used to disappear in the constantly rising steam and in the clouds of endless washing, flapping in the breeze on miles of clothes-line. She was always working, mending, washing, cleaning, cooking and always caring: an absolute saint,' Bob said. 'I cannot imagine how my mother coped.'

'I could never, ever do anything right for my father,' said David Woodward, 'but my mother was such a kind-hearted, lovely lady; she had a heart of gold and it was a very hard life for her.'

Their galvanised bath was brought into the house twice a week, on Mondays for washing clothes and again on Fridays for washing bodies when the winner of the weekly rough and tumble was rewarded with the sought-after first dip while the bottom of the bath was still visible. One bath night, during Alan's turn, the family received a visit from their cousin Doreen, who settled herself on the floor by the side of the bath and chatted away to him for several hours. When finally she left, poor

Alan emerged, dignity intact, but curiously blue and somewhat wrinkled. This became a favourite family story over the years and one that Alan has never been allowed to forget.

The Woodward household did not boast an outside 'coal hole'; it was indoors and formed part of the kitchen. There were times when the coalman dumped up to two tons of coal during mealtimes and black dust settled over their food—providing unwanted flavouring and minerals to their inadequate diet.

Their house backed on to well-stocked market gardens and acres of open fields where Bob and his siblings spent the long summer days and evenings, playing endless cricket matches until they dropped. The fields that were planted with artichokes provided an adventure playground. Just before harvest, when the crop was at its most abundant, the boys fashioned long, winding tunnels through it, leading ultimately to their den. How proud the market gardener must have been of his neighbours' engineering prowess.

One day an unusual sight caught the boys' attention. 'We had never seen a tent before, not a proper tent,' said Bob. 'Shepherd and his brother were camping out, sitting round their campfire, and roasting chestnuts. We offered to look after their tent while they went down to the hayfield for some more hay to keep the fire burning. When it looked as if it might go out, we tried to keep it going with extra sticks. The next thing we knew, the tent flaps caught fire and before you could look round, the whole blimmin' thing went up. We could hear the Shepherd boys screaming out from the hayfield; they had spotted the flames and realized that it must be their tent. We made sure that we didn't bump into them over the next six months.'

In the winter, the market gardens and surrounding fields turned into a blinding white wonderland where the children, in their element, delighted in wading through deep drifts of snow completely oblivious to the freezing temperatures.

Bob was taught an early lesson in life when a friend brought an impressive toy into school: a lead soldier on horseback. Bob thought it magnificent and got the boy to show him where he had bought it—F.W. Woolworth—and he wished he had enough money to buy one. To his amazement, his friend brought several more into school the next day and, after classes, the two boys hurried into Woolworth's to gaze at the figures displayed on the open-topped counter.

'Where on earth do you get the money from to buy these?' Bob asked.

'You don't buy them,' the boy said. 'Watch! The girl's going up there.' While her back was turned, he snatched two toy soldiers and scarpered.

Caught up in the excitement, Bob grabbed two figures for himself before running after his friend, straight through the back door of the store and into the lane outside. He could hardly believe that in his little hands he held two mounted horsemen: the cavalry. Fantastic. He took them home and hid them. He hoped that they would go unnoticed if he brought them out slowly, over a period of time

To his horror, not all went according to plan: there was a man waiting at school the next day, dressed in silver-buttoned navy-blue serge, complete with helmet and truncheon.

'I suddenly realised what I'd done,' said Bob. 'Did it ever frighten me? It was so different then. If you saw a policeman walking towards you, it was like a dose of opening medicine. And if he actually spoke to you, you were petrified. When they found out that it was me, all hell was let loose. I vowed I would never ever take anything that belonged to anyone else ever again. It was a good lesson.'

Cyril gave him the mandatory hiding, one that Bob felt he deserved. He was so frightened and ashamed he considered running away from home and never coming back. 'I felt like a leper. It was a horrible, horrible feeling.'

Aged seven, Bob left Manor Road infant school, followed in his older brothers' footsteps and became a pupil at Dr Bell's junior school nearby.

The youngsters at Dr Bell's were presided over by the terrifying figure of Mr Cook, a man who used the cane for nearly all misdemeanours, such as simply talking in class or being late. Bob experienced this heavy-handed and inequitable discipline on more than one occasion.

One dramatic incident involved a boy called Mervyn Hughes. Following heavy rain, a large puddle formed at the end of the playground and the area was declared out of bounds. During one playtime, Mervyn, not realising the consequences of his boyish delight, threw stones into the pool before stamping and jumping around in it.

Later that afternoon, Mr Cook burst into Miss Packer's class waving his cane wildly in the air. This instrument of chastisement was feared with good reason: Mr Cook had increased its efficiency by splitting its end and inserting a small piece of metal to add weight to the swish action. Unapologetic for his disruption to the class and the distress and consternation he was causing, Mr Cook roared out that somebody had dared defy his order. 'I want the boy Hughes,' he bawled.

He marched in among the desks, seized the nine-year-old Hughes and dragged him bodily to the front of the class. 'I'm going to make an example of you, boy, with six of the best,' he bellowed.

The first three strokes thrashed down; the pain was too much for Hughes to bear. He screamed out, 'Please … I can't take any more, sir,' and tried to pull away. But the out-of-control headmaster held on tightly and continued the attack, caning the boy's neck, back and bare legs—every blow witnessed by the terrified, dumbstruck class.

Miss Packer, through her tears, attempted to halt the battering but Mr Cook was relentless and the onslaught continued.

Greatly disturbed by the frenzied caning of his friend, Bob was unable to come to terms with the unfair brutality of it. Not long after, he bought a bamboo cane, which cost him a whole threepenny bit out of his precious pocket money. He carried this cane with him whenever he walked through the fields behind his home and, as he made his way through the abundant wild flowers, stinging nettles and artichokes, he lashed and flayed the innocent plants until they fell to the ground.

'I have always carried with me a terrible amount of aggression,' said Bob. 'This memory is so vivid it lives with me to this day, more than sixty years on.'

The one and only holiday the family ever took—three whole days—was to nearby Weston-super-Mare, a traditional, Victorian seaside resort on the Somerset coast twenty miles south-west of Bristol. They stayed in the front room of Mr and Mrs Barrington's boarding house, a cheerful little B&B situated in the pink, mop-head-hydrangea-lined Locking Road, Weston's thoroughfare from Bristol to the Grand Pier.

The family walked the mile or so into town, then on to the seafront where a long debate took place between Beatrice and Cyril about whether they could afford to take lunch in the Grand Central Hotel where Mr Barrington worked as a chef. The children were so excited about eating out, they could hardly contain themselves, and eventually Cyril marched his troops into the restaurant and sat them down at a table. Overawed by their smart surroundings, they eagerly awaited the promised feast. It was a long wait. A lengthy discussion over the menu sadly ended their anticipation when Cyril and Beatrice rose from the table and told the children to follow them. It proved not too much of a let down because they all scoffed fish and chips steeped in salt, sand and vinegar, in newspaper, on the beach.

Immediately afterwards, bellies full, they streamed into the open-air swimming pool for a dip in the freezing cold water. It was the only time Bob saw his father dressed in a swimsuit—a knee-length model complete with bib and shoulder straps. He was amazed when Cyril climbed the diving stage steps higher and higher, before plunging some 23 feet into the sparkling surface of the water below.

3

Pied Piper

During the Second World War, Bristol came under heavy bombing from the German Luftwaffe. The main targets were the city's aircraft factories and port but the bombing was inaccurate and, over a four-year period, nearly 90,000 properties suffered damage or were destroyed and the city experienced considerable loss of life.

When the Woodward children were at school, in their innocence, they looked forward to hearing the air raid sirens; it was a signal for their teachers to dispense ginger biscuits in the rabbit warren of underground shelters beneath the tarmacadam of the school playground—to distract young minds from the immediate danger.

'Although we were frightened when the planes came over, we could still run around and play cowboys and Indians afterwards. The bombing didn't stop Father going out for his pint but I was always afraid that a bomb would fall on the pub and he wouldn't come home to us. Although I never really knew how I felt about him, he was still precious to me,' said Bob.

At night, when the sirens wailed, the Woodward children left their beds and, warmly wrapped in blankets, slept alongside their parents under the stairs because they all disliked the uncomfortable, wet and musty government-supplied Anderson shelter in the garden. If the air raid was expected to be longer or more destructive, Bob and his brothers were woken up, told to dress quickly and ushered across the road to Wendover, a large imposing old manor house, where they slept in its cellars, as did many of their neighbours.

The prospect of heavy bombing over London led in August 1939 to the migration of children to safer parts of the country. Families were torn apart when their offspring were dispatched to small villages in the countryside. The exodus began at 5.30 a.m. and affected over one and a half million youngsters. The children were instructed to take no more than one set of clothing, a toothbrush, a comb, and a handkerchief—and just enough food to last them for that day. Few parents knew where their children ended up on that first night and although most were anxious in the extreme, they were forced to accept the government message informing them that they would be told 'as soon as possible.'

Country folk were shocked by the verminous condition of the children from city slums while the city-bred youngsters were both fearful and alarmed by their strange surroundings: for many it was their first sight of the countryside and 'scary' farm animals.

In 1941 it was the turn of Bristol's mothers to suffer heartache and, inevitably, the awful reality hit the Woodward household. Of the four boys, John, David and Bob would have to be sent away but Alan, just a toddler, would stay at home.

The evacuation caused a lot of administrative and organising work, as the fearsome headmaster, Mr Cook, in his usual forceful manner, reminded the pupils of Dr Bell's: 'The decision has been made for you and there is no going back on it.'

Bob felt sick at the thought of leaving his family. 'I still remember some of the conversations at home and the unhappy look on my mother's face when we discussed the plans for the evacuation.' He was heart-broken and worried for the safety of his parents and baby brother. What might happen to them while he was away? He fretted that if anything did happen, no one would tell him and when he returned home, the house would be silent and empty. This sense of foreboding was not universal among his peers: as the day of departure grew nearer, many of his friends felt great excitement about their new adventure.

The dreaded day arrived and the Woodward boys picked up their battered cases along with the cardboard boxes containing their gas masks and, clutching these few belongings, they reluctantly trudged to Alexandra Park school to join the other children before boarding the charabancs that were to bear them to darkest Somerset, some 30 miles to the south.

'When you're by the side of the coach and you're going off, you do wonder if you'll ever come back. It was a dreadful thought,' said David.

Throughout the country, those who witnessed the brave smiles, the not-so-brave tears, the frightened and the scared, the courageous little lions, will not forget the sights, sounds and smells of that day. Mothers and fathers said their goodbyes to their children and the children said their goodbyes to their parents—disconsolate thoughts of never seeing each other again so very close to the surface. For Bob and his brothers, only Beatrice was there at the send off and her final contact ended when the charabanc turned the corner at the end of the street, cruelly severing their anxious stares. As the journey began, the boys suffered a horrifying sense of separation but were comforted because they had each other—at least for now.

Later that day, they arrived at a village hall near Taunton for tea and buns. Each child, identified by the label tied to the strings of their gas mask box, filed past the administrator for registration before being allocated to local volunteers who had offered to take them into their homes for the duration of the war. Of course, placing three boys together was always going to prove a problem.

'Difficulties began to arise when first John was paired with David and I was left out. I went berserk! Then John and I were paired and David started to howl. And then David and I were put together and John broke down. It became very clear there was no way anyone could split us up.'

'We all cried—we didn't like the idea of being away,' said David. 'It was being away from Mother really. We knew jolly well that she didn't want to be parted from us.'

There were benefits for billeting more than one child, albeit only pecuniary: 10s. 6d. a week was paid for the first child and 8s. 6d. for each subsequent guest. Mr and Mrs Saunders—a courageous couple— stepped forward and offered to give a home to all three but not before pointing out that their spare room housed only two single beds and the boys would have to make the best of it. A shortage of beds was not a problem—at least they would be together. With that settled, they started the journey to the Saunders' bungalow on the Trull road, south of the county town.

Later that night, the boys witnessed flashes in the sky and immediately thought of home. How were their parents and little Alan? Were they safe? Was their home being bombed right now? The solution to their problem was obvious: the boys crept out of the bungalow in the dead of night without food or proper clothing to walk the fifty miles to Bristol. It never crossed their minds that, in the blackness, danger could be lurking. Fortunately, they were captured before getting too far and put back to bed where they remained until morning.

Mr Saunders ran a small haulage business and, the next day, in an attempt to settle them, he gave the boys a ride in his lorry. It was to no avail as identical flashes in the sky again that night prompted another unsuccessful dash for home. Once again, the patient Mr and Mrs Saunders rounded up the errant boys and returned them to their beds but it was not lost on them that they had not one but three problems on their hands. In another effort to settle them, Mr Saunders came up with the idea that they could take a few days off school to help him with some deliveries. The boys had a whale of a time on that Monday morning but trouble awaited them back at the bungalow.

The boy living next door had reported them for not attending school and, at lunchtime, he delivered a note from the headmaster stating that the Woodward brothers must turn up that afternoon without fail. For his trouble, the boy received an unwelcome reward for squealing. The Woodwards certainly made their mark on the quiet community they had just joined—and not least on the boy next door.

The rest of the week continued in much the same way; it was evident that being cared for by strangers was not going to work and arrangements were made for the boys to return home to Bristol. They were beside themselves with joy at the prospect—while the Saunders probably thought that their war was over.

An angry Mr Cook, along with another teacher, Harry Herbert, met the boys at Temple Meads Station and ordered them to be at school first thing on Monday morning to receive their punishment for the immense amount of trouble they had caused in just one week. The huge relief at being home, however, was dominant and Mr Cook's threats were soon forgotten.

When they got home, Cyril ticked them off in such a manner that they could tell that he was not really annoyed with them at all. From their mother there were just countless hugs and kisses. They were all back together as a family once more.

4

Boys will be Boys

Cyril and Beatrice sent their children to Fishponds Baptist chapel although they never attended themselves: even so, they called themselves Baptists. It was a simple matter of location; had the closest church to home been Methodist they would, in all probability, have called themselves Methodists. Being made to go took on great significance as, in Bob's early life, the church became the only place he felt truly secure and marked the beginning of a lifetime as a committed Christian.

The Woodwards were responsible for the local chapel experiencing something of an unusual event. As their first-born, John, was the only child they had christened, Cyril and Beatrice asked the Revd Bernard Stapley if he would hold a service for the remainder of their brood and dedicate them in a 'job lot'. It was a one-off for Fishponds chapel and much talked about at the time. When the embarrassing news leaked out, their school friends ribbed them unmercifully.

As soon as the children could walk and were able to make the journey, Sunday school became a weekly ritual come rain or shine. It was a thrilling moment when Mrs Ford, Bob's Sunday school teacher, presented him with his first Bible, awarded for reciting the books of the Old Testament in the correct order. Sunday school also played a welcome part in Beatrice's life: it meant that during the afternoon the children were out from under her feet.

In keeping with the times, Sunday was a special day for the Woodwards: it was the Sabbath and a day of rest and there were things they would not dream of doing. However snowed under Beatrice found herself with the endless laundry, none of it ever found its way to the clothes line on the Sabbath.

John was always quiet and reserved with his own circle of friends—unlike Bob who was completely the opposite and becoming a bit of a prankster: his mischievous nature went unsuppressed even in church. On one sunny, summer afternoon, at the carefree age of eight, the lure of a multitude of grasshoppers inhabiting the field at the side of the church encouraged Bob to make a special effort to arrive early for Sunday school. He and his friends crawled underneath the fence into the field to collect as many grasshoppers as they were able to cram into their trouser pockets before heading into church. During prayers, the boys opened their eyes, lifted their heads and waited for a signal from their leader before releasing their captives. Unholy pandemonium broke out when a choir of chirping grasshoppers zip-zip-zipped freely through the Sunday school class.

Attending Sunday school was a pattern the Woodward children followed until they started work and only then were they given the choice to continue or not. The other boys happily abandoned this activity but Bob remained with his church; his faith strengthened and several years later he became a lay preacher.

While the family lived in Overndale Road, Bob and his friends loved to play cowboys and Indians in the long garden of the house opposite where his best friend Frank Henderson lived. One day, when Frank's parents were out, the privilege of playing Bob's Wild West hero, Roy Rogers, fell to Brian Winterson, while Bob played Hop-along Cassidy. There were, of course, always two sides: the goodies and the baddies.

The day went badly for Roy Rogers. A posse of baddies captured and handcuffed him to a vice in the fort (the Hendersons' garage), before galloping off to capture more goodies who were hiding out on the prairie. Soon after, the sounds of Roy Rogers's screams were clearly heard across the open range but went unheeded at first until one of the cavalry thought he should check. The words he shouted to the others made them all turn tail and hoof it back to camp. Roy Rogers was in heap big trouble. Hop-along Cassidy can still recall his disillusionment when he heard the yell: 'Roy Rogers has messed himself.'

In his final year at Dr Bell's, Bob sat the 11-plus exam for the grammar school. Always a bright pupil and always in the A-stream, he dreamed of going to a posh grammar school and wearing a smart school uniform but, during one of the many heated exchanges that occurred night after night at home, Bob overheard a conversation about the approaching exam and only then did he realise the concern it was causing. The extra money to send him to grammar school was way beyond his impoverished parents, so he eliminated all thoughts of passing the exam.

A year later, Bob followed his older brothers into Alexandra Park senior school, known locally as 'Alex'. It was the pattern that all of the Woodward children followed.

At the end of his first year at 'Alex', two vacancies were offered for late entrants to the grammar school and the headmaster, Mr Stacey, told Bob that both he and Freddie Uzzell would 'walk it'. Bob wished long and hard for them to choose someone else but fate decreed that he should sit the scholarship again. As predicted, Freddie Uzzell 'walked it' but as circumstances at home were much the same as before, Bob delivered the same result as he had done at the first sitting. Mr Stacey was most annoyed because Bob deliberately wasted the prospect of a better education.

A favourite playtime activity at 'Alex' was for one intrepid soul to collect a few ha'pennies from the others and act as a runner to smuggle edible contraband into school. When it was Bob's turn, he would squeeze through a gap in the railings, sprint to Ford's bakery to buy a crusty bun-loaf and return, hell for leather, to share the treat with the rest of the gang. The bun-loaf would be flattened against his stomach beneath his shirt in an attempt to hide both the shape and ároma of the bread; it was a painful experience, as the loaf, straight from the ovens, burned hot against his skin, but the scrumptious taste of the freshly baked bread made the discomfort all the more worthwhile. This was always a risky venture because should he arrive late for the next lesson, he would be in serious trouble.

At the age of eleven, Bob started a paper round, again following his older brothers' examples. At first, he delivered evening newspapers but, blessed with an abundance of energy, this soon developed into morning, evening and Sunday morning rounds. A hard worker, he got on extremely well with his employers, Mr and Mrs Stevens: so well in fact, that it was Mr Stevens who gave him his first bicycle, a thrilling gift in spite of its dilapidated state. The sight of its unfashionable, over-sized 28-inch wheels caused much amusement among the locals but, for Bob, it mattered not one jot because he was always hopeful that the local girls would notice that he owned a bike. He went everywhere on it including trips to the unkempt estuary-side resort of Severn Beach, some fifteen miles from home.

Bob's childhood included a fair share of 'boys will be boys' episodes and demonstrated promising leadership qualities as he became a ringleader among his peers. Often, on winter evenings, he and his friends waited at the rear exit of the Vandyke cinema and, like boys before and since, took the opportunity of free entry when someone walked out. Sneaking into the cinema and sitting quietly in the first available seats—usually in the front row—became a polished manoeuvre, which never stopped there. When the attention of the audience was held by some dramatic incident on screen, the boys moved to better seats at the rear—but even these were not good enough. During the interval, they hid in the lavatories before scaling the stairs to settle themselves into the posh seats in the circle. Mission impossible? Not for the Woodwards: mission accomplished.

The Woodward boys were the proud owners of a much-envied collection of glass marbles, and the harsh reality of worn-out shoes was used to advantage when playing marbles with their friends on the daily walk to school. As the marbles collided and spun off in all directions, it seemed only natural to step smartly onto the biggest and most colourful and wiggle it through a hole in their shoe. Little time was spent hunting for the elusive marbles lest they should be late for school. In some discomfort, the 'winner' made his way to the classroom where, furtively, he removed the cause of his pain to add later to their prized and ever-growing collection.

On another occasion, after church one evening, Bob, David and his friend, Michael Keeler, made their way through the Cleeve Tea Gardens to the riverbank where they jumped into a punt piloted by Reggie Sims and his cousin for a free float up the river, out of sight of the boathouse.

'On the way back, the perishers wouldn't let us get out,' said Bob.

As the punt floated under a tree, David and Bob grabbed an over-hanging branch and swung themselves up into the tree before jumping onto the riverbank. 'Poor old Michael Keeler grasped a branch that was too thick to hold on to and he just hung there until he fell in. The state he was in when he finally clambered out of the river in his best Sunday suit was unbelievable. We followed him all the way to his home until the door slammed behind him. Reggie Sims and his cousin were frightened to death that someone would tell Michael's parents that they were responsible, so they asked David and me to give Michael two Rupert Bear annuals to keep his mouth shut. Well, we went up there three times to deliver those books but each time the door was slammed in our faces. After about 10 days, we thought it would soon be all forgotten so we kept the annuals. We were stinkers really.'

Bob also cheerfully led his friends in a potentially fatal pastime at Vassall's Park, part of the Oldbury Court estate, an area that was, and still is, a delightful corner of Bristol set in several thousand acres of lush green parkland bisected by the river Frome. After Sunday school the boys ran to the quarry end of the estate before scrambling through fences bearing 'Keep Out' warnings. There they eyed the heavy trucks that, on weekdays, carried stone along the railway for tipping over the edge to the quarry floor some 120 feet below. On quiet Sunday afternoons, the trucks were always empty and ready for use by young tearaways eager for excitement. They pushed the truck along the track until it gathered sufficient momentum for them to jump on, grimly hanging on to its sides as it rattled towards the quarry edge. They had dared each other to see who would be last to drop off before it tipped over the precipice. Luckily, not one of these foolhardy souls ever got seriously hurt.

While the boys were out causing mayhem, their only sister, Diane, spent most of her time demurely pushing her dolls' prams around until she was old enough to take the neighbours' babies out for walks. 'My greatest ambition then, was to become a mother,' she said.

Cyril always worked hard in his vegetable garden and the readily available fresh fertiliser, which his sons reluctantly collected, enhanced its abundant yield. The chore of lifting recently dropped horse manure from the road always fell to the first boy to arrive home from school.

'I've just passed a fresh dump in Stanbury Avenue,' their father would say. 'Get going before it disappears.'

The smelly deposit was often still steaming when, armed with bucket and shovel, the boy scraped up the offensive load to take home. The boys detested the job; it was a humiliation they all shared, but their greatest worry was that their friends might see them doing it.

In 1947, aged 14, Bob reached school-leaving age. His headmaster made a strong case for him to stay on for one more year to attain some qualifications in order to get a better job but, driven by the lack of funds at home, he chose to find work to contribute a few shillings a week to augment his mother's housekeeping. There was a bonus, however: now that he had left school, he was allowed to wear long trousers every day, not just on Sundays.

Bob was growing in both stature and confidence, as were all the boys. As a result of this, and the fact that they were now providing their parents with a better standard of living, Cyril became less autocratic. Aunt Joyce remembers an occasion when, after stripping to the waist in the scullery to wash, Bob deliberately walked back into the kitchen to flex and show off his muscles. Joyce always felt that Bob was a good talker and that, although he followed his father in strength of mind, he followed his mother in loving and caring.

5

Out of Pie Tins and into Glue Pots

Bob's first job was at Pople's butcher's shop in the St Werburgh's district of Bristol where he greased pie tins, scraped floors, washed up and did other menial tasks. He worked there for just three weeks because his father had arranged for him to start at the cardboard box factory of the large, well-established company, E.S. and A. Robinson.

Mr Pople obviously thought highly of Bob and did not want to lose him. 'My boy, if you stay on, in just a couple of short years, you'll be working on the ovens,' he said. Evidently, this enticing offer did not tempt Bob sufficiently because he promptly took a cut in wages of 2s. 6d. a week to work at Robinson's.

His new job took him out of pie tins and into glue pots. 'I broke open the barrels of glue and cut the sticky mass into chunks for boiling in the pots to be used by the lines of girls making up the cardboard containers.'

After spending some weeks in glue pots, he was moved to the loading bay area where he pushed the rear of a hand-pulled forklift truck. At an age when he was becoming aware of the opposite sex, he felt self-conscious doing this in front of hordes of attractive girls and he was relieved when they moved him into the artist department, even though it meant that he was at the beck and call of the artists. It was there he enjoyed the occasional spell of relative freedom when called upon to deliver urgent plans to other Robinson factories in the city. Bob looked forward to breaking off from the routine chores and travelling into town.

Robinson's did not pay overtime but gave time off in lieu. Bob always tried to arrange his time off for Wednesday afternoons to coincide with half-day closing at Hodder's chemists in Fishponds, to spend time with their shop assistant, Mavis Jones—his first girlfriend.

One Wednesday, Mr Andrews, head of the artist department, came rushing round with an urgent delivery for Bedminster in the south of the city. It was already one o'clock and Bob had arranged to meet Mavis at two o'clock in Fishponds in the north of the city. Although it was unheard of to refuse, he remonstrated with Mr Andrews but his boss remained resolute. Len Howlett, the foreman of the printing section and a man some ten years Bob's senior, eavesdropped their discussion; he delighted in Bob's predicament, knowing full well that Mavis was about to be let down.

Bob was not at all amused and felt some anger towards the leering

Len. 'I remembered that only a few days before, he had been calculating the scale of several articles in his office by holding up a pencil, lining it up and marking the pencil with his finger.'

With this in mind, Bob turned towards Len, held up the long roll of plans, adjusted them into the horizontal and closed one eye as if to gauge the size of the foreman's head. Len went potty and, not wishing to be made a fool of by a mere boy, rushed headlong through the department after the cheeky young assistant. Bob turned tail, flew towards the fire exit, pitched head first into the panic bolts and the doors burst open. He continued to run until he reached the road where he swivelled round to check Len's progress. Risking capture, he lifted the roll of plans once again to check Len's cranial diameter before racing over the railway station bridge where, defiantly, he repeated the impertinent manoeuvre.

Moving quickly down Station Avenue to the main Fishponds Road, Bob prayed for a city centre bus to whisk him away from the onrushing Len. With exquisite timing, his prayer was answered and he hopped on the first bus that came along without checking its destination. It pulled away just as the red-faced, out-of-breath Len came round the corner. In a final display of showmanship and some triumph, Bob held up the roll of plans once more to measure the now apoplectic foreman's head.

Bob's reward was an almighty row with Mavis for not turning up on time but this altercation merely took his mind off the consequences that were certain to befall him next day.

The following morning, Bob clocked on as usual and made his way through the maze of tall paper stacks on the factory floor to the artist department. As he rounded one of the bends, a huge pair of powerful hands tossed him into a corner.

'The blows came thick and fast to my stomach and ribs, though not to my face of course, so that any injuries would be hidden,' Bob said. 'I really thought something was broken; I was sore for weeks. Len is in his eighties now and still lives in Fishponds. To this day we laugh about it when we meet.'

Bob's courtship with Mavis turned out to be an on and off affair. They often disagreed and sometimes parted company for several months but, in spite of this, Mavis gave him his first watch—for his sixteenth birthday.

It was at this age when Bob undertook a brief dalliance with cigarettes. Peer pressure ruled and, when many of his friends started to smoke, he followed suit, even though he had witnessed the effects of his father's addiction. In a Western he saw at the 'threepenny rush', the toughest cowboy extinguished his cigarette by stubbing it out in the palm of his hand so Bob tried it with his first cigarette. Although he burnt his hand quite badly, it proved not too painful and this encouraged him to repeat the exercise but the excruciating pain that followed the stubbing out of a second cigarette onto a rapidly forming blister, dissuaded him from becoming a regular smoker.

Bob's brother John left school and trained as a painter and decorator. National service interrupted his life for two years, which he largely spent stationed at Catterick, North Yorkshire. It was bleak and cold and he hated it. His absence strained the family finances further as his father's earnings continued to wane due to his deteriorating health. David followed John into the same trade but he detested it and to the fury of his father gave up his apprenticeship. David's passion for cinema resulted in him becoming a projectionist at the local picture house.

'The movies fascinated me,' said David. 'It went right back to the time when I read about William Friese-Greene in Bristol. He invented the projector. He was the first ever, his studio was up in Whiteladies Road; his plaque is still on the wall there.'

After Bob had worked at Robinson's for two and a half years, the call of the outdoors drew him into the building trade and he took up a job with Ken Warne, a local builder. His first task was that of a brush-hand and he primed all the new timber on the site. 'If it didn't move, I'd knot it and paint it pink.'

6

Young Love

Prompted by a friend's attendance at baptism classes, Bob resolved to make his own public proclamation of faith. He and Frank Henderson undertook full baptism at Fishponds church. Then, with religion playing an ever more important role in his life, Bob became a Sunday school teacher at the age of sixteen. He took further responsibility by becoming treasurer of the Young People's Fellowship. The YPF met socially on Wednesday nights to arrange outings, cricket and football matches, hikes and similar healthy pastimes. Whenever he could, Bob attended its activities and he made a wonderful circle of friends there, including Harold Neal.

'It was a friendship that was to last for the rest of my life,' said Bob of the person who was later to be his best man. 'Harold was the leader of the YPF and has been a tremendous influence.'

'When Bob was asked to speak at some of the YPF meetings, he would have us in fits of laughter telling us of his experiences at work,' said Diane, Bob's sister, who had also joined the YPF. 'He was a very entertaining speaker but he always got his message over.'

The following year, the Bristol and District Association of Baptist Churches' Itinerant Society invited Bob to join as a lay preacher. After accepting, he took Sunday services in the smaller churches of the area that were without a resident minister. Sundays were now busier than ever. Typically, he rose early to cycle the twelve miles or more to Old Sodbury to take the morning service; afterwards, he pedalled home for lunch before taking an afternoon Sunday school class followed by a five-mile round trip to the children's TB ward at Frenchay hospital. Still finding the time to get home for tea, Bob then covered a further two miles to take services in the wards of Snowdon hospital in Manor Road. As if that was not enough for one day, he frequently managed to turn out for either a football or a cricket match to represent the YPF. He possessed inexhaustible energy.

'There was a fellow in the church called Alec Roberts whose father was a local barber,' said Bob. 'Mr Roberts was a dear old chap and knew his Bible inside out and upside down and I went to him for help with my sermons. The week before my sermon, Alec and I would spend the whole evening sitting in his barber's shop over some bread and cheese where Mr Roberts brought life into biblical stories. He always went through it with me first and then I asked questions. I can remember the first time he told me the story of Elijah: how it had not rained for years, how they put up sacrifices and called on God for fire and how the fire was sent down to earth. He brought the whole thing to life: I felt almost scorched by the flames. It was now my story and the sermon for the following Sunday. I gave the same sermon in different churches over and over again and the more I told it, the better it got. When I needed a new one, I visited Mr Roberts again. After Elijah there was the story of the tax collector, which I used for a while before visiting him again to get another story.'

Responses to Bob's inspiring sermons were both popular and positive; however, one incident demonstrated that there were those who may have been motivated by other considerations and were not necessarily present just to hear Bob's golden voice. On a chilly Sunday evening, at the tiny church in Woollard, he delayed the start of the service because the congregation amounted to just two elderly women. Ten minutes later no more worshippers had turned up, so he announced the number of the first hymn to the sparse assembly when one of them arose and walked towards him.

'Can I help?' Bob asked, surprised at the interruption.

'Before we start, can I just ask you to step down from the pulpit? Now would you mind just lifting the pulpit aside? The coalhole is underneath,' she explained.

Bob lifted the pulpit and stood aside; the elderly woman stepped forward, removed several lumps of coal and carried them over to re-fuel the boiler in the centre of the church.

'They were not only there for the service they were there for a warm as well. I still can't decide which was more important to them,' Bob said.

At the age of eighteen David Woodward was called up for national service in the RAF at Old Sarum, near Salisbury.

'I loved every minute of it in the RAF,' said David. 'But I can remember coming home on leave and finding my father having a go at Alan in the lane by the side of the house. There was a terrific row. I got a bit upset and said something I shouldn't have and when my back was turned, Father threw a poker at me. If it had hit me, it would have killed me. I said, that's it, I'll leave home and I lived rough for a long time. So I know what it's like to sleep under the stars.'

The following year, Bob's national service papers arrived; always the home bird, he dreaded the thought of leaving the nest and departed miserably for his medical. During a test for Babinski's sign, the doctor stroked a sharp instrument across the sole of Bob's foot. Normally, toes curl downward: Bob's did not. Lack of reaction to reflex tests had already raised eyebrows but his perverse reaction to the foot-scraping test stopped proceedings altogether. It seemed to show a problem with his central nervous system and his certificate was marked grade four; he failed the medical.

It was a blessing because his father, aged just 45 and in worsening health, had recently given up work altogether. The failed medical was a tremendous relief to Bob: now he could stay at home to look after his dear mother and family.

Unlike their father, the boys remained free of TB but, although she was not told about it at the time, Diane was found to have a spot on one lung.

'I remember having to have sun-ray treatment, taking lots of cod liver oil and malt and having lots of rest,' she said. 'Throughout my child-hood, I can remember them coming in to fumigate my parents' bedroom after they took my father to the sanatorium.'

Younger brother Alan, now a painter and decorator, met and courted Margaret Edmonds. One evening, at the YPF, Margaret showed Bob a photograph of her sister Judy. After admiring the photograph, Bob persuaded Margaret to bring Judy along to make up a foursome, and the big date was set for 5 December 1953 outside Eastville Methodist church.

The boys arrived at the church on time, but Bob's face fell when he saw that Margaret was alone. His disappointment soon quieted, however, when Margaret explained that her sister was shopping in town but would definitely join them later. As promised, Judy met up with the group as they queued outside the Odeon cinema in Fairfax Street. Bob remembers how lovely Judy looked in her brown corduroy-velvet coat and pillbox hat; she was just seventeen and 'looked like a film-star.' They shook hands before going in to watch *The Caddie*, a Jerry Lewis and Dean Martin comedy. Bob thought it incredible that this beautiful young girl sitting at his side was actually with him.

'It was love at first sight and the start of the rest of my life.'

7

The Gospel according to Billy Graham

As Bob grew better acquainted with Judy's family, the disparity between their home lives became more noticeable. Cliff Edmonds, Judy's father, was warm, easy to talk and laugh with—things that Bob had never been able to share with his own father. He revelled in the Edmondses' generosity and Cliff made a lasting impression upon him.

'The warmth and love in their house had to be experienced to appreciate it,' Bob said. 'The games we used to play—such fun. It was magic.'

Judy's parents welcomed him into their midst with open arms while he became increasingly fond of them and he was overjoyed when they invited him on their family holiday in Cornwall. Bob strapped a few things to his bike and set out for Newquay where the family was staying in a caravan. He got as far as Crediton where a strong headwind forced him to stop for the night in Okehampton. The next day, he took the train to Padstow and from there cycled on to Newquay. 'But I felt a failure for letting the weather conditions overtake me. The following year I repeated the trip but this time on a racing bike and I cycled all the way to Newquay where I stayed in a B&B and visited Judy every day. It was a marvellous holiday, all that surfing on the rolling wake. Judy was very good at it but I wasn't.'

In his new job as a novice painter and decorator for Rodgers of Bedminster, Bob was only allowed to distemper walls, as he was not yet experienced enough to hang wallpaper. Rodgers also ran a small builders' merchants business and, when the manager fell out with Mrs Rodgers, she offered Bob, her new blue-eyed boy, the position of shop manager. He accepted with some surprise, as he was only just eighteen. Cyril shared in his surprise and boasted to his mates that his formerly distemper bespattered son now wore a collar and tie to work; indeed, the whole family was overawed. For Bob, however, it was not quite that glamorous; having to run the shop single-handed the position turned out to be a lonely one.

The shop was kept afloat by the popularity of paraffin heaters—its one successful line. When the spring came and demand for heaters and paraffin fell, the shop failed; nevertheless, his time had not been wasted. He had become acquainted with some commercial travellers who seemed to chase around the countryside all day long in company cars. Their carefree lifestyle appealed to Bob.

After passing his driving test, he applied to several firms to realise his new ambition. He was short-listed for a job with Magnet Paints but unsuccessful due to his age and lack of experience. His disappointment was short-lived when one of his regular travellers, whose father owned Horwoods, a hardware business based in Three Queens Lane in the St Mary Redcliff area, told him of a vacancy in the company—albeit not for a travelling salesman. Bob accepted their offer only to find that his first task on Monday morning was sorting chamber pots before packing them into tea chests. On Tuesday, he did the same again but the thought of doing that for the rest of his life did not enthral him and his father's words, 'Starting at the bottom as a po packer', did not help at all. At high noon on the third day, he resigned.

He next took a job with a building sub-contractor working at the nearby municipal swimming baths but, during the persistent snow in the long hard winter of 1953, he was laid off. Fed up with having so many different jobs, he confidently told his father that he was never going to work for anyone else ever again and that, at the age of nineteen, he intended to join the ranks of the self-employed. With just enough savings to cover his household contributions for three months, he struck out on his own and did anything and everything to bring in some money.

Someone else who dreamed of striking out on his own was Harry Tudor (Judy's uncle) who, although he had a health problem, wanted to set up in business as a flooring contractor. Harry was diabetic and because his condition had affected his eyesight, he asked Bob to chauffeur him around to search for contracts. After giving Harry's proposal some thought, Bob agreed to it, as he felt that he might pick up a few painting and decorating jobs for himself on the way round.

Harry hired an Austin 10 and they headed towards Nailsea where they were referred to a firm in Clevedon a few miles further on. They parked their car at Hawkins the builders where, smartly dressed in Sunday best and brimming with confidence, they asked to see someone in charge. Yes, they were told, Mr Leslie Hawkins would see them if they would like to wait. Eventually, they were called into Mr Hawkins's office, where Harry made his pitch. Sadly, Hawkins did not require his flooring products but, seizing the moment, Harry exclaimed, 'We also do painting and decorating!'

'Well, that's more interesting. All our men are busy and we desperately need painters and decorators to finish off a house,' Leslie Hawkins replied. 'Could you give me a price for the whole house?'

Harry nodded.

'How many painters do you have?'

'Seven,' said Harry without hesitation and with more regard for the commercial imperative than for the facts. There was, of course, only Bob who did not even own a paintbrush.

Leslie Hawkins suggested that they follow his car—a smart Vauxhall Velox—to view a house in Edward Road South. Even though Hawkins was a fair-sized company, Bob was surprised to note that the old-fashioned, lashed timber-pole scaffolding was still being used on a row of newly built detached houses. Leslie ushered them into a smart, three-bedroom detached house, which would see the birth of Bob's first business.

'I'll wait outside while you come up with a price,' said Leslie.

Bob and Harry were in a quandary. Should it be £50 or £500? In an effort to appear professional, they told Leslie that they would telephone him later with the figures. Bob had no equipment, no materials and, more to the point, no choice; he wanted the job so badly he made up his mind to decorate the whole house on his own.

The two men deliberated without consequence until, finally, after spinning a knife, they let fate decide—and fate decided £68 10s. 6d. When Leslie Hawkins accepted the price immediately, they knew that fate had advised them poorly. Then, Harry, scared he was about to lose money, developed cold feet and pulled out, leaving Bob as sole proprietor.

Full of enthusiasm, Bob visited his Uncle Wally on the bank holiday weekend with a proposition. 'I'll paint your house if you lend me your van for this weekend in part payment; you can pay the rest in cash when I've finished.'

Wally agreed to lend him his van and offered some money on account but Bob politely refused it: his first business contract needed to be to his uncle's full satisfaction before payment became due.

Bob was now 'in business' and, while temporarily mobile, he bought buckets, brushes, paint and a hundredweight of distemper to transport to the Clevedon site. Then, swiftly but efficiently, he painted Wally's house and, after washing his brushes and buckets, marched straight into the house to collect his money—only to be told that his uncle was not feeling too well and was sleeping. Eager to get away but reluctant to leave without his money, Bob hung around outside killing time; he whistled, slammed a gate and kicked a dustbin before charging inside to wake his uncle. Wally was not best pleased and, under the pretence of locating his false teeth, made Bob wait even longer before finally writing him a cheque.

The next morning, Bob, a fully experienced tradesman after just one weekend's work, took a bus from Downend to Clevedon to paint and decorate the new house.

When Leslie Hawkins turned up to inspect the site, he asked when the rest of the men would be arriving. To save face, Bob said they were busy elsewhere.

Hawkins was taken aback. 'We've got a completion date for this property in four weeks,' he said, 'and it normally takes *us* four to five weeks with *two* decorators on site.'

Bob was determined not to let Leslie Hawkins down and he completed the work in three and a half weeks—top to bottom, inside and out. The speed and quality of the work left Leslie dumbfounded and delighted and he asked Bob to look at another job—a bungalow in the West End district of Clevedon. Having under-priced the first job, and with bus fares eating into his meagre allowance, Bob put aside his reservations and said, 'I'd be delighted to look at it.' This time, with some experience under his belt, he quoted a realistic price.

'That sounds reasonable but it's a lot more than the job you've just finished,' Hawkins pointed out.

'It does make the other quote look silly, Mr Hawkins, but I'm not happy with the situation I find myself in,' said Bob. 'Harry told you that we had seven painters but, actually, there's just me. This is the first job I've ever done. Maybe I could build up a squad by recruiting my brothers. I must confess that when I quoted for your other house I didn't know what I was doing.'

'OK, Mr Woodward, if you were pricing the other job today what would you quote?' asked Leslie.

'£105,' Bob answered.

'To be honest, I've never seen anyone work as fast as you so I'll pay you the £105 for the first job and I'll accept today's quote for the bungalow. Perhaps we can build a good working relationship.'

Some weeks later, Leslie asked Bob to take on another painting job, this time at the Hale's Home Bakery factory in Clevedon. The contract was too big for him alone so Bob asked his brother for help. 'John was a much better tradesman than I could ever be,' he said.

With his brother on board, they completed the work earlier than expected and Leslie asked them to give him a price for some more painting at the same factory.

'Before we do that,' said Bob, 'my quote of £140 for the last job was too high. £100 would have been nearer the mark, so here's £40 back.'

Leslie appreciated Bob's honesty. 'Tell me; how much money are you looking to earn?'

'£20 a week,' was the quick response.

'I tell you what, Mr Woodward. If you would like to continue with this job at Hale's, I'll happily pay you and your brother £20 a week.'

Occasionally, Bob preached at Nempnett Baptist chapel in the Chew Valley where he made friends with a number of parishioners in the local community, but he was especially close to Farmer Evans. He and Judy visited the farm on Sunday afternoons to enjoy the Evanses' teatime hospitality before setting off for the evening service, with most of the villagers following in their wake. Whenever Bob preached at these country chapels, Judy played the keyboard or small organ. It was a gentle time.

In 1954 Britain witnessed a spiritual phenomenon: the Billy Graham Crusades. This American evangelist preached the Gospel face-to-face to those seeking a personal relationship with God. The fanaticism within the religious community resulted in record attendances wherever Billy Graham evangelised. A three-month tour in 1954 and a further six weeks in 1955 attracted audiences totalling nearly three million.

Bob and his friends were able to join in these events thanks largely to Charlie Lee, an ex-Marine Commando who was then a flooring contractor in the enviable position of owning an Austin Devon A40 van. Their paths had crossed in the building trade and Bob knew him to be a 'hard nut' but a devout Christian. Charlie—a member of the struggling Eastville Baptist Mission—had a lovely voice and often sang solo (accompanied by Judy who was a fine musician) when Bob preached at country churches. Making full use of his van, Charlie regularly ferried the group to church services around the country and on three occasions drove them to London to attend the Graham rallies, twice at Wembley Stadium, where they were part of an enormous 180,000-strong audience, and the other at Earl's Court a year later. Suffused with the energy of these meetings, the group sang hymns all the way home to Bristol.

'We wanted the rallies to go on and on,' said Bob. 'They were incredible. If we had not already been baptised, we would have been first up there to profess our faith in God.'

Bob was deeply affected by Billy Graham's message, his personal magnetism and the whole compelling experience. He adored the rallies and he still listens to the recordings of the sermons: they remain an inspiration to him. During his life, three great speakers have inspired him and Billy Graham was the first of these.

Bob also attended church youth weekends, one of which was in Weston-super-Mare. A coach took the young Christians from Fishponds to the Highbury Hotel in Weston where they met like-minded folk from other churches; Judy, although less keen and less socially minded than Bob, went along with him. Preoccupied in this way, the Church and its teachings enriched his consciousness. It was not all serious preoccupation: once, in a light-hearted moment, to entertain the others, Bob climbed to the top of the hotel stairs where, in prone, plank-like attitude, he tobogganed downhill to cheers from the spectators; not one took up the challenge to copy him.

But Bob's irrepressible sense of fun did not diminish the significance of the business in hand. So moved was he that he was inspired to become a missionary, although he may have been put in mind of this because Fishponds Baptist church supported two missionaries serving in the Congo. Bob found that people were receptive to his speaking, which reinforced his conviction that his vocation was definitely that of a missionary. When he told Judy about his inner feelings, she was shocked: she did not think it right for him; he was too impulsive; he should think it through. Nevertheless, his enthusiasm led him to discuss it over and again with their minister, Ivor Tomlin, but this also bore no fruit. Only in maturity did Bob come fully to appreciate Ivor's profound influence.

'At the time, I couldn't understand why Mr Tomlin wasn't elated,' said Bob. 'I thought he was negative but I know now it was his way of testing me. Although I felt I was being called, on reflection, I was not. It took some years for me to recognise that if I had really wanted to be a missionary, no one could have stopped me.'

Ivor Tomlin's interest in Bob led him to lend him the book, *Timothy my Son*; he suggested that it would increase Bob's knowledge of the Bible. Judy recently came across *Timothy my Son* and chided Bob for not returning it.

'There were two reasons why I never returned it,' he said. 'Fifty years on, I still haven't read it and, sadly, Ivor Tomlin is now deceased.'

Bob admits to not being much of a reader.

8

The House that Bob Built

In 1956, another milestone year, Bob became the proud owner of his first motor car: a 1938 Ford Popular. It bore the registration number 210 EHP and his friends pulled his leg, telling him that it broadcast the fact that it was on 'Easy Hire Purchase'. Bob was very excited to have his own car at last and he was unable to sleep for nights thinking about it. The world was now his oyster. 'It was fantastic to be so independent. It was ever so rare to have a car in those days ... ever so rare.'

Having got used to her daughter's boyfriend arriving on an assortment of bicycles, Judy's mother Gwen was amazed the first time he drew up outside their house in a motor car. The Edmondses had never owned a car and Bob felt that Gwen wondered whether he could truly afford one; nevertheless, over the coming weeks, he and his car were frequent visitors. Others enjoyed the benefits of Bob's car too.

'Just before I was married I'd arranged to take my fiancée on a trip to Aberystwyth,' said Alan Woodward. 'On that particular morning, I didn't hear the alarm go off and I got up at five to eight, when the coach was leaving at 8 o'clock. Bob came straight to the rescue by diving out of bed to fetch Margaret in his car. She lived three miles away so that was six miles in all. If it hadn't been for Bob we certainly wouldn't have made that trip. I can remember it was a very quiet coach journey because no one spoke to us after delaying the departure for twenty minutes.'

Love was in the air and it was not long before Bob asked Judy to marry him.

'From the beginning, it was always serious,' said Bob.

A year or so before his wedding, Bob found a splendid half-acre building plot in Claverham just one and a half miles from where he was born and, with no experience whatsoever, he decided to build their first house on it. The land was up for sale at £350 and he and Judy paid an equal share of the deposit to secure it. After some help with the design of their new home from Harold Neal, his friend from the YPF, Bob budgeted £2,000 to cover both land and building costs. He spent his evenings and weekends digging trenches and doing whatever he could to help, but he employed contractors to do the actual building.

Robert Woodward was no longer just a painter and decorator: he upgraded himself to clerk of works to supervise the building of his own home. He put in endless hours of hard work and admits to making many horrendous mistakes; when it went well over budget, he wrote it off as part of learning new skills.

The marriage of Mr Robert Norman Woodward and Miss Judy Edmonds took place at Eastville Park Methodist church on 15 February 1958. This date was also significant in that it marked a rare local event: an FA Cup tie between Bristol Rovers and their rivals, City, at Ashton Gate. Bob was a great Rovers supporter but his brother John, followed City. By the end of the day, Bob had married the girl of his dreams and Bristol Rovers had won their match. Result!

Judy looked radiant in her white wedding gown and was attended by four bridesmaids: Bob's sister Diane and Judy's cousin Mary wore green velvet; Judy's sister Margaret and her best friend Miriam were resplendent in red. Bob's best man Harold Neal, along with the rest of the men, looked dashing in their hired Moss Bros morning suits. Bob's morning suit, however, concealed underpants and vest borrowed from his brother John, because he could not find his own in the family's airing cupboard. The Life Boys, the junior section of the Boys' Brigade, provided the happy couple with a guard of honour, after which a smart reception for 100 guests was held at the Berkeley Hotel at the top of Park Street. Aunt Joyce clearly remembered how much in love the couple were; she had also not forgotten that it was a Methodist wedding where not a drop of drink was evident.

Harold delivered the best man's speech, which included a joke that no one laughed at, before Judy's Aunt May, a lady well into her eighties, rose to her feet. She admitted it was unusual for a woman to stand up and speak at a wedding but she felt she must. Registering her approval, she said that Bob and Judy were well suited and were tireless workers; wherever the couple chose to settle, the community would surely benefit from their efforts.

A cine-camera recorded the wedding day and, rather like the *Wizard of Oz*, showed the outdoor scenes in colour but the interior sequences were in black and white.

'Judy looked absolutely gorgeous on our wedding day,' reminisced Bob. 'I shall never, never understand why she was interested in me.'

Mr and Mrs Woodward chose to honeymoon in Newquay, the setting of several summer holidays with Judy's family, where they now experienced the delights of a Cornish winter. When they returned to Bristol a week later, the newspaper placards reported the latest news on the Munich air disaster, in which several Manchester United players had died.

After the honeymoon, the only cloud on the horizon was Bob's anxiety about his mother. He missed her and, knowing that Beatrice did not have the happiest of lives, the thought of not seeing her every day was difficult for him to cope with. He was her liveliest, most unpredictable son; he felt he used to brighten her day and now he was no longer there for her. 'I thought I was contributing to her unhappiness.'

Bob and Judy moved into two sparsely furnished rooms in their new bungalow at Claverham. For fifteen months, they lived in a meagrely equipped kitchen with just a table, four chairs and a second-hand tea trolley on which stood a black and white, 12-inch television set—a wedding present. They slept in a simply furnished bedroom and cold linoleum covered both kitchen and bedroom floors.

In spite of their frugal lifestyle, finding the monthly mortgage repayments of fifteen guineas eventually became too much of a struggle and they had no choice other than to sell their new home. This turned out to be a significant step as the sale showed an impressive £1,100 profit and was the foundation of exciting things to come. Proud though surprised at the size of the gain, Bob held on to the cheque for a week before banking it, as a daily reminder of a successful first foray into the housing market.

For their next home, they moved into a scruffy little flat in the Staple Hill area of Bristol. After six long weeks, they bought a house overlooking the green pitch of the Co-op cricket ground in Overndale Road (the same road Bob had lived in as a child) and were in the satisfying position of being able to find a third of the total cost. The house needed some attention and so Bob worked on it in the evenings and at weekends, always taking care not to intrude on church time. Two years later, after making another successful sale, he financed two-thirds of the cost of a semi-detached house in Frenchay.

1. Bob in 1937 aged four.

2. Bob and Judy on a day trip to Brighton.

3. Bob and Judy leave Eastville Park Methodist church in Bristol after their wedding in 1958 *(Western Daily Press)*.

4. Judy with Robert aged six months. *(J.L. Matthews).*

5. Hugh aged three months.

6. Rachel aged three months *(Navana Photos).*

7. James aged three months.

9. Bob with his demolition gang *(David Iddles)*.

8. Market Street, Wotton-under-Edge, in decay *(David Iddles)*.

10. The first two phases of the Parklands development at Wotton-under-Edge *(David Iddles)*.

11. Bob surveys the start of demolition at Market Street in Wotton *(David Iddles)*.

12. Market Street rebuilt, for which Bob and John received a European Architectural Heritage Year award in 1975 *(David Iddles)*.

13. Judy, Bob, Rachel, Robert and James in the Tabernacle at the beginning of the mosaic project in 1974 *(David Iddles)*.

14. The central section of the mosaic with an overhead drawing of the original *(David Iddles)*.

15. The Great Orpheus Pavement in its new home at Prinknash Abbey. *(Gloucestershire Gazette Series)*.

16. Robert aged six and in his Wolves football kit.

17. Sister Frances Dominica, the founder of Helen House in Oxford, the world's first children's hospice.

18. Professor David Baum, Head of Child Health at the University of Bristol and president of the Royal College of Paediatrics and Child Health.

19. The Duchess of Kent, patron of CLIC, with Bob at the opening of the CLIC Annexe *(Malcolm Simmonds)*.

20. CLIC House, Fremantle Street, Cotham, Bristol *(Malcolm Simmonds)*.

21. Judy and James with Bob after he received an honorary degree from the University of Bristol *(Malcolm Simmonds)*.

22. John Nickolls is crowned `King of the Jumble' at the CLIC Shops Conference at Bristol Grammar School *(Malcolm Simmonds)*.

23. HTV news presenter Bruce Hockin opening the CLIC shop at Downend with Bob, John Nickolls and the manager, Hazel Wilson *(Malcolm Simmonds).*

24. Jane Seymour, Father Christmas and Bob with children at a Christmas party held at her home, St Catherine's Court *(Malcom Simmonds).*

25. Paul Newman greets Bob at the Hole in the Wall Gang Camp in Connecticut.

26. Lesley Gesa, her mother Margaret and Bob after Lesley's sponsored walk.

27. Mikhail Gorbachev greets David Baum and Bob at the Gorbachev Foundation in Moscow.

28. Mikhail Gorbachev signing the documents to become president of CLIC International.

29. Mikhail Gorbachev and Bob in a bear-hug embrace.

30. The 1994 Channel Tunnel charity walk.

31. Bob carries three polystyrene children around the London Marathon course in 1995.

32. Kate Jeffery with her brother Eddie and Bob.

33. Bob with the ageing owner of the dacha shown below.

34. The timber dacha in Minsk which Bob visited.

35. Daniel Palumbo enjoying his yellow balloon *(Palumbo Family)*.

36. Bob, Charlie Dobson and Mary Dobson with the Jack and Jill Appeal chairman David Giles at the presentation of £1 million from the Starfish Trust to the new children's unit at Frenchay Hospital *(Gloucestershire Gazette Series)*.

37. Bob has lots of help laying the foundation stone for the Barbara Russell Children's Unit at Frenchay Hospital *(Western Daily Press)*.

38. Bob receiving the Freedom of the City of Bristol from the Lady Mayor and Lady Mayoress *(Paul Gillis)*.

39. Outside the CLIC flats in Budapest the head of the children's unit, Professor Gyorgy Fekete, presents Bob with a medal of appreciation, accompanied by Professor Dezslo Schuler *(Warren Linham)*.

9

To Judy and Bob, a Daughter, Rachel

Bob and Judy both longed for children and their wish became reality when their daughter, Rachel Judith, was born on 10 November 1962 in the old Bristol Maternity Hospital. Rachel offered her parents fulfilment of the purest kind.

Bob was elated with his new daughter but it never occurred to him to take flowers into Judy when he visited her. 'Someone mentioned it afterwards and I tried to make up for it but it just wasn't the same as taking flowers in straight after Rachel's birth. I was so disappointed with myself that I now have a fetish for giving flowers. I have given Judy so many baskets of flowers that several times over the years we've had to clear out our store of baskets and return them to the florists.'

The Woodwards' business grew steadily and soon they needed to recruit: enter Johnny Drinkwater, John Woodward's best friend. 'Johnny was a great character but he cut corners. He was the type who would miss out the undercoat and go straight to the gloss whenever he could get away with it,' said Bob.

Even so, Johnny joined the company, which then became Woodward Bros and Drinkwater. Their first job was to cover the vast expanse of ceiling in the large office suite at Hale's cakes factory in Clevedon with ninety rolls of paper. From their elevated working positions on the scaffolding, they were treated to a spectacular view right across the moors to Clevedon and the sight of the fields criss-crossed by water-filled trenches—known locally as rhynes—proved a major distraction for both Bob and Johnny.

'You always reckon you're so flippin' clever, Johnny. See those two pipes spanning the rhynes? I bet you can't walk across those pipes without falling in,' said Bob, laying down an irresistible challenge.

'I bet thee casn't,' retorted Johnny, revealing his strong Bristol roots.

'I bet I can.'

'Bet thee casn't,' repeated Johnny.

'Well, what would you bet me that I can't cross those pipes without falling in, then?'

'Bet thee five bob thee casn't,' said Johnny confidently.

Challenge accepted, they downed tools and marched over the fields to the nearest rhyne. From the muddy bank, they could see that a central collar encircled the larger pipe and that the narrower pipe sprouted green algae along its surface. Bob, smartly attired in painter's white bib and brace, crept gingerly along the slimy pipe and over the collar. Loudly guffawing, Johnny leapt about, jumped up and down and made a huge effort to distract his workmate but Bob reached the far side without mishap.

'Thee's gotta come back on that litl'un now,' laughed Johnny in demented glee.

Bob considered the dicey return journey and started out for the middle; he was barely two feet across when Johnny's continuous hullabaloo finally took effect and he too began to laugh; he lost concentration and started to wobble. Dropping through the reeds into the fetid, thigh high water, it took him several attempts to scramble up the slippery, muddy bank when, defeated, he squelched his sodden way back to work followed by the hysterical Johnny.

'I watched the whole thing in amazement,' said Bob's brother, John. 'I just couldn't believe that people of their age could be quite so dopey.'

By now, it was lunchtime and the humiliation of being seen by the young girls leaving the factory was unavoidable. The girls stopped in their tracks to stare and giggle at the approaching apparition fetchingly draped in green pondweed, but the apparition kept its head down and quickly made its way back to the office where it took off its bib and brace to remove its soaking wet underpants and socks. Climbing back into his soggy bib and brace, Bob was horrified to see Leslie Hawkins approaching.

'Bob,' Leslie called out. 'I just wanted to catch you. There's an urgent job I want you to see.'

Reeking strongly of pond slime, looking at an urgent job was the last thing Bob wanted to do. Leslie glanced quizzically in the direction of Bob's shoes but the absence of socks was the least of Bob's problems. 'I was more worried that my overalls might come apart and he would see that I was not wearing underpants. How embarrassing that would have been.'

When he was not causing mayhem, Johnny Drinkwater had his uses: for cash flow, he was indispensable. Johnny kept chickens in his backyard and when customers were slow in paying their bills, Woodward Bros and Drinkwater lived on Johnny's egg money. The partnership dissolved when the daily grind of travelling from Bristol got too much for John and Johnny who decided to work closer to home, so the business (Bob and one painter) reverted to R.N. Woodward.

In the meantime, Bob's business relationship with Leslie Hawkins continued to flourish. Phase one at Hales factory was completed and, although there would be a delay of four months before work could start on phase two, Leslie, keen to retain Bob's services, offered to pay him and his painter to remain on site rather than risk losing them.

It was not long before they became bored with the inactivity. Bob's painter Bob Osmond—'King of the Portishead Teddy Boys'—was always ready for a bit of fun and they constructed a small raft and sailed it up the rhynes for something to do. But the devil soon found other work for their idle hands.

'We made brown paper-bag water bombs and waited quietly on the rooftop during lunchtime for the factory workers to leave the tea-hut,' said Bob. 'As they passed below us, we dropped the water bombs on to their unsuspecting heads. Then we scooted down the ladder, pretended to come out of the lavatories and innocently asked them what had happened.'

The two Bobs got away with it; they thought it was a howl.

On the financial front, things were looking up for Bob and Judy. There was money for extras and it gave them great pleasure to purchase a brand new three-piece suite from Maples, an up-market furniture store at the top of Park Street. The indulgence of sitting comfortably in their own home is not forgotten and that same suite, now re-covered, is still in use.

Colourful adverts proliferating in the press for the Charles Atlas Body Building Course caught hold of Bob's imagination and he became an enthusiastic purchaser of a twelve-week correspondence course with its promises of a muscular body. As enticing as the photographs of Mr Atlas were, however, Bob did not possess the necessary discipline to complete the programme. More than fifty years on, it still resides, in mint condition, in the loft of his home; Bob never attained the physique that Charles Atlas promised.

In business too, things were looking up: John rejoined him and, after a soul-searching discussion about making only average wages from small jobs, they considered buying land and becoming property developers. To this end, they bought their first pick-up truck, a Morris Oxford, which ran beautifully when empty. 'Great truck providing there was nothing in it,' said Bob.

Harold Neal introduced them to J.W. Ward, a firm of solicitors, and suggested they see Vic New, one of the senior partners, for business advice and finance. Bob immediately donned his only suit and naively called at the solicitor's home that evening. He was told to go away (nicely, of course) and make an appointment to see Mr New at his office.

'I met him at his premises in Small Street in the centre of Bristol, and

I will never forget the padded door between the reception area and his office,' said Bob. 'I fully expected this door to lead straight into his office but instead, a second door confronted me, which threw me and made me a bit nervous; it was a double office door, with the outer one padded for soundproofing. When the inner door opened and a six-foot three-inch beanpole thrust his hand towards me and said, "Good morning, Mr Woodward", I smartly echoed, "Good morning, Mr Woodward."'

Vic New was charming and soon put Bob at ease. They discussed the Woodward brothers' plans to become developers and the predicament of not having enough money to carry out these hopes and dreams. Bob built his case persuasively; he and John would put in endless time and effort and would not draw on the business until they had proved themselves builders of quality. From that moment, the firm of J.W. Ward became their financial backers and handled all their property dealings. This was a tremendous triumph because, being such small fry without any assets, it would have been most unlikely for the High Street banks to consider them for an overdraft. Woodward Bros was on its way.

Although Bob had worked as a labourer on his own bungalow, to build a complete house from scratch was new to him so he sent Judy to Downend library for books on how to become a builder. She brought home two—*How to Plumb* and *How to Build your own House*. Bob showed no interest in the book on plumbing but read *How to Build* twice, an example of commitment given his disinclination 'to waste valuable time reading'. He was now prepared for anything the building trade might throw at him.

His resolve to succeed, coupled with his mother-in-law's words, 'Bob will never make a builder,' spurred him on. When he saw an advertisement for three plots of land at Charnhill near Mangotsfield, on the outskirts of Bristol, even though it was eight o'clock at night and too dark to see anything, he hared off to look at them. The owner, who lived next door to the land, obligingly pointed out the three building plots by the light of the moon. Bob shook the man's hand, insisting that the land not be sold to anyone else until he returned in daylight. At 6.30 the next morning he was back. J.W. Ward came up with the money and the foundations were laid—but a bitter lesson in building quickly followed.

Impetuosity, coupled with lack of experience, led them to fail miserably when constructing a steel reinforced, concrete-capped, external chimneystack. After laying sheets of asbestos over floor joists in the sitting room of the first house, concrete was poured into the shuttering and left to harden. A week later, after removing the shuttering, the cap looked splendid. Two men attempted to lift it up the ladder to the top of the chimneystack; then, four tried to lift it; then, eight men attempted to haul it up. It was too heavy—and it was an absolute failure. They could do nothing with this concrete behemoth other than break it up and let it drop between the joists. 'It is most probably there to this day,' Bob said.

They made another cap outside at the base of the ladders but the finished product could only be lifted as high as the first rung; that cap too ended in pieces. Finally, they bowed to the inevitable, re-read the drawings and followed the plans carefully. They carried the materials up the ladder, erected the shuttering and floated the concrete in situ. 'Another lesson in life,' said Bob. 'Never cut corners.'

The Hoare family purchased the house on completion and Woodward Bros became known as the builders of the Mangotsfield Hoare house. The partnership now attracted quality craftsmen from the locality such as Geoff Bateman and Wes Bond, who worked with the company for sixteen years.

Woodward Bros bought a sizeable property called The Mount at Frampton Cottrell from their cousin Terry. They demolished it and built ten homes in its grounds. This development was quickly followed by another twelve houses in North Road, Yate. Then came their chance of a lifetime: an opportunity to buy eighteen acres of land in Wotton-under-Edge for £54,000, a giant leap and by far their biggest challenge. It could make or break them.

10

The Houses that Bob and John Built

In the 1960s major developers were gobbling up great tracts of building land in Yate, which became the fastest growing urban development in Europe. These large housing estates often used the Radburn scheme, where the layout of the site was pedestrian segregated. New developments up and down the country looked strikingly similar and featured clusters of homes grouped around central blocks of garages and tarmac parking areas. This style of building originated in the United States in the 1920s but had been sensibly abandoned there by the time it was adopted by UK planning authorities. John and Bob had no desire to succumb to the Radburn scheme of building sixteen houses to the acre, as was common practice in Yate; they sought to stamp a seal of quality on everything that carried their name and, wanting to create distinctive homes, they looked elsewhere to build.

Bob viewed a parcel of land that had been up for sale for two years in Wotton-under-Edge and, being familiar with the area, it really appealed to him. The asking price was £54,000; it consisted of eighteen acres, a prime site for building an upmarket development of seven houses to the acre. In spite of the fact that it was gloriously situated, with a wooded backdrop, the land had attracted little interest because there were complications.

There were three areas of concern. Other developers considered it to be too far from the city—eighteen miles—although this did not trouble Bob and John. There was also a particular challenge regarding the water supply: the Wotton watercourse ran downhill through the swampy site and the land would need extensive drainage work before a single brick could be laid. But by far the biggest challenge lay in how they could overcome the Radburn scheme.

Dick Pearse, a tenant farmer, bought the land in the 1950s not realising for some time that planning permission for housing development had been granted a number of years before. Later, armed with this knowledge, he decided to sell and took on local firm Howes, Luce, Williams and Panes as agents. A condition of the sale was that a purchaser would inherit the existing architects' bills from Richard Kingscott and John Kendall and be committed to using the Radburn scheme. Then, Tom Parker, a developer from Yate, took up an option to buy the site.

'What a dilemma for us,' said Bob. 'There was this beautiful parcel of land but it was far from a straightforward purchase.'

At the risk of losing their money, Woodward Bros offered Tom Parker £2,000 for an option on the land—but he stipulated that they had to complete the transaction in six weeks. There was no time to waste.

They began to research styles of properties to build on Parklands, the chosen name for the development. To this end, Bob and the selling agent, Jim Panes, racked up 2,000 miles in Jim's Jaguar Mk X exploring the Cotswolds and beyond for new ideas; a vital exercise if they were to present a convincing argument to overturn the current permission.

After making noises to the council about the Radburn scheme, Bob went straight to the chief planning officer, Norman Collins. Then he and Jim Panes recruited sympathetic local figures to support their argument. The persistent duo pestered Sir Alan Durrand, known locally as the Squire of Wotton, two or three times a week until he came on board, and soon, the vicar of St Mary's in Wotton, the Revd Freddie Sillett, followed suit.

'Because we made such a rumpus,' said Bob, 'I got a telephone call from Norman Collins's office agreeing to a half-hour meeting at the planning offices in Barnwood, Gloucester, at 8.30 the following morning.'

He arrived in plenty of time and took two hours of his allotted 'thirty minutes' to talk about their alternative plans; initially, they would build terraced houses at the front of the site with rear access (Bob and John's only compromise to the Radburn scheme); bungalows and houses would follow as the development progressed. When eventually the Radburn scheme was overturned, Bob's success stuck in the craws of more established builders in the area. He was viewed as a young upstart.

The Woodward brothers were now ready to take on the next challenge: the Wotton watercourse. In order to drain the site effectively they would have to channel water down the hillside, across the main road, through a business car park and into the local stream, a disruptive course of action that needed to be closely managed.

Bob approached Philip Brooke, of the Brooke Bond family, who owned the affected business, Collotype, to explain the problem and the solution of draining Parklands, which would affect access to Collotype's car park. By scheduling the work to begin on Maundy Thursday with a promise of completion by the Tuesday after Easter, they agreed a plan that allowed the minimum of disruption. So with everything lined up, they went ahead and bought the land.

But unseasonal snow at Easter and other delays ruined their timetable and in the end, Collotype's car park was closed for six weeks. Its employees were forced to leave their cars outside in the road and a director's car suffered accidental damage. Things got worse when Collotype was unable to take delivery of bulky loads of paper and Woodward Bros found themselves paying for transport and storage at nearby Charfield village hall.

'It was a nightmare,' said Bob, 'but there was something so exciting about it all. How fortunate we were to be able to deal with Philip Brooke, who was delightful and a perfect gentleman. He was so helpful and understanding; after all, we adversely affected his business for several weeks.'

Because of the size of the projected development, Woodward Bros approached Lloyds Bank for finance. Although the brothers considered their business small (but with sights aimed high), they struck out and committed to high capital expenditure; against their normal practice, they purchased plant from Reed Bros and Bailey instead of hiring it. They were now into the bank for a lot of money.

This beautiful location called out for sympathetic building and plans were drawn up in a variety of designs for the site. Much thought went into the layout of the landscaping, leaving existing mature trees to enhance the common areas. Work started on the terraced houses built of Bradley Stone at the front of the Parklands development. All the homes featured an innovative central heating system called the Brick Central Flue System by Husqvarna that distributed heat to all rooms from a central brick chimney shaft and a single giant Shell-Mex oil tank fuelled the whole site from the top of the hillside.

This was a financially scary time. Woodwards Bros had flown in the face of more experienced builders and it had been a brave step to take when no one was sure how it would go. Moreover, the houses at Parklands were different: Wotton had not seen the like before.

Norman Collins, chief planning officer, inspected the standard of work on the terraced houses and was delighted with the quality: a good start, but it was early days. Only in the selling phase would they discover whether Parklands had been a good investment, and everything now depended on the selling expertise of Jim Panes. Four houses were offered for sale at £2,600 each but they stood empty for weeks.

'For heaven's sake sell some of them,' Bob told Jim.

'Stick some of your brickies in them, and then there'll be curtains in the windows. If it looks like some have sold then you are more likely to get sales,' the agent retaliated.

Sham curtains never hung in the windows, however, because suddenly the new properties at Parklands began to sell.

'Thankfully, they sold,' said Bob. 'Ten terraced ones to begin with, and then sales gained momentum as interest in Parklands grew.'

Gradually, the Woodwards built a reputation for their quality houses and Parklands attracted professional people from all over the country. Many of the buyers worked in Bristol but had no wish to live in the city. As the houses filled, the local community benefited economically and socially as new residents set up branches of Rotary and Round Table.

Parklands became the yardstick by which other developments were judged and the firm's proud workforce often took their families for a drive around the estate to show off the new homes. Most of the sub-contract builders remained loyal to the Woodwards. 'We had a great team of around 20 who all enjoyed a sense of belonging.' Extremely fit, possessing boundless energy, Bob led by example and ensured that he worked as hard as his workforce: delivery drivers were astonished when he pitched in, helping to unload the lorries.

One of the great selling features of Parklands was that they accommodated requests for alterations or additions, and some were sizeable: a granny annexe for example. On one occasion, to help a new buyer, Bob found himself driving to London to pick up a 90-year-old man to bring him back to Wotton. On another he agreed to raise the roof level of a bungalow to increase the ceiling height throughout—no small feat—so that the owner's collection of grandfather clocks would fit in without recourse to a hacksaw. It mattered to Bob that people enjoyed living in the homes that he and John built. 'I've always felt that where people live influences their lives from the moment they get up in the morning to the time they go to bed.'

He often visits Parklands to relive happy memories and enjoys chatting to some of the original residents who, after more than thirty years, still live there.

'We frequently did extremely well when we took on things that no one else wanted. Until we got rid of the Radburn scheme, no one wanted Parklands. After that, of course, everyone said how stupid they'd been not to have done the same.'

During these successful years, John and Bob moved their parents to a nice little house in Westbourne Road, Downend. Later on, they moved them into a smarter house in the same locality before finally settling them into a bungalow when Cyril and Beatrice became frail.

They also bought them a car, a Hillman Minx; on the day it was delivered, Cyril drove straight over to the Parklands site. He had mellowed over the years and got a tremendous kick out of his sons' success. Not only had his sons 'made it', they had made it in Wotton-under-Edge, where he had spent most of his early years. Nothing could have given him greater joy and he was very proud of them; however, it also became one of Cyril's few topics of conversation and this pride manifested itself as boasting, which led to family misunderstandings and, indirectly, to an estrangement between Bob and John and their brother David that continued for a number of years.

'I wouldn't have anything to do with them but it was only because of that,' said David Woodward. 'Every time you went there, Father was always talking about my brothers and how they were doing. No disrespect to them but maybe I got a bit jealous at times. I probably did because I wasn't doing as well. That friction was there and it's a great shame really, it stays with you all through life.'

David and his wife, May, emigrated to New Zealand in the late spring of 1973, and although the detachment between the brothers had continued, Bob felt quite broken-hearted. 'Here was my brother whom I didn't know terribly well, leaving to live on the other side of the world. I got quite upset about it.'

11

To Judy and Bob a Son, Robert

In 1965 Judy gave birth to their first son, Robert Clifford, a brother for Rachel.

'He was 10 lb 3 oz so it was easy enough to spot him in the hospital,' said Bob. 'He was everything we could wish for, strikingly handsome with blue eyes and blonde hair.'

Relatives said that Robert would be a heartbreaker. Little did anyone know how accurate that description would turn out to be and in which way Robert would break so many hearts.

In 1966, in appreciation of a valuable client, Shell-Mex gave Bob two tickets to see the World Cup semi-final between England and Portugal at Wembley and he took Clifford, his father-in-law, along with him. It was an evening to remember, watching the greats like Charlton, Eusebio and Moore battle it out for a place in the final. England won and when three more tickets arrived from Shell-Mex for the final, Bob invited his brother-in-law Don to join them. The events of that day are part of well-documented sporting history.

'The atmosphere was incredible and afterwards we saw the cup and got to speak to some of the players. Everybody was on a high.'

Following this momentous footballing occasion, Bob took regular trips to Europe to see England play, including France, West Germany, Greece and Belgium. A notable aspect of these sporting excursions was the lack of hooliganism; he and his friends enjoyed the travel and the atmosphere at the games in peace and safety.

Meanwhile John's life took a more committed turn when he met Carol Organ, who made grocery deliveries to the new residents on Parklands. Their relationship grew serious and they became engaged. Carol's father, who ran the local grocer's shop, gave his blessing on condition that they marry on half-day closing. So, on one Wednesday afternoon in 1967, John married Carol in St Mary's church, Wotton, directly opposite Parklands. Their reception was held in the Moore Court Hotel, Minchin-hampton, and after their honeymoon they moved into a Woodward Bros house on Parklands.

Bob, ever the practical joker, was best man and could not resist playing a trick on his brother. John thought that he had made sure that no one could tamper with his suitcase but Bob found it and removed all of his brother's underpants and pyjama bottoms. When John discovered that Bob had been the culprit, he told him that the hotel staff had displayed Carol's nightie on one pillow and his lonely pyjama jacket on the other, both fashionably pinched in at the waist.

Although Parklands was a success, Woodward Bros continued to buy and sell parcels of land elsewhere, working alongside Jim Panes. Not everything turned into a pot of gold; indeed, land at The Hackett in Thornbury and Wick at Downend turned out to be extremely poor investments. Nevertheless, in 1968 when he was 35, Bob was able to build his growing family Spruce House in Frenchay—their family home to this day.

Then a guesthouse in Malmesbury, Wiltshire, with a stable block suitable for conversion, came on to the market. It also had two building plots, one at the side and one to the rear. Both Bob and Jim Panes liked it, so Bob bought it for Woodward Bros, and work began almost immediately in the stable block, which was to be used as a studio for the Woodward's new venture: mosaics.

Bob had renewed an old acquaintance in a talented mosaicist named Brian Bull and, after visiting his studio, Bob and John bought Brian's business, (lock, stock and mosaics). The three of them then started a company called Abbey Studios, named after Malmesbury Abbey. It was suggested that they form a limited company—a new venture for Bob and John as they both held strong beliefs in the ethics of personal responsibility.

Brian Bull specialised in table tops and used a new type of polyester resin in which he cast his finished mosaics. The tops looked most impressive. Another member of Judy's family, Ken Barrett, designed the bases for the tables, which, after assembly, were displayed in the newly converted studio in the stable block.

The new venture started well: there were enquiries from Heals in Tottenham Court Road and from Harrods of Knightsbridge (via Reg Snow at Kandya, the kitchen supplier for Parklands), but problems loomed. The smart new tables were taken to Heals for perusal. The first table top survived the scratch test of a two-shilling piece drawn across its surface: the resin face remained smooth and even. Unfortunately, to the embarrassment of the company, subsequent table tops fared somewhat poorly and showed clear signs of scratches and indents.

What seemed to have happened was that the resilient resin mix for the first table top had been chanced upon and could not be reproduced for later batches. There must have been many attempts at finding the original resin mix formula because, some time later on, batches of discarded mix came to light in a variety of unlikely places. They were found buried in the studio garden and some filled old Victorian urns dotted around the property in Malmesbury. No one was ever sure where the next cache would be discovered.

The mosaics themselves were rather beautiful but the finished products did not satisfy the retailers' demands and production of the tables was abandoned. This was not one of Bob's finest moments.

The company went on to produce a number of mosaics including one of the arms of the City of Bristol for the Bristol 600 Exhibition staged to celebrate the 600th anniversary of the city receiving its charter of incorporation. Nowadays, visitors to Bob's garden shed may come upon some original table tops as well as a number of homeless artistic mosaics.

A number of people made strong impressions on Bob and amongst the most notable of these was a deacon of Fishponds Baptist church, Sigmund West, who years earlier had encouraged Bob to become a Sunday school teacher. Sigmund asked Bob to take on the role of assistant fabric officer and Bob, with his band of volunteers, kept the church to the finest standard during his office. The role involved turning his hand to anything that needed doing: repairs to the church gates, upkeep of the roof, and both interior and exterior works as well as decoration and general maintenance. His responsibilities also covered sourcing reliable contractors and negotiating the best deal on behalf of the church. Other local churches called on Bob for his expertise and he was happy to oblige. He fulfilled this role at Fishponds Baptist church for a period of 27 years.

Bob remembered his time with Sigmund with great affection. Once he asked Bob to report to the church committee about transplanting some laurel bushes from the front of the church to the graveyard at the side. When the laurels did not survive, Sigmund took Bob to one side and asked him to inject some humour into his monthly report. Looking into the faces of the gathered church members, Bob delivered the report.

'I am terribly sorry about the loss of the laurel bushes but, being realistic about it, when they found themselves moved into the graveyard, perhaps they thought they *should* die. Unfortunately, the laurels proved not to be hardy. But then ... would you expect a Laurel to be Hardy?' This quip produced a few laughs and the atmosphere lightened.

Bob's use of humour helped him on another such occasion. There were constant complaints over the poorly documented plan of the graveyard and so a new plan was drawn up using letters for rows and numbers for columns. Every grave could now be quickly identified and located. In his usual fashion Sigmund took Bob to one side and asked him to explain the plan in a humorous way.

'We have now numbered the graves on a grid pattern basis but we have taken the liberty of excluding some letters. You will soon realise why,' Bob began. 'Only last week, a lady came here to find where her relative was buried. I looked at the old plan and had to tell her that her relative was in "L". When another lady arrived, I had to tell her that her husband was in "L" too. So, forgive me, but there is no longer a row "L".'

Over the years, Bob became known as the Fishponds church estate agent and, with Sigmund, found the first manse for their church. It was a deal that had to be done quickly, leaving no time for formalities. Despite Sigmund's anxiety and the lack of committee approval, driven by the thought of losing such an opportunity, Bob went ahead to purchase the manse on behalf of the church anyway.

'I thought they would be so pleased,' said Bob, 'but what a risk. Once or twice I thought what have I done?'

Nevertheless, he had full confidence in his judgement and, over the years, he located around thirty houses, negotiating both purchases and sales, for a number of the congregation who gave generously to the church fund for his services.

One day Sigmund told Bob that he thought he had strained himself carrying some lights into the church. They had been far too heavy for him but he had not asked for help. Within 48 hours, on 16 April 1969, Sigmund West died. He was 57. It came as an immense shock to Bob who suffered the loss of a loved and valued friend. Sigmund's sudden death affected the whole church; he was a very special man and much loved by them all.

12

Brazil 1 England 0

England defended their World Cup in the summer of 1970 and Bob made an eventful trip to Mexico.

The aircraft experienced engine trouble over Maine and was forced to land in Bangor, USA. The passengers, who were on a bonded flight, had to remain in the hangar while the engine was being repaired. As there were no plans to stop off in the United States, no one had any dollars to pay for snacks when they were offered them; their foreign currency consisted entirely of Mexican pesos. This unscheduled stopover increased their journey time to a wearisome 36 hours and, even then, their troubles were only just beginning.

Although the group of football supporters were under the impression that they would be staying in Mexico City, they were transferred by coach to Cuernavaca, a small city in the mountains some 50 miles from the capital. The exhausted England fans arrived at midnight Mexico time, six hours behind GMT.

England's match against Brazil, their second of the tournament, was scheduled for the next day but if the supporters were to arrive in time for the match they would have to travel by coach back to Mexico City to catch another flight to Guadalajara, some 350 miles to the north-west. Most of the group could not face more travel but Bob and Ken Barrett, tired but determined, set off at 2.30 in the morning. Once in Guadalajara, they made their way to a hotel to pick up their tickets from their contact, a travel agent who worked for James Vance Travel Agents in London. They were disappointed: the agent had absconded. What were they to do?

Close to the football ground but with no means of entry, the intrepid duo ignored the warning that armed police were intent on cracking down on ticket touts and strode into the midst of the throng. They soon found a tout with a single ticket and then another who sold them one more but for a different part of the ground. Even though they were in some doubt as to the authenticity of the tickets, they separated and went off to their respective parts of the stadium. The dense crowd filled the gangways and prevented Bob from reaching his seat. When he tried to push his way through, he witnessed a man setting fire to a rolled up newspaper before lobbing it into the multitude—instantly creating a space where before there was none. This novel form of crowd clearing was being used successfully throughout the stadium.

Unused to the altitude and such high temperatures, the sweat poured off the England players. Nevertheless, the game was remarkable: the Banks save, the Astle miss and England losing 1–0 to a Jairzinho goal. Bob had never experienced an atmosphere quite like it and, despite the result, there was no crowd trouble to contend with. The Brazilian contingent freely displayed their passion for both the game and the victory.

After the arduous return journey, the lack of sleep, the extreme heat and the punishing altitude all took their toll and the two friends collapsed with exhaustion. Late that same evening the oppressive Mexican humidity enticed the unhappy band of cheated supporters into the cool water of the hotel swimming pool until three or four in the morning where they reflected on the unresolved problems of the stolen tickets and the errant travel agent.

England's progress to the quarter-finals against West Germany involved a further 700-mile round trip to Leon—but they had no tickets. In a nearby bar they met a party of Swedes who said they could arrange tickets to the match if Bob and his companions could find enough people to fill a coach. When they demanded payment up front, several in the English camp heard alarm bells ringing and declined the offer in fear of losing more money but for Bob it was an opportunity not to be missed and he came up with a plan to keep an eye on the Swedes around the clock. Even so, only four of their party decided to chance it. All looked lost until a party of Germans turned up to stay at the same hotel. Bob was quick to rally support among them. The Germans were more amenable to the Swedes' offer and, more important, there were enough of them to fill the coach.

'We now had four English and 38 Germans sharing a coach. The Germans joined in the surveillance and we never let the Swedes out of our sight,' said Bob.

The coach left for Mexico City and, on arrival, the Swedes picked up the tickets, accompanied by a posse of English and German football supporters. Those who waited anxiously on board heaved a collective sigh of relief when the Swedes emerged shortly afterwards to hand out the tickets. But it was not over: the supporters insisted that the Swedes accompany them all the way to the stadium gate just in case the tickets turned out to be counterfeit. All was well, however, and they entered the ground without incident.

The game began well for England and, at 2–0 up, the four English supporters, undaunted by the unfavourable ratio, treated their newly acquired German associates to some friendly banter. Events soon turned the score on its head and a 2–0 lead ended in an agonising 3–2 defeat. Bob's heart dropped into his boots; it was unbelievable.

The exultant Germans quenched their thirst in the local bars before filling the central aisle of the coach with crates of beer. Several of them picked on Bob because he was not drinking beer and they thought he was insulting them by not joining in but he stuck bravely to his 7-Ups. As the journey progressed, bottles were smashed, beer flowed down the aisle and the deterioration of the *entente cordiale* inevitably led to some fighting talk. When they arrived back at the coach depot in Mexico City, a forbidding welcoming party awaited them: La Policia had been tipped off about possible trouble and they surrounded the coach.

'As soon as we pulled in we thought, that's funny, there's a lot of police cars here,' said Bob. 'They ringed the coach and I thought what the flippin' hell's going on here? Having said that, I wasn't sad to see them. Some of the Germans were out of their minds because they'd won and I felt threatened. There was no way we were going to come out of it terribly well—there were just too many of them but I considered I stood a better chance because I hadn't been drinking. If I had to swing my fists it would be far better to aim at faces that weren't blurred.'

The police told the occupants to vacate the vehicle and to wait quietly while the broken bottles were cleared away and the coach was hosed down inside and out. By the end of another long day, Bob and his companions were delivered safely back to their hotel, but even though their lives were intact they were inconsolable because England were out of the World Cup.

The holiday package included a week in Acapulco where the heat was yet more intense and every day their clothes were drenched in sweat. It was a beach holiday, which suited Bob because, although not a great swimmer, he loved the open sea. On their first day, after being warned of strong currents, the group did no more than paddle ankle-deep in the Pacific. Next day, the boldest lured some of the others further out, where, with the relentless sun beating down on their backs and daringly far from shore, they watched a wall of water surge towards them; before they could take evasive action, they all disappeared beneath a freak wave.

'I couldn't really say just how high the wave was and it is easy to exaggerate these things but it must have been at least fifteen feet,' said Bob. Whatever its true dimensions, it was certainly more than his five-foot nine inches and it quickly carried him away. 'As I was dragged along the sea floor, the shingle filled my mouth. I could feel its sharpness ripping at the skin on my face and body.'

Suddenly, he broke the surface of the water and gasped for air. 'My heart pounded and there was a deafening echo in my head. I was completely disoriented.'

His eyes searched wildly for the shore; he heard a shout before slipping beneath the waves a second time where his stomach and lungs filled to bursting with seawater. When he broke the surface again, he began to vomit.

'Get him now,' he heard before he disappeared again. Barely conscious, Bob felt strong arms encircle him and a hand lift his chin clear of the water as his rescuer hauled him through the treacherous surf to the shore. A crowd gathered to watch the powerful young swimmer pump seawater from the prone Bob's lungs. Meanwhile, the others had fared somewhat better: a Peruvian tourist dragged Ken to safety while the instigators of the misadventure swam ashore under their own steam. Bob's knight in shining armour turned out to be a Mexican Olympic swimmer by the name of Pedro Hernandez. Without him, Bob would have drowned.

At home, the account of Bob's dramatic rescue hit the headlines in the *Bristol Evening Post*. But the frightening incident left its mark and he suffered a nightmare that haunted him for many years. In his dream he wakes to find his home filling with water; then, panic mounting, he tries to escape the swelling torrent by making his way to the loft. At first, he cannot locate the hatch because, inexplicably, it is in a different place in every nightmare. When at last he finds it, entry to a warm, dry and safe haven is denied him; the hatch is always locked. His near-death experience was a constant reminder of how lucky he was to be living in such comfort with his wife and children when Hernandez and his family lived in such poor circumstances.

Bob talked to his bank manager, Norman Watkins, about sending a gift but how much is enough to give to the man who saved your life? He considered a sum of £5,000 but Norman advised him to send a smaller amount. Although Bob felt he could be more generous, he heeded the professional advice and sent a more modest sum in spite of his misgivings. Soon after, a four-page begging letter from Hernandez dropped on to the doormat. It graphically described a catalogue of misfortune: his brother had been killed and his mother was bereft; she relied on her two sons for her living; if they could not scrape together enough pesos to pay their rent, their home would be taken from them. A second letter followed on the heels of the first, which detailed more hardship and misery:

> On that day when you almost lost your life, my immediate thought
> was to go home and leave you but, as a good Mexican, I plucked
> up courage and dived in to save your life. In those moments of

great anguish, near to death, I am sure you thought of how much your life is worth. In all my heart, I wish you great success but in my present situation, I am very short of money. My mother weeps for my dead brother and I have to comfort her because she is the only thing I have in my life, next to God. She is everything to me and I have dared to bother you because I have no other to whom I can turn. Answer me quickly.

More letters followed. Bob realised that whatever he did, it would be impossible to satisfy this man's needs and so he took the difficult decision to ignore any subsequent communication, even though this distressed him.

A possible resolution, for Bob at least, presented itself. Alterations were being made to Fishponds Baptist church and, as ever, there was a shortage of funds. There had been some talk about replacing the dilapidated rose window above the church organ, a once stunning, multicoloured, stained-glass casement. In order to save money, the church committee had sanctioned a replacement in plain glass. Bob felt that after the beauty of the original, clear glass would be a poor substitute and so, to thank God for being saved from drowning in Acapulco, he made a donation so that coloured rose panes could be fitted. Over the years the original window had given so much joy and its replacement continues to do so to this day.

Alas, the now desperate Hernandez took a different approach: in his letters, his tone changed from pleading to darker, emotional demands. He had saved Bob's life, he said, he had appealed for help but his pleas had been ignored. Bob searched for other ways to resolve the situation. He wrote to the Mexican tourist board and offered to pay for lifebelts for the beach providing it would send photographic evidence of the installation. He heard nothing and tried again. No reply. He wrote a third time but never got a response from the authorities.

What should have been a wonderful trip of a lifetime almost turned out to be an unmitigated disaster. Bob's bank manager, Norman Watkins, displayed a darkly fiscal sense of humour and summed up the whole episode with the words. 'It doesn't surprise me at all. You always did have trouble keeping your head above water.'

13

To Judy and Bob a Second Son, James Sigmund

James, Bob and Judy's third child, was born on 26 May 1971. This date had a happy coincidence; it was also his grandmother Gwen's birthday. James's middle name, Sigmund, was given in memory of Sigmund West, Bob's great friend.

At eighteen months, little James fell sick to a common infant ailment but it quickly developed into something more serious.

'I could see that Judy was frightened and that really frightened me. Judy had been a nursery nurse; she knew when a child was desperately sick and she could tell immediately that James's cough was very serious,' said Bob.

He rang their GP, Dr Peter Powell, catching him just as he was leaving home. Peter said that he had two calls to make before he could get to them but, within a quarter of an hour, he rang their doorbell. He decided to visit James first because, as a registrar, he had encountered two children with croup in need of tracheotomies but both died before they could be operated on. One look at James was enough. Peter was not one to panic but he came straight to the point.

'Bob, we don't have time to wait for an ambulance. You have to get James to the children's hospital now,' he said.

After carefully settling James into the car with Judy, Bob drove at speed to the city centre. It was rush hour and, in his haste, he hit two cars on the way. He jumped out, gave them his card and told them that he accepted full responsibility and would pay for the damage, whatever the cost. At the hospital, James was put straight into an oxygen tent and within two or three days he turned the corner. 'He's never looked back but we really did come that close to losing him.'

In gratitude for the full recovery of their son, Bob and Judy made a donation to Bristol University and, after talking with Professor Neville Butler, head of the Institute of Child Health, it was given to the Leukaemia Research Fund, which undertook innovative work in childhood leukaemia. Neville would play an important role in the lives of the Woodward family in the not too distant future.

The money for the donation came from a successfully fought court case when Bob, on behalf of Ken Barrett and himself, forced James Vance Travel to account for their Mexican debacle. The travel company's errant employee had still not surfaced. The case took over two years to reach the court in which time the 54 other plaintiffs dropped proceedings. Bob stayed the course and eventually won; his determination to fight the case was a matter of principle and the damages provided a generous gift to charity.

In the early 1970s Lloyds Bank considered Woodward Bros financially over extended; their overdraft was not being reduced anywhere near fast enough for its liking. To Bob and John's consternation Lloyds foreclosed and ordered the sale of Parklands. Jim Panes produced a brochure for the forthcoming auction, promoting Parklands to the full, but such was the economic climate only a handful of prospective buyers turned up. Skilfully, Jim offered Parklands at a non-acceptable figure—to absolute silence. Not a single bid was voiced and the lot was withdrawn. Bob and John breathed sighs of relief. Parklands was still theirs.

14

The Street that Bob and John Rebuilt

A new venture presented itself in 1971. Some time earlier, Market Street in Wotton, the hub of the town, had been closed when the top floor of a four-storey building fell into the road below. It had been a quaint street lined with shops, which boasted architecture spanning some four centuries, and the council's scheme to bulldoze the site and turn it into a car park generated some local resistance. As part of his protest against this potential act of municipal vandalism, Donald Milner, a noted artist and president of the Royal West of England Academy, painted an interpretive watercolour showing a fully restored Market Street. Then, the local *Gazette* featured the forlorn sight of the crumbling street and called out for someone to restore it to its former glory. Until now, there had been no takers.

Jim Panes tempted Bob with the challenge of rebuilding the area and the opportunities to which it could lead. 'Why don't you go there and buy up all the properties?'

'At the time, no one wanted to touch Market Street,' said Bob. 'All those rickety old properties in the centre of Wotton-under-Edge, the one in the middle had fallen into the street—no one wanted to know. I wasn't motivated by the money but I thought it would be lovely to recreate that street. Our bank manager and accountant didn't think it was a good idea at all. It was tricky and it might be difficult to get people to take the shops and get good rents on them. It turned out to be a tremendous amount of hard work, but in the end it was worth it.'

One by one, Woodward Bros negotiated with the owners and bought the properties. Many of the shops had been boarded up for years and in amongst this crumbling structure there still lived some elderly residents. One, a 'dear old spinster', Miss Organ, had lived in Market Street all her life and was desperately worried about what was going to happen to her. She thought that Market Street would never be the same again. A house for sale on the opposite side of the street provided the perfect solution. Bob and John bought it to accommodate Miss Organ and she was able to sit in her front window to watch the old street being pulled down and then rebuilt again. When the work was finally completed, Miss Organ moved back into her renovated flat on the first floor on the other side of the street.

In Bob's opinion, demolition contractors had quoted ridiculous prices to pull down Market Street, and so he assembled his workers from Parklands, showed them the site and asked them if they could do the job. Even though they had never attempted anything like it before, their reaction was positive: with the right equipment, it would be a bit of fun to do. They demolished the street in ten days without mishap.

'For the rebuilding, we hunted around for some local stone and we found a water tower built with the most gorgeous Cotswold stone in a hamlet called Owlpen, just outside Wotton,' said Bob.

The tower belonged to a farmer who wanted to keep the tank but was quite happy for them to take the stone. After removing the tank from the top of the tower, the builders dismantled the structure stone by stone before transporting it to Wotton where the stone was cut and re-dressed to rebuild the whole of one side of Market Street. It was magnificent.

When the council granted planning permission for the reconstruction of Market Street, it made a proviso. 'We had a bit of a run-in with the council over an archway,' said Bob. 'They wanted a central car park in Wotton and insisted that we build an archway in Market Street to provide access to some land at the rear. We put an awful lot of work into that arch and, to give the path a cobbled effect, we floored it with granite cubes. When we asked the council where we should send our bill, they said, "We don't know. Who instructed you to put in the archway? We don't have anything in our minutes." It turned out that the council had never acquired the land for the car park, so we were stuck. After we had gone to all that trouble and left out a unit, we had an archway that led nowhere.'

Apparently, during the council reorganisation of the early seventies, when confusion reigned, the new authority had overlooked buying the land for the car park and no records could be found concerning the archway.

To draw attention to the unpaid bill, Bob got someone to make an eight-foot white elephant out of polystyrene and, late one night, it was loaded onto the back of a truck and taken to Market Street. When the people of Wotton awoke, they found a white elephant blocking the archway with a big sign on it displaying the amount the council owed the Woodwards.

'Even then, we finished up having to take legal action to get our money. Two weeks before we were due to go to court, they paid up. They strung us along for a couple of years on that one.'

The local community followed the reconstruction of Market Street with great interest; after all, it had been a no-go area for over a year. At last, someone had come forward to return the street to its former role of a busy thoroughfare. Work started and the original architecture was

copied as closely as possible. The Market Street redevelopment consisted
of six shops and the archway leading to the council's non-existent car
park. Ten bedrooms and a new reception area were added and leased to
the Swan Hotel.

Above the shops they built two flats, one on the first floor, which
Miss Organ eventually occupied, and a top floor that was divided into
two offices: Woodward Bros used one and J.W. Ward, the solicitors,
moved into the other. The brothers took great pride in their new offices
and furnished them accordingly with velvet tasselled-curtains, leather-
topped desks and matching studded-leather chairs from London. The
entrance hall floor featured a mosaic of the Woodward business crest.
Such was their confidence in their ability and regard for business ethics,
they designed a logo, the 'Woodward Bros Seal of built in quality',
which they used on all stationery and promotional material. Market
Street was an enormous success and, in 1975 won a European Architectural Heritage Year Award: quite a coup, as the coveted civic trust award
had never before been granted to private enterprise. This honour was
given to a firm run by a man who built his first house after reading a
book borrowed from Downend library. In protest, as they were still in
conflict with the council over the archway, the Woodwards did not pick
up their award in person but allowed their architects to do so on their
behalf. The firm retained ownership of the Market Street shops and flats
to let as a source of income.

Cyril showed great interest in the reconstruction because he had lived
in Market Street as a child. He was also hugely impressed that his son
was best friends with Jim Panes, predominantly because Jim lived in the
White House, an eminent address in Wotton. Cyril and his brothers had
played on the building site of the White House in the 1920s and, after
the builders left, the boys had crept inside the builder's tea-hut to
scavenge any leftover food, usually discarded crusts of bread, which had
fallen to the ground. Cyril became a regular visitor to Parklands and
Market Street and Bob thinks that his father's last years were probably
some of his happiest.

Cyril Woodward died at home on 27 November 1971 aged 67; Beatrice,
John and Bob were with him. He rallied enough to ask what the Bristol
City score was but died in Bob's arms soon after.

'I was terribly sad when he died,' said Bob. 'I always thought it was
a shame that he couldn't have made more out of life and enjoyed it
more. I was sad for him and sad to think that if he believed in God he
never owned up to it. There was a part of him that wanted to be
involved, to be a nicer person but he just wasn't able to do it for some

reason. I never had a huge problem with my father and neither did John. It was always the others who came off the worst.'

After their father's death, Bob and John donated a two-acre field to Wotton town council in his memory. It was set aside for a playground at the end of Parklands estate: a fitting memorial, they thought, as it was where Cyril had played as a boy.

A few years later, Beatrice suffered senile dementia and, more than once, her neighbours called her children to tell them that she was unable to get into her bungalow. On one occasion, Beatrice had tried to open the front door with a penny, pushing the coin in the lock, not understanding why the door would not open. There were other problems: she tried to light the bedside lamp with a match and caught the shade alight, scorching the bedroom wall. It was obvious that Beatrice could no longer live alone and she moved in with John and Carol for a while. Unfortunately, her condition deteriorated so rapidly she needed full-time care. Her final days were spent in Clarendon House, a nursing home in Frenchay.

Clifford, Judy's father, died aged 72 on 13 March 1973 after suffering repeated attacks of asthma. He had been ill, on and off, for some time and Bob regularly made a point of calling in to see him. On one of these days, he found himself alone with his father-in-law.

'I think, Bob, I'm right when I say that if anything did happen to me that you would look after Gwen,' said Clifford.

Bob readily agreed, of course, but took this to be a casual remark because Clifford was feeling low and just needed reassuring that everything would be taken care of. He is still not sure whether Clifford really knew or just suspected the worst, because he died the next day.

'On the day of his death, "Pop" got up as usual but then he went back to bed for a sleep and he didn't wake up again. That was absolutely wonderful for him—a way of departing this world that he fully deserved,' said Bob.

There was no question that there had been a very special relationship between Clifford, Bob and Robert, his seven-year-old grandson, a bond between three generations. Clifford's death left a gaping hole in their lives.

'It hit me very, very hard when "Pop" died and I know it hit Robert as well. There are people who believe that a nasty shock of this kind may have triggered the problems we had later. I have no idea ... but I do sometimes wonder. Robert was just seven when "Pop" died.'

Now well ensconced in Wotton, Woodward Bros purchased the manor house in The Chipping, a charming old property set in spacious grounds but in dire need of renovation. When it was finished Jim Panes leased the whole of the ground floor, where he auctioned furniture and antiques while other businesses rented the rest of the house. It was a good buy because, in addition to renovating the house, they built nine smart townhouses in the grounds in the same style as Parklands.

Bob attended an auction at the Swan for another piece of land at the back of Parklands. It sold for an astronomical sum and Bob did not make a single bid but, just as he was leaving, Jim Panes called him back.

'Whatever you do, don't leave now,' said Jim. 'You must wait for the next lot. You'll be amazed.'

Bob could not recall anything on the list that had taken his fancy but he stayed and soon realised why Jim had delayed him. 'Jim wasn't expecting to sell the next lot. He described it as the beautiful church at the top of the hill—in natural stone with a slate roof and leaded lights. The way he described it, I thought everyone would bid for it because it sounded as if everybody should have one. How could anyone live without one? He made it sound absurd that there was only the one for sale. And so, after a lot of huffing, puffing and pleading with people, he called for a starting bid of £1,000.'

Thinking that Jim was in a bit of a hole, Bob put in a bid of £1,500: a building like that could be worth at least £10,000 or even £15,000. Bids mounted slowly. He began to wonder whether some were genuine: even so, Bob made one more bid of £2,000. The room fell silent. The Woodward brothers were now the proud owners of a disused Congregational church, the Tabernacle, even though neither had ever crossed its portal.

Curiously, the next day, Bob neglected to mention the business's new acquisition and John asked how the auction had gone. Had Bob bought the piece of land at the back of Parklands?

'No, we didn't,' Bob said. 'We bought the church, the Tabernacle church, instead.'

'What the devil have we bought the Tabernacle for?' asked John.

'I don't know but I'm sure we'll find a use for it.'

'I was just flabbergasted,' said John, 'because he didn't go there with any intention of buying it.'

Bob always liked to return the hospitality extended to him from Reg Snow, the managing director of Kandya Kitchens, who regularly invited Bob on a number of 'thank you for your custom' days out. He looked for something unusual and exciting, and in August 1973 he read in the local *Gazette* that a Roman mosaic had been unearthed in Gloucestershire and was to be opened to the public. He decided to take Reg there: it sounded rather special as the mosaic only saw the light of day every ten years, and people travelled from all over the world to see it.

The pavement once graced the floor of a Roman villa, which was probably the luxurious home of someone important such as the governor of the region. As Roman Britain fell into the Dark Ages, the villa's crumbling remains vanished without trace beneath leaves, scrub and earth. The mosaic pavement, a classical masterpiece with its marvellous pictures of Orpheus charming wild animals with his music, lay unsuspected for more than a thousand years while the village of Woodchester, near Stroud, grew over the site. When this area was consecrated as the village churchyard, gravediggers exposed the first hints of something unusual beneath the surface when their spades uncovered coloured squares of stone.

In the late seventeenth century, after countless tons of earth were removed to expose the astonishing treasure, the pavement was carefully drawn by antiquaries, then re-covered again to preserve it. The Great Orpheus Pavement became so well known that the church agreed to occasional public viewings when the site was re-excavated to reveal the breathtaking beauty of the hidden stone carpet: the most complex, beautiful and fascinating Roman mosaic to survive in Northern Europe.

During the open days that year, 141,000 visitors made the same pilgrimage for a brief viewing before the mosaic was covered with 300 tons of soil and sand. The village shuddered under a siege of milling people and the graveyard's neighbouring fields overflowed with visitors' cars. Bob and Reg joined the untidy queue and filed past the perimeter of the sunken pavement that lay in the graveyard two feet below ground level. Roman Britain's most fabulous buried treasure stunned Bob the moment he saw it and he determined there and then to bring it to the world. 'I was absolutely bowled over by it. I had never seen anything like it before and it really caught my imagination.'

The artistry, the workmanship, the detail and the sheer scale of the Woodchester treasure thrilled him. 'To think you could build something as beautiful as that and people would still be looking at it 1,700 years later. Just imagine being able to build something like that.'

On the way home, he could think of nothing else. Random digging and neglect had destroyed almost 40 per cent of the original pavement and the missing pieces of this gigantic mosaic jigsaw intrigued him. What would those missing sections have shown? He felt upset that so much of it was missing and he felt that he would love to build a replica of this masterpiece, complete, as the owner of the Roman villa had seen it. It could be an exciting new project and he asked Reg for his opinion.

'Just imagine this stone carpet—in its entirety,' said Bob.

'Yes, it would be fantastic but there's no way anyone could ever do it,' said Reg.

'Well, I think I might have a go at it.'

'You'd have to be crazy to do that,' said Reg.

Taking the last statement as a personal challenge, Bob set to work. He could hardly wait to get started on his new passion and he invited the rector of Woodchester, John Cull, to lunch at the Swan in Wotton. During their meal Bob asked him what he thought of the notion of making a replica of the mosaic.

'You'd have to be crazy to do that,' said the rector. 'You obviously haven't got a clue about what you'd be taking on. The task would be enormous; could you do it? That's not to demean you: I just don't think anybody could do it.'

That remark did not put Bob off; he explained to the rector that he intended to research the missing pieces so that everyone could enjoy the whole pavement in its full glory.

'It would be magnificent but I don't think you could do it,' he repeated.

'Do you have any objections to a professional photographer recording each section of the mosaic?' asked Bob.

'No objections,' said the rector. 'And, if you are really serious, I'll help you. When the pavement closes to the public it will remain uncovered for ten days and you can come along to take your photographs then.'

Next, Bob talked to his brother, John, about their building business in Wotton. 'I think we've achieved as much as we're going to,' he said. 'We've finished Market Street, we've retained ownership and we've got the rental income coming in. As far as Parklands is concerned, we've built on the best parts of the site and there's just twenty or so plots further on up the hill. It might be the right time to make a change.'

'What would we do?' asked John.

Bob enthused about his visit to the mosaic in the Woodchester graveyard.

'I know what I'd like to do,' said Bob.

'I know what I'd like to do too but you'll think I'm crazy. I'd like to have a go at making that mosaic,' said John.

'That's absolutely unbelievable because that's exactly what I'm thinking. You're game then, are you? That's fantastic. Let's do it. Let's change course.'

And so it was that two men, both in their forties, who had never laid a piece of mosaic in their lives, took on the task of recreating a stunning work of art, the Great Orpheus Pavement, the largest mosaic ever constructed in Britain, indeed, the largest north of the Alps. In AD 325 the Romans used a team of experienced artisans to complete the original at Woodchester but in late 1973 this work fell to Bob and John Woodward. Looking back, Bob now agrees with both Reg Snow and John Cull's assessments that one would have to be crazy even to think of building a mosaic of that magnitude. He and John thought the pavement would take just a couple of years to complete. They could never have imagined that this hasty resolution would keep them busy for ten long years.

15

The Mosaic that Bob and John Built

The first step in this labour of love—which must have sometimes felt like a life sentence—was making a complete photographic record of the pavement: mounds of coloured slides, 289 in all. This proved straightforward compared to what lay ahead. Their most pressing concern was to find a workshop in which to construct the mosaic. They needed premises of at least 2,500 square feet.

'Why don't we put it in the Tabernacle church?' said Bob.

'Is the Tabernacle big enough?'

'There's only one way to find out,' said Bob. 'Now, where did we put the key?'

After some searching, they found it and made their way up Tabernacle Pitch. Could their least researched purchase be just the place they were looking for? They walked into the church and immediately saw the possibilities, but would the mosaic fit? Bob placed one end of a tape measure on the wall behind the pulpit where the Revd Rowland Hill used to preach, while John pulled it taut to the front of the gallery. They checked the result and were astonished. The original mosaic pavement measured 48 ft 10 in. square and their tape measure showed exactly 48 ft 10 in. The church was only 38 ft wide, but this could easily be overcome by using the wall space on either side. As luck would have it, the angle from floor to wall would fall on one of the straight lines running through the mosaic. The church boasted a delightful viewing gallery on three sides; it seemed that the Tabernacle had been purpose-built for the mosaic.

Both the redevelopment of Market Street and the replication of the Great Orpheus Pavement had become a talking point all over Wotton and, mindful of the value of publicity, Bob alerted the local media to the new role of the Tabernacle. He and John became hosts to television crews and newspaper journalists eager to report on both the recreation of the Woodchester pavement and the remarkable coincidence regarding the dimensions of the mosaic and its new home.

They were interviewed by Clive Gunnell, a roving journalist for local television, and by Brian Johnston, from the radio programme *Down Your Way*. During the rehearsal, 'Johnners' walked around carrying a stack of papers filled with prompts and questions; after each question, Bob, not realising it was Johnners' practice to toss these papers over his shoulder, followed closely behind him picking them all up.

'Well, Bob,' said Brian, 'we're about to go live and I'm going to interview you right now. So, just concentrate on me. I'll blurt out the questions and you just hit me with the answers—that sort of thing. Ready? So, we'll start with just a short introduction.'

The recording began. 'We are here today in the Cotswold town of Wotton-under-Edge. Bob Woodward,' Johnners said, turning to Bob, 'I think I can say without fear of contradiction that you've been responsible for boosting the population of Wotton-under-Edge by 25 per cent.'

Bob started to laugh.

'What was wrong with that?' asked Johnners.

'You just stop and read that through again slowly,' said Bob.

'Oh yes,' laughed Johnners. 'Oh yes, I think we'll change that, don't you?'

Preparations for building the mosaic breathed new life into the Tabernacle church. With a new slate roof and sunlight streaming through the replacement leaded lights, work began on the floor area. They removed all the pews bar one, which remained upstairs.

'I knew that some day I would be giving talks on the mosaic and I'd want to say, when I spoke in the Tabernacle, there was never more than one empty seat,' said Bob.

The church, known locally as the Revd Rowland Hill's Tabernacle, held one of Wotton's great mysteries: no one had ever found the final resting place of the preacher's wife.

During the preparation of a new concrete base for the mosaic, Bob, John and their digger-driver, Jim Berry, ripped up the existing church floor and exposed a flight of steps that disappeared into the darkness below. They descended into the gloom, waited until their eyes became accustomed to the meagre light, and were astounded to find themselves in the midst of a quantity of coffins, stacked three high; spookily, the coffins began to deteriorate under the weight of their gazes. After a long creak and an eerie groan, a brass coffin handle fell to the ground, before several of the old caskets crumbled into the ones beneath.

'We were up those steps and out of there like scalded cats,' said Bob. Further investigation revealed that the Tabernacle had been built on top of the crypt of a much older church.

'It just seemed so strange that we were building the Orpheus pavement in there. Orpheus at Woodchester is in the graveyard and now we were going to put our version in a graveyard as well,' said Bob. 'And we solved another mystery: the name on a brass plaque on one of the old coffins was that of Mr Hill's wife.'

In spite of the renovation, the Tabernacle turned out not to be the easiest place to work; although the light was good, it was huge and cold.

After informing the authorities of the new use for the church, the planners referred Bob to the Highways Department. It stated that should the church become an exhibition hall attracting volumes of visitors in cars, the road leading to it, Tabernacle Pitch, would be inadequate.

The strip of land opposite, part of the old, deserted Tabernacle schoolroom, seemed to provide the answer. Bob and John approached the trustees of the school and purchased both the schoolroom and the land; then they widened the road. The Highways Department demanded more, and so they re-sited the graveyard wall to accommodate a footpath and built a two-and-a-half-acre car park on adjacent land that they already owned. Still the Highways Department was not satisfied: officials brought a coach to the Tabernacle and found that the junction at the bottom of the hill was too tight. The only way to widen the junction was through some gardens belonging to the almshouses situated on the corner of Old Town and Tabernacle Pitch. After successfully negotiating with the trustees to truncate these gardens, all services to the almshouses (electricity, gas etc.) were re-directed with most of the work completed by, and at the expense of, Woodward Bros. Following all this groundwork—they were yet to start on the mosaic itself—the planners granted them permission to exhibit their Great Orpheus Pavement for just five years rather than on a permanent basis. This disappointment led to some lateral thinking. Bob and John looked to the future: should the authorities refuse to extend permissions for the exhibition, it would be prudent to construct the pavement in transportable pieces: a mobile exhibition, a giant jigsaw.

The purchase of the two-storey schoolroom also provided a solution to the poor working conditions in the Tabernacle; they converted the upstairs into a storeroom and the ground floor into an office and workshop. Discussions ensued with Ron Bean, who lived next door to the Tabernacle, and Alan Wilson, a sign maker: both gave practical help in the setting up of the workshop. During the refurbishment of the schoolroom Bob and John found a quantity of Sunday school registers, some of which listed their father and uncle, both pupils many years before.

'I think that must be why Father sent us to Sunday school,' said Bob, 'because he was made to go.'

Now, with a workshop and an exhibition hall, the real work could begin. It seems incredible that two complete novices could even imagine taking on such a gargantuan project but, by trial and error, they mastered mosaic-building skills.

The original mosaic had been fashioned in stone but as this would be difficult to find and too heavy for a mobile exhibition, they decided to make the copy out of clay. Then they had to determine how much clay would be needed to build a 2,500 square foot Roman mosaic and they pulled a figure out of thin air: twelve tons. For specialist help, they contacted a potter, Bob Blair, from South Wales, who suggested firing the clay in strips before chipping it into tiles for laying.

Colour too, was of vital importance and there was some difficulty in matching the blue lias shade to depict water. Bob Blair, however, developed a process he called 'body-staining', which allowed him to produce authentic colours; varying shades of blue could be achieved according to where the clay was positioned in the oven.

John confessed to being colour-blind. 'Doesn't make sense does it? We used to stand up there in the Tabernacle making that mosaic with Bob telling me the colours all the time.'

To help them in laying the tiles, they engineered all manner of contraptions but one by one they were discarded. They preferred at first to lay the individual stones, or 'tesserae', on a type of drawing board—at an angle—rather than lay them flat. This idea was soon ditched when the tesserae insisted on following the laws of gravity.

Next, they devised a more sophisticated method using a slide projector where images of the original work were projected onto paper before outlining in pencil. This method too was rejected as the image distorted the measurements of the tiles. They experimented with placing the projector in the middle of the ceiling pointing downwards, which removed the distortion but threw up another problem. It was impossible to place a tile in the correct position without getting in the way of the projection and losing sight of the image. Finally, they came up with a solution. What if they floor-mounted the projector and pointed it upwards to an armour-plated glass work-surface covered in tracing paper? They could then lay the tesserae on top of the tracing paper. This almost worked, except that to achieve a clear image the top of the work-surface was now only nine inches from the ceiling. To overcome this they removed some of the upstairs floor and reached down through a hole in the ceiling to the work surface below. Another rejection: it would be too uncomfortable to operate in this way especially during the winter months and almost impossible if one of them was working alone.

'So, we got in touch with the people who made the projector and asked if they could supply us with a short-throw lens,' said Bob. 'But no, they couldn't: not for that type of projector, so we had to buy other projectors capable of utilising short throw-lenses. Then, we were not too far away.'

Even using the new lenses, however, the focal point was still too high, so Bob and John excavated a coffin-shaped hole in the floor and sited not one but two projectors in it.

'With the help of our cousin Basil, who was an architect, we contacted some engineers who confirmed that by using Bowden cables, we could move the projector cage, making it possible to alter the focus and tilt or shunt the projectors to the left and right or to the front and back. We were now in complete control of the projectors.'

The benefits of using two projectors were numerous. When the two slides, side by side, covered the glass work-surface, the joint image would measure from 18 to 24 inches wide and about five to six feet long, depending on how much overlap there was on the original photographs. All of the sections varied in size and shape, which meant that the joins in the 'jigsaw' of the mosaic would be less noticeable.

'This was great,' said Bob. 'We had a picture of two pieces that merged together perfectly; we had the size, we had the shape and we had the colour. We could work without getting in the way of the projected image and we could make the whole thing at workbench height.'

Having perfected the method of laying the tiles in each section, moving them became the next problem. There appeared to be three possibilities but only one proved satisfactory.

'We came up with the idea of using clear sheets of acrylic so that we could lay the tiles straight onto the plastic,' said Bob. 'That didn't seem too bad an idea but then we had to think about trapping the tiles into the plastic. We did all sorts of research and eventually found a German company that could supply an adhesive that fused clay to plastic.'

This process involved placing the tesserae into the adhesive, which, after a chemical reaction, melted the surface of the acrylic, creating a bond. But this reaction had a drawback: obnoxious fumes. Bob and John rigged up an extractor using elephant trunking (huge flexible piping) and set it into clear Perspex hoods (two redundant baby cradles from the children's hospital with one side cut away so that they could get their hands inside). After turning the cradles upside down onto the acrylic sheet, they cut a hole large enough to take the elephant trunking, connected it and extracted the fumes away from the mosaic.

'Sometimes, when we opened up first thing in the morning, we could see a chemical mist floating a foot above the ground. It was pretty potent and could well have been damaging to our health over the years,' said Bob.

After completing each section of the mosaic, they grouted it with cement and added a chipboard backing. At last, two segments of an area close to the centre of the pavement were finished: one pictured birds, the other a run of guilloche, the chain pattern that featured throughout the original mosaic. After four months work, Bob and John were thrilled when they viewed the fruits of their industry lying before them on the workbench. They raced across the road carrying the weighty panels and placed them on the floor of the Tabernacle church before tearing upstairs to the gallery to view them from above. When they peered down at the dinky little pieces of mosaic, their faces fell; the result of all their work resembled two pimples in the middle of the floor.

'This is going to take for ever,' said Bob.

It was at that moment they realised the scale of what they had taken on and, only slightly overwhelmed, over the following weeks they continued to make several more pieces, including one of a leopard. Their excitement undiminished, they charged over to the Tabernacle to add another segment; to their disappointment, it did not fit.

'Let's pack it in and come back fresh tomorrow,' said Bob. 'Let's go home and forget about it.'

After considering what might have gone wrong, they found that some of the slides still showed distorted images and Bob immediately realised why.

'My mind went back to the uneven floor of the original mosaic. At times, the photographer's tripod must have been slightly tilted, skewing the camera angle, which accentuated the unevenness. We were in possession of 289 colour transparencies of which an indeterminate number gave us a distorted picture. The challenge was now: what could we do about it? How could we find the distorted slides?'

Ingenuity met the challenge: six projectors, in two rows of three, one above the other projecting six images on to the wall. It was obvious then which slides did not marry up. The projector showing the distorted view was adjusted to correct the aspect, the new image traced in pencil and the slide marked accordingly.

Then another problem reared its head: the inexpensive equipment lacked internal cooling fans and was prone to overheat, which resulted in a number of warped slides. No strangers to adversity, they improvised with the help of a hosepipe, a length of copper pipe and a vacuum cleaner.

'Our cooling system involved running a hosepipe underneath the projectors; then, using a piece of copper pipe, we attached the hosepipe to a vacuum cleaner and reversed its action so that it blew rather than sucked. We made holes in the hosepipe and directed a jet of cold air onto the slides to keep them cool. That's how we got over that one,' said Bob.

Weeks passed and work continued in the same vein. There were now half a dozen pieces laid out on the church floor but, when Bob inadvertently stepped on the edge of one segment, the opposite edge lifted off the floor. The acrylic base beneath the tiles had warped into a shallow saucer—yet another threat to the project.

More deliberations: they contacted the acrylic sheet suppliers. Could the warping be caused by the floor temperature? Or by direct sunlight? The supplier's response was simple: as no one had ever used their products for laying mosaics before, they would like to observe the problem first hand. When the 'acrylic men' visited Wotton, they were mesmerised by the sight of a partly reconstructed Roman mosaic laid on their panels and immediately identified the problem; however, they were not so quick to provide the solution.

'Because the pull of the adhesive over the surface is just on one side, there is nothing to counterbalance it on the other,' they said. 'So, to rectify it, you really should be laying tiles on the other side as well.' They went on to make a further suggestion. 'You either need to do something to compensate or you need to bake the sheets to anneal them to remove internal stresses.'

'Do we roast them for five minutes or ten minutes or what do we do?'

'Experiment with them,' they replied. 'We can't help you there.'

With this less than helpful advice, Bob and John rigged up a makeshift tent over the mosaic panels and, oblivious to the fire hazard, belted heat into it using an industrial space heater of the rocket-style Calor Gas type. When they checked the acrylic panels some time later they were even more bent and twisted. 'Let's go home and forget about it,' said Bob again.

Next morning, to their amazement, the panels were straight and true. They had found the answer. All they needed was a special type of oven to anneal the panels correctly, and a firm of electrical contractors in nearby Stroud tailor-made it for them. In due course a gleaming new oven featuring asbestos shelving to withstand extreme temperatures arrived, but its installation had to wait. When they struggled to carry it to the entrance of the schoolroom, they found that it was an inch too wide for the doorway; consequently, the door and its frame were removed to accommodate it.

'John was absolutely incredible,' remembered Bob. 'Sometimes he stayed there all through the night playing around with the acrylic sheets. He found that after annealing a sheet, a month or so later, it started to curl again. I don't know how he got it right in the end but eventually he found out exactly how long was needed to bake each sheet. He played around with the timing and with different temperatures until he solved the problem and then every sheet was successfully annealed. Some of that mosaic was laid more than a quarter of a century ago and it is still as flat as when we first made it ... he put in so many hours, so many hours.'

While John was busy with the practical side of making the mosaic, Bob took on the research. He abandoned his opinion that 'reading always seemed to be such a waste of time when you could be doing something really productive' for a second time and visited a number of local libraries. Then, as his compulsion grew, his odyssey led him further afield to explore book auctions and, later, to an association with the Bristol and Gloucestershire Archaeological Society. He acquired anything and everything he could find relating to the Woodchester area and to the pavement in particular. He bought a copy of a book by Samuel Lysons, the son of a Gloucestershire clergyman, who excavated the Woodchester villa over a four-year period in the late 1790s. Lysons is still an acknowledged authority on the subject and his book includes some outstanding illustrated plates of the pavement.

'It really is a very impressive piece of literature, dedicated to George III and first printed in 1796,' said Bob.

With the help of the city archivist Bob gleaned yet more knowledge of his chosen subject. Then he was granted permission to research his subject at the Bodleian Library in Oxford. '"Find your way around the catalogue," they told me. I didn't know what they were talking about. I had no idea. I didn't even know how to order a book. Here was a kid who left school at fourteen thrust into an academic world that he knew nothing about. I just had to find my way through it all.'

He found some unpublished manuscripts at the Bodleian that supplied some interesting new information about the Orpheus mosaic. From there, his studies took him to the Ashmolean Museum, also in Oxford, and that, in turn, led him to London and to the British Library.

'The British Library had just opened a new building, so the first day I just sat there and looked at it. I didn't even take out a book; I just looked at the building.'

News of the Woodwards' replica spread through academic circles and Bob was invited to present his findings to the Association for the Study and Preservation of Roman Mosaics in London. In spite of his experience of public speaking, he had never before addressed such a distinguished, knowledgeable audience and, as they appeared sceptical, he felt the need to win them over. Armed with a couple of segments from the mosaic, he told the scholars about the time, commitment and energy he and John were pouring into the project. His depth of knowledge was obvious and Bob soon won the respect and attention of his audience.

One of the most challenging theories for them to accept was the water feature in the centre of the pavement, because there had been no precedent for a geometrical Orpheus mosaic to have water at its centre.

'My research allowed me to come up with all of the reasons why I felt absolutely convinced that there had been water in the centre and, in the end, they agreed,' said Bob. 'I did some of my research in Burlington House, the home of the Society of Antiquaries, in Piccadilly. It is a wonderful place, a wonderful building, and I found things in there relating to the pavement that even they didn't know they had. It was quite amazing to have found all these different illustrated plates and I referred to them when I made my presentation. They helped to explain why there was water in the centre, how it got there and why the trenches of damage to the mosaic are in the position they are—it is where the lead pipes carried the water supply into the centre of the pavement.

'The property next to the site of the original mosaic has a fountain in the garden, tapped into the original Roman water supply, which runs even in the most excessive droughts. The hilltop springs provided the source of the water, which ran down into the centre of the mosaic; today, it runs right through what is now the Manor House in Woodchester. The evidence is there.'

Bob promised that should firmer evidence come to light regarding the design of the missing sections, he and John would remake any areas that were in question: in fact, none had to be remade.

Given Bob's feelings about his educational background, the presentation of his findings and the acceptance of his arguments about this unique feature of the Woodchester pavement was a major accomplishment. He put a paper together that was read by David Smith, keeper of antiquities at Newcastle University, who came to Wotton for his own research. He was most complimentary about Bob's work and, when Dr Smith published his work relating to the Woodchester pavement, he credited Bob for expert advice. Bob was delighted. 'I was quite chuffed about it really and I must say that once I had won the academics over, they were very gracious.'

It is to Bob's credit that his diligence elevated him from enthusiastic amateur to an internationally acknowledged antiquarian: deserved reward for so many painstaking months of research at some of the country's leading libraries and museums.

While Bob found that that the most oft-quoted authority was Samuel Lysons, there was another name linked with the Woodchester pavement, that of the modern-day mosaic draughtsman, David Neal. At the unearthing of Roman mosaics Dr Neal plotted and drew them before painting them for posterity. His painting of the Woodchester pavement was stored in Acton and Bob asked if he could borrow it to demonstrate to academics how close the replica was to the original.

When permission was granted, the brothers hired a large van to travel to London to pick up the painting to bring it home. Alan drove the van while Bob and John went by car. At Acton they were horrified to find that the painting was stored on the seventh floor and the building had no lift. Morale did not improve when they carried the large painting, complete with heavy brass frame, down seven flights of stairs to the awaiting Bedford van. It was not until they were at the door of the van that the three exhausted men discovered just how rough the 'rough measurements' they had been given turned out to be. The painting was two inches too large.

They fell about laughing, not believing that all three of them could be so stupid. After hiring a larger van they stowed the painting securely inside and that evening the M4 witnessed a convoy of returning Wood-wards.

Bob considers the most embarrassing moment of his life was when he appeared on BBC's *Blue Peter* in 1980 to talk about the Woodchester pavement. Although work on the mosaic was still unfinished, Bob, John and Alan took the completed central section to the television studios at Shepherd's Bush. They were welcomed and shown into a dressing room, where, in spite of a scheduled appearance of just five to six minutes, their names adorned the door.

Bob found the rehearsal process an alien and painstaking affair. The production team rehearsed the interview about ten times over and timed it to the second; then they asked Bob to do it all over again but this time, ten seconds faster; by the end of the rehearsal, his head buzzed. Biddy Baxter, the show's producer, spoke to Bob just before going on air. 'We want you to do it again, Bob, but this time six seconds faster than last time.'

The show started to the sounds of the famous theme tune and almost immediately after the introductions, Bob's interview began.

'You have set this on Perspex,' said the presenter, Sarah Greene.

'Yes,' replied Bob. 'There are two reasons for doing that. The first is that the image is clearly visible through the Perspex on which we place the stones.'

'Oh yes. And what's the other reason?' asked Sarah.

There was a pause. 'I can't remember the other reason,' Bob said regretfully.

'Of all the flippin' times that I had to forget, I did it on live tele-vision,' he said. 'I felt as sick as a parrot.'

On the way home, the brothers stopped at Membury Service Station on the M4. 'I want to go to the loo and I want to get some petrol,' said Alan. After buying the petrol, he stopped and looked at Bob. 'Now, what was the other thing I needed to do?'

The family will never let Bob forget the *Blue Peter* interview and still rib him for his untimely lapse of memory.

In spite of being let down by his memory during his interview, Bob was invited back to the show in 1988 when Caron Keating was host. This time Bob was word perfect. The completed pavement was displayed in the BBC studio where Dr Timothy Potter, assistant keeper of the Roman Britain section of the British Museum, valued it in situ for insurance purposes at £1 million.

Because the original pavement was due to be unearthed again in 1983 and to be sure that their version was ready for comparison, Bob and John set their sights on completing their Great Orpheus pavement by 1982. Part of their dream was fulfilled: they managed to complete their pavement on schedule but were disappointed when the original mosaic was left undisturbed in 1983. The final presentation of the original mosaic turned out to be in 1973 when it attracted 141,000 visitors in just 50 days; the projected figure for 1983 was 250,000.

The approach to the Woodchester churchyard is narrow, as are all the roads in the village, and the challenge of thousands of visitors proved one hurdle too many for local residents. They voiced severe doubts as to how they could possibly cope with such numbers and a plan was put forward to ease the congestion by making the site a year-round attraction. They asked the Department of the Environment for consent to erect a permanent cover over the mosaic in the graveyard but were told that the Ancient Graveyards Act states that permission must be obtained from the last known relatives of the interred before any changes may be made; efforts to trace these relatives covered the globe. Ultimately, the plan was abandoned because some descendents refused permission and, as the mosaic is an ancient monument and cannot be re-sited, there was no other solution. The Great Orpheus pavement at Woodchester has not seen the light of day since.

'We got into the 1983 *Guinness Book of Records* as the largest mosaic made in this country,' said Bob, recalling the pride that he and John felt at receiving such official recognition of their ten-year project.

16

Robert, a Most Promising Footballer

The decade in which Bob and John were busy with their extraordinary labour of love coincided with the unfolding of a terrible tragedy that increasingly overshadowed Bob's family. Because of this, the intensity of Bob's involvement in the day-to-day business of the mosaic lessened as time went on. 'It was good that I did the research in the early years,' said Bob, 'because John carried on working on it when I wasn't there. I don't know how many dozens of times the telephone rang telling me that something had cropped up and then I would have to go back to Bristol. He would just carry on; never once did he ever so much as murmur a single word of discontent. Someone once said that John was one in a million. Rubbish. You could trawl the whole of the world and never come across anyone more loyal.'

It began in 1973, when Bob took a trip to Spain with Chris Stokes, the local baker in Wotton. But bakery was not Chris's only interest: he had other irons in the fire. He owned three villas and some land in Spain, just north of Alicante; Calpe was still a fishing village but was fast becoming a delight to sun-seeking tourists. Chris told Bob about the property opportunities that lay waiting and about one in particular. A British buyer had run into financial difficulties during the building of a holiday villa and Chris thought that Bob might be interested in it.

The villa, comprising four bedrooms, two bathrooms and two reception rooms, was located in the lower foothills of Calpe, about a mile from the sea, next door to terraces of vines. It was the first in a development of five and was on offer at a very good price. The views were outstanding from all rooms, a panorama of the mountain slopes to the rear and, to the front, the Peñón de Ifach in the Bay of Calpe. Bob fell for the house, bought it and immediately took a liking to the Spanish way of life. He had wild ideas about having his own gang there and building more villas alongside his own. Albeit wild, Bob thought seriously about these plans.

'Judy was not that happy about a house in Calpe; she didn't think we needed a place abroad—couldn't really see a reason for it,' said Bob.

Nevertheless, Casa Spruce was built but, sadly, what should have been a dream fulfilled turned out to be a source of disappointment. During the family's only holiday there, storm water poured through the roof and they were forced to decamp into a hotel in nearby Benidorm.

'It was not long after Clifford's death and Judy's mother's first Christmas without him, so I thought let's all go to Spain for a holiday and stay in our new house. It was a disaster. I had paid the Spanish builders an awful lot of money to complete the work to a good standard but they left it unfinished and demanded even more money to put things right. I ended up giving it to them; it seemed to be the only way to get them back to work but after paying them they still didn't turn up. I had to find someone else and pay for it all over again.'

It was while the family was making the best of their holiday that a rather more serious and frightening situation arose.

'It happened in January 1974 and was the first indication that there was something not quite right with Robert,' said Bob. 'He and I used to play for hours and hours on the beach; we played all sorts of ball games. We'd been racing each other across the sands and I could see that Robert was in trouble; I had to take his hand so that he could keep up with me. I knew there was something wrong. He woke up a couple of times that night and complained; we thought it was growing pains and we rubbed in some embrocation. But it went on and we knew that something was worryingly wrong. It made us jump a bit.'

On the way home, Robert complained about a sore throat and said he felt unwell. Bob and Judy's concerns subsided when he seemed to get better although he was reluctant to return to school, which was most unlike him. Soon after, he took part in a cross-country race of 33 runners; he finished last, which was also unexpected. During the race Robert's hip locked and he needed the help of friends to carry him some of the way. Bob and Judy were deeply concerned about their son.

'Within days, he became desperately ill, his colour changed and he looked really, really sick,' said Bob.

In February Robert was admitted to Bristol Children's Hospital for a series of tests. Hospitals can be bleak places; their very structure can increase the sense of foreboding. Four days later, Bob received a telephone call at work telling him that the senior paediatrician, Dr David Burman, wanted to meet them both at two o'clock that afternoon. The journey from Wotton-under-Edge to Bristol was an emotional one. What on earth could be wrong with Robert? Bob thought he had the answer. He somehow convinced himself that it must be a kidney problem and he knew what he could do about it: Robert could have one of his. This thought comforted him as he arrived—a little late—at the hospital.

David Burman was already leaving by the time Bob arrived but returned to the ward after they bumped into each other on the staircase. He delivered the grim news to the fearful parents; Robert had stage 4 neuroblastoma. Bob and Judy had never heard of this ferocious disease, had no idea of its implications and struggled with this information.

'Dr Burman explained that they had found one of the most deadly tumours in one of Robert's adrenal glands and it was pressing down on his kidney. We were told that if it wasn't treated he would most certainly die within six weeks but there was a chance that something could be done for him. They told us about a brilliant young doctor at the hospital, named Martin Mott, who looked after all of the young cancer patients in Bristol and throughout the South West of England. Martin would be seeing Robert within a few days.'

There was hope.

The time had come to talk to Robert; he was only eight years old. Bob remembered telling him that it was neuroblastoma.

'What a funny name that is. What does it mean?' asked Robert.

'The only way I can explain it to you is if someone asked me to choose any illness for you, neuroblastoma would be the last I'd choose.' Bob thought this was the kindest way of telling his son that it was 'really nasty'.

'Oh dear,' Robert said, 'it doesn't sound very good. What's going to happen?'

'I'm not sure what's going to happen,' said his father, 'but I guess that you might need an operation. And you'll need some drugs and that's going to mean needles; I know you don't like needles but I can promise you that whatever treatment you need and wherever you go, I can arrange to be with you all of the time.'

'Well, that makes all the difference and I don't mind,' Robert said.

Bob and Judy were utterly devastated: terrified that they might lose their child to a life-threatening illness, they also had to face breaking this unimaginable news to Rachel and James.

'It was so difficult telling them,' said Bob. 'They were so concerned for Rob and they were so wonderful for us.'

Over the next few days, Bob visited their family and friends; he found it particularly difficult telling the older generation as he feared it would hit them hardest.

In the meantime Bob and Judy waited to hear from Martin Mott. People spoke highly of Martin in terms of his knowledge, dedication and commitment to the task. Parents who are or who have been in similar circumstances will recognise the Woodwards' anxiety: their son's very life would now be entirely in this doctor's hands. When Bob and Judy met Martin Mott they found him to be sensitive and comforting but the discussion was frightening; in his gentle way, they felt that he was preparing them for the worst. Martin described Robert's condition openly and told them all the things that they did not want to hear, alarming things that they did not want to even think about. Robert's tumour was one of the most difficult to treat; there were very few survivors of neuroblastoma and as yet no long-term survivors of stage 4.

In this advanced form, Martin could not—and would not—provide an unrealistically positive outlook; it would depend so much on how Robert responded to the regimen. He went on to say the best they could hope for was that Robert would survive his two years' treatment; by then, new research might give him a further extension of life. They talked about surgery, about radiotherapy and about chemotherapy. To Bob and Judy, it was all 'pretty ghastly stuff'; thoughts of their little boy undergoing such brutal procedures were unbearable.

'There were no specialist children's oncology wards in those days and it was easy to pick out the children with cancer. There was a boy there from Stapleton who had neuroblastoma and he looked so terribly, terribly sick. That really frightened me,' said Bob.

As if things were not bad enough, Martin delivered yet more disturbing news. He would be leaving the hospital within two or three weeks to take up a position as visiting professor at the Stanford Cancer Centre, California, where research and treatment into childhood cancer was advancing rapidly. Bob and Judy's fragile hopes were dashed in a single second. They had placed their complete faith in this doctor and now they felt that their son's only possible chance of survival was lost. Martin would be 6,000 miles away and there were no other childhood cancer specialists in Bristol at that time. In despair Bob spoke to Neville Butler, the head of the Institute of Child Health at Bristol University, whom he had met the previous year following James's illness, but neither could find a solution. Bob could not rest; there must be something he could do.

Two days later, on his drive to Wotton from the hospital, he came up with the idea of setting up a travelling fund for Martin Mott. If the young cancer specialist travelled freely between Britain and America, the benefits were obvious; he immediately turned the car around and sped straight back to the hospital.

'If I set up a travelling fund, would you put your seal of approval on it?' Bob asked Neville.

'If Martin is responsive, we will be delighted,' said Neville. 'It will mean that we shall be able to keep in close touch with him and he can continue to see the other children in the South West.'

Bob arranged a meeting with Martin who, as predicted, was receptive to the idea. So, having had the go ahead, Bob paid a sum of £2,000 into a fund at Bristol University to pay for Martin's flights to and from California using Milton's Travel of Fishponds; the fund allowed Martin to come home whenever he wished.

Quite often, Bob picked Martin up at Heathrow and sometimes he was able to give Martin one of their firm's cars for the duration of his visit. On one occasion, when there were no cars available, John gave Martin his car. This act of unselfishness demonstrates the bond between Bob and John and is just one of the many things that Bob has always appreciated about his brother.

From all over the South West, families with children stricken with cancer benefited from the travelling fund. Martin's presence undoubtedly made an incalculable difference to the quality of the treatment throughout the region. His regular visits to England enabled him to hold clinics in Exeter, Plymouth and Cornwall as well as in Bristol.

Bob and Martin got on famously, became good friends, and often shared meals together. There were, however, differing opinions about the travelling fund. Some of Bob's family were not too happy with it and neither was his accountant. Bob, of course, was totally committed to the idea because the travelling fund had a direct bearing on his son's life.

Every day, Bob and Judy drove to the children's hospital to be with Robert. Observing other families in the ward, it struck Bob that parents living away from Bristol faced additional difficulties to those living in the area. Some parents travelled long distances to be with their children: from Cornwall, from as far away as the Scilly Isles, even from the Channel Islands. He and Judy witnessed their tired and anxious peers sleeping on chairs in the wards: one father attempted to get some rest curled up in one of the cots; another slept on a mattress in the corridor. Bob and Judy could only imagine what this extra hardship must be like; they felt for these strangers and finding a way to reduce this burden was constantly in Bob's thoughts. Then it came to him: he and John owned a bungalow at the bottom of his road in Frenchay. At one time, they had considered demolishing it to build a new house there. Now, Bob thought, the situation had changed and the bungalow could be used as a home for tired parents to stay in. John agreed.

The bungalow needed renovation and furnishing but, again, Bob had the solution—Casa Spruce. Now the family had lost all interest in their house in Calpe they intended to sell it but, as all of the brand new furniture was of good quality, it was decided to put it to good use in the Frenchay bungalow. It became the first Home from Home for parents who lived away from Bristol and Judy, as housekeeper, and Bob, as maintenance man, shared the work. Although the Home from Home concept was pioneered by McDonalds in Philadelphia in 1974, few in England were aware of it and Bob had certainly never heard of it. The Frenchay bungalow was the first such property in this country.

Bob visited Colston School in Bristol with the news of Robert's diagnosis.

'Mr Jameson, the headmaster, was like a character from a book: a real Mr Chips, one from the old school. When I told him the terrible news, this genuine, kindly man just stood there with tears rolling down his cheeks,' said Bob.

'What can I do? What can I do?' said Mr Jameson. 'The only thing I can do is pray. That is all I can offer.' He struggled for the right words. 'I am devastated ... and that it should be Robert ... he's such a lovely looking lad ... we all thought he was destined to be a great sportsman.'

From October to December 1973 Robert had scored 22 goals for his school team: he was a most promising footballer.

Through the dark days and the torment, Helen and Gerry Davies were there for Bob and Judy. Gerry, a GP, and his wife Helen, a nurse and health visitor, were members of Fishponds Baptist church.

'Sunday nights after church, they came home to be with us and also during the week if they thought we needed a bit of moral support. Our family GP, Dr Dougal Dickson, and his wife Pat were just the same; nothing at all was ever too much trouble for any of them. We talked and talked; we were ever so close. They were all absolutely outstanding people, more than friends, an extension of the family. I could ring them any time of day or night and they always came at a minute's notice,' said Bob, in tribute to the value of true friendship.

Friends at church were equally supportive although Bob found that viewpoints and reactions varied tremendously. There were times when he tried to analyse other people's approach to the difficult subject of terminal illness. One friend took the trouble to call in to see him.

'I've heard your news,' said the friend. 'You should feel very proud. God only allows this sort of thing to happen to very special people.'

'If you follow the logic of that,' said Bob, 'I have just the one prayer for God. Please, please, please don't make me special. That's what my prayer would be.'

Looking back, Bob considered the feelings of other people when faced with this type of situation.

'I think some people feel awkward and clumsy; their hearts are so heavy, they just try to do their utmost to convey how they're feeling. It reminds me of the story of the Good Samaritan. A man lay injured in the road: when a Levite comes along, he crosses over to the other side of the road. I know that people have deliberately avoided me because they haven't known what to say. We're always very hard on that Levite who walked away to avoid the situation. But was it that he didn't care, or was it that he cared too much? He might have been just like those people who avoided me. They care so much that they can't cope with the situation. So that might be why people cross over to the other side.'

He accepted that, faced with such difficulties, people find different ways to cope. 'I thought Judy's strength throughout was quite remarkable. She's a very different person from me in all of these things. She's got such a sound, basic belief in God that she doesn't really question anything. She accepts whatever comes. The strength of her belief is remarkable and I am often envious of it. Perhaps, if I was like that, I might cope far better. Her belief was stronger, maybe still is stronger than mine is but I think her strength comes from the way she was brought up and the love that surrounded her; it was there for her from day one. If you believe that God is in control, Romans says, "All things work together for good to them that love God."'

Fishponds Baptist held a number of special prayer meetings for Robert and his family and, after one particularly well-attended meeting, Mrs Dunn, the church organist, told Bob that he would not believe the power that their prayers had generated that evening.

'I did believe it,' said Bob. 'After all, we had been on the receiving end of it—we felt we were plugged into it.'

After some discussion both at home and at church, it was decided to perform a service that is described in the New Testament: the laying on of hands. In the hushed, calm atmosphere that prevails after visiting times in the Bristol Children's Hospital, Bob held a service around Robert's bed with a small group of friends who prayed and effected the laying on of hands. They explained to Robert that this was their way of letting God know how much they wanted him to get better. His reaction was one of surprise but acceptance.

'Robert, like every child I have ever met with cancer, had some very special qualities. He had a firm belief in God and the thing that he loved doing as much as he loved his football was to take the hymnbooks off the piano, tune in to *Songs of Praise* on a Sunday night, and join in with the hymns. He absolutely loved doing that and because of his great belief, it wasn't really difficult to tell him what we were doing. He accepted it.'

It was the first time that Bob had been involved in such a practice. It was a strange experience and difficult for him to work out just what he expected from it, which led to feelings of confusion and guilt. How was he to know what God wanted? Was he going against God's wishes by praying for Robert's recovery? Given that the others fervently believed in the power of the ceremony, was his personal faith enough to make it happen? Or was he the weak link?

Therapies for the treatment of cancer can be barbaric. While radiotherapy uses various forms of radiation, chemotherapy uses cytotoxic drugs and chemical compounds designed to prevent normal cell replication and so inhibit the growth of tumours or of excess cells in body fluids. In many cases, the treatments can destroy healthy cells alongside the cancerous ones and produce devastating effects on the patient, some hidden, some distressingly visual.

As soon as Robert started his course of chemotherapy, he suffered hair loss. As difficult as this may be for a child, it can be almost unbearable for the parents. For Bob and Judy, the sight of Robert's beautiful blonde hair falling out on to his pillow was dreadful: a poignant and shocking sign of the extreme effects of toxic poisons coursing through their son's body.

When he was not in hospital, Robert's attendance at school was sporadic; from time to time, he was only just well enough to attend classes. Sometimes, on Saturdays, after undergoing the trauma of chemotherapy, administered by injection in those days, he still managed to turn out to play his beloved football in the afternoon; his illness and its treatment put immense limitations on his game but, although he could no longer play in the way he used to, he never wanted to give up.

'Robert was magic with a football.'

The day before Robert's ninth birthday in August 1974, Bob drove to Aust, a small village by the Severn Bridge, to visit the renowned rugby player, John Pullin. Although they had never met, Bob intended to ask John to autograph a white rugby ball as a special surprise present for Robert. Bob found his way to the farm where John lived and recognised him standing at the gateway. Bob introduced himself and apologised for turning up unannounced. The two men talked for some time; Bob told John about Robert and asked if he would sign the ball for him. John asked for more information and his sincere interest touched Bob deeply.

'So, it's Robert's birthday tomorrow?' said John.

'Yes,' Bob said.

'I'll sign it tonight,' said John, 'and if you tell me where you live, I'll come over tomorrow and give it to him personally.'

The next day, he arrived as promised and met Robert on the front lawn. They had a photograph taken together and John gave him the signed rugby ball: but that was not all.

'I have something else for you, Robert,' said John as he took out an England rugby shirt from his bag. 'I thought you might like this as well.' It was one of his own shirts proudly emblazoned with the red rose of England on the front and the number '2' on the back. It also sported the badges of England, the British Lions and the Barbarians.

'What an incredible thing for him to do,' said Bob. 'When you play for England, those shirts must be so precious and such great mementos. I had known John for less than 24 hours and here he was, at our home, giving one of his shirts to our boy. What an incredible thing.'

Earlier that day, Bob and Judy had given Robert their present—a Leeds United football strip; Robert was football crazy and Leeds was his passion. Even on the morning of his birthday, Robert had to go for radiotherapy treatment but he went happily, showing off his new football gear.

John Pullin became a regular visitor and, at moments of crisis, he would stop everything to be at Robert's side. Years later, when Bob introduced John to the Duchess of Kent, he told her of John's kindness but John refused to accept the praise, saying that it was only what anyone would have done in the same situation.

John's interest led Bob to other sportspeople who brightened his son's life. Robert met Kevin Keegan and Ray Clemence when the Liverpool team was in town and, following contact with Alex Stock, then Fulham manager, he met Bobby Moore and George Best. In fact, Robert, Rachel and Bob were invited to lunch at the Unicorn Hotel to meet the whole of the Fulham team.

Closer to home, Bob went down the road to see Bristol Rovers and when he told their assistant manager, Bobby Campbell, about Robert, Campbell invited them to all their home games and introduced them to the players. For Robert's tenth birthday, Campbell brought the whole of the Rovers team along to Robert's party.

'We rounded up all the kids in the neighbourhood to give Bristol Rovers a game. We erected portable goal posts in the grounds of Frenchay Hospital and we played them there. James was only a tiny nipper then and he called himself Neeskins after one of the Dutch World Cup players; Rachel joined in the football games too. We had a special birthday cake made for tea after the game. It was a fantastic day. And some of those players stayed in touch with Robert,' said Bob.

Bobby Campbell, a former Scotland international, was another who gave one of his prized shirts to Robert. Later, he put Bob in touch with Liverpool and their legendary manager, Bob Paisley. Paisley wrote a 'lovely letter' and arranged for Emlyn Hughes, David Johnson and Terry McDermott to come to the house to see Robert. They stayed and chatted with him for some time.

'If I could give you just one thing, Robert, what would you like?' said Emlyn.

'I'd like the shirt that Kevin Keegan will be wearing for his last

Liverpool game before he leaves,' said Robert.

Within a few days, the shirt arrived in the post. The Liverpool number 7 shirt was now part of Robert's collection.

Bob wrote to Bertie Mee, then Arsenal manager, and enclosed a cheque for three seats in the stand (for himself, Rachel and Robert) to see Stoke play at Highbury. The cheque was returned in pieces accompanied by a personal letter from Bertie insisting that the seats were complimentary and that there would be an opportunity to meet some players after the match. They met Pat Rice, Don Howe and Alan Ball; even Geoff Hurst was there. On another occasion, Robert met Don Revie, the England manager, and he also had several calls from Jimmy Armfield, who had recently taken over as Leeds manager.

Bob remembered these sports celebrities, and others too numerous to mention, with affection; they gave their time, their support and their friendship to Robert.

'It's absolutely wonderful, Dad,' said Robert. 'All the people we've met. I don't know how you managed it. But it would be nice not to be ill, wouldn't it?'

Bob realised but for Robert's terrible illness, it would have been unlikely for his son to have met any one of them. 'He'd never have met them, would he? You can't argue with that, can you? But he really did enjoy meeting them; there was no question about that.'

Robert underwent five operations in all: three major and two less so. His first operation was the one that Bob will never forget. It took place on 14 May 1974, Judy's birthday. Gordon Glover, their minister, and his wife, Doreen, insisted on being with them in their usual supportive way. While they waited, Gordon's feelings became so intense he almost passed out. Then Martin Mott emerged with the news that the surgeon 'was very, very pleased' with the way things had gone: the whole tumour had been removed. For Bob and Judy, coming after the laying on of hands, it was the answer to their prayers and a wonderful birthday present for Judy.

It looked as if Robert had turned the corner but cancer can be a cruel and relentless disease; gradually, the warning signs returned and his battle went on.

17

Infinity Times Infinity

There were some good days for Robert but there were some tough days too.

The horror of watching and hearing your own child undergoing cancer therapy is a punishing, waking nightmare. It is impossible for anyone who has not experienced it even to try to imagine what it must be like.

'Three-year-olds went down for radiotherapy treatment with eighty-year-olds,' said Bob. 'Although they were dear old people, I just wondered what it must have been like looking at them through the eyes of a child. I wondered what little children might have thought about going in alongside these old people. They must have thought, "Am I going to look like that?" Of course, I realised that hospitals couldn't possibly have radiotherapy equipment just for the use of children.

'They marked Robert up; Jill Bullimore, the consultant radiologist, was there—she was wonderful. When it was over and we went to the car, as I tried to help Robert into his seat, he stopped me and said, "Dad, whatever is the matter with you?" I said, what do you mean, what's the matter with me? He said, "Dad, you look awful. You look as if you are going to collapse." It was just how I felt, but I said, no, no, I'm all right. He repeated, "Are you sure? You look awful." I said, well, I think I got myself in a state when you went down for your radiotherapy, sitting there watching you go through it. He said, "You mustn't get like that. Do you remember that first day when you told me what was wrong with me?" I said, yes, I remember. He said, "You made me a promise that you would be with me all the time through the treatment." I said, yes, that's right. He said, "I know you will keep that promise so nothing else matters." I thought, golly, the trust of a child in his father. When I came to be a believer, I got that same promise from God but now to be told almost the same thing by an eight-year-old.

'When Robert was on chemotherapy, he stayed in overnight. They used three different drugs and they were all pretty ghastly. In those days, you had to drink so many pints of water before you were allowed to go home because one of the drugs could cause the bladder to bleed. With vincristine, you also had to be so careful because it could affect the heart. His chemotherapy was very regular: all the time—bang, bang, bang. The drugs were given intravenously with needles and he hated needles. There were no Hickman lines in those days. Later, CLIC paid for the pilot scheme for the first Hickman lines but there were no lines then for Robert.' (A Hickman line is a tube inserted by operation into the chest and directly into the major blood vessels to administer chemotherapy to avoid continual, distressing use of injections.)

'And then there were the side effects—there would be all sorts of things that had to be dealt with. Ulcers in the mouth: he had one ulcer the size of a half-crown. He was very, very good but there was an awful lot of vomiting which seemed to go on forever. Robert hated the needles, absolutely hated them. We tried so hard to make it easier for him and invented the needles game where we counted the injections and finger pricks. When we reached 100, the staff at the hospital made him a cake. The needles went on, of course. He got to 872.

'I tried every conceivable route to the hospital just to go a different way because, as soon as he saw the hospital, he vomited straight out: it would just shoot straight out of his mouth. He couldn't do anything about it. I got special permission to take him in the back door; I tried every conceivable thing.

'On the way in, we used to play games. "Derbies", we called one of them: who could spot the first VW Beetle. We called them "Derbies" to be different from everyone else who called them "Herbies". The first car we see is mine, the second is yours. We would play anything at all, anything to distract him on our way in to the hospital but as soon as he got the smell of the place ...

'In the ward, when he was given the drugs, I couldn't even look at him. I'd just look away.

'Because of the circumstances, my relationship with Robert was unreal, almost uncanny. I remember when I had flu; Robert sat all day on a chair at the end of the landing outside the bedroom door. That was the sort of relationship we had. He tried to tell me how much he loved me but he couldn't put it into words. He tried top express his love for me on a rising scale. Then, one day he said, "I've worked out how much I love you. Infinity times infinity."'

18

Something will Click

In the meantime, Bob and John's business continued to prosper; they sold the remaining 20 Parklands plots for more than double the amount they paid for the whole site some ten years previously. When no one else seemed interested, 13 acres of land in Tetbury, bought for a ridiculously low sum, also turned to gold. To others, it had seemed a foolish gamble; the acreage was landlocked and the only possible entrance was through a nursery but Bob was aware that a developer already owned the nursery and therefore had access to the site. After acquiring the land, the Woodwards sold it to the developer at an enormous profit. With his drive and an eye for opportunity, Bob's prowess as a businessman was certainly augmented by the fair hand of good fortune. 'We took chances but things seemed to turn up trumps,' he said.

Having done it once, Bob tried to do it again and, after sounding out the developer, he bought 20 acres of woodland in Dursley. This deal was different because it stretched Woodward Bros' finances. It was also different because the developer pulled out leaving Bob and John with a piece of land they did not want. To cover their costs they looked for another buyer; then, completely out of the blue, they received a telephone call with an offer that was exceptional: twice the amount that they would have accepted for it. Triumph snatched from the jaws of defeat.

'It was like giving a donkey strawberries, really,' said Bob.

The travelling fund that allowed Martin Mott to return to Bristol on a regular basis was proving to be a success, as was the first Home from Home in Frenchay, but Bob wanted to do so much more. He sought advice from Professor Neville Butler and Duncan Guthrie, the founder of Action for the Crippled Child, about setting up a charitable trust. After speaking with his solicitor, Vic New, Bob hunted for two trustees to join him and invited Neville to be the first. For the second, he turned to Gerry Davis, his friend and GP.

At a Fishponds Baptist church luncheon, Bob arranged to be seated next to his longstanding friend Jim Carbines where he asked him whether he would like to do a little bit of bookkeeping for a worthwhile charity.

'It was amongst the best approaches I ever made,' said Bob. 'Jim's meticulous accounting skills and the time and effort he gave for CLIC were second to none. He has accompanied me on CLIC journeys over many hundreds of thousands of miles.'

'I couldn't have wished to do anything better in retirement,' said Jim.

Bob knew Jack Lyes, a solicitor and a fellow trustee of Unity Home, an old people's home in St Paul's, Bristol, and asked him to attend CLIC trustees' meetings for guidance and advice. Jack later became a trustee of CLIC and served for many years.

Of Neville Butler, Bob said, 'I only had one fall-out with him. I suggested he should be chairman but he would not hear of it. He said, "It's your idea; it's your vision; you've got to be the chairman." Well, I'd never chaired anything in my life, so I felt I couldn't possibly do it. I'd be the secretary and the general dogsbody but I didn't want a title like chairman. In the end, Neville agreed to be the first chairman and he stayed in the post for several years.'

The new charity was now up and running and received its first funds. John readily agreed that their firm should be the first to make a donation of £1,000 to open the bank account.

On 16 January 1976 the CLIC Trust was founded. Its simple but powerful name undoubtedly contributed to its success and was conceived following a conversation at Heathrow, when Bob shook hands with Martin Mott before his departure to the States.

'I do hope that by the next time we are in touch, you will have a name for the charity,' said Martin.

'You know,' said Bob, 'we have thirty or forty already and if we keep on coming up with new names something will click.'

'I hope so,' said Martin as he left to catch his flight.

Driving back to Bristol, Bob mulled over their conversation and thought about how much he was looking forward to setting up the charity. He had to find a name ... something will click ... something will click ... click ... click. It was so obvious. Drop the 'k' and it could be an acronym for 'Cancer and Leukaemia in Children'. Or perhaps it should be 'Cancer and Leukaemia in Childhood'? Neville Butler preferred 'Childhood', and so it was.

Having found the name, Bob set to work on a CLIC logo. He took his sketches to Nigel Green in Wotton-under-Edge who designed the Woodward Bros letterhead. Nigel played around with the logo and came up with the final design that featured a blood-red teardrop dotting the 'i' of CLIC; stationery and branded items proudly bore this logo into the late 1990s. The charity's watchword, 'The fight to save young lives', was coined by PR man Richard Bladen and adopted in 1976; it inspired CLIC's volunteers and fund-raisers for over twenty years.

While travelling to and from Heathrow, Bob and Martin talked excitedly about the future prospects of CLIC. They talked about a new consultancy post that would give them leverage to open a daybeds unit, complete with nursing staff. Both men shared the vision that Bristol Children's Hospital should be a centre of excellence. Even at this early stage, they planned to have domiciliary nurses to provide wider care beyond the bounds of the hospital. They only disagreed on the provision of Homes from Home. Martin would have preferred the money to be used on care and treatment but Bob, as a parent, could see the enormous benefits that the homes provided.

Late in 1975 Bob's interest in providing funds for advancing knowledge, research and teaching in the field of childhood cancer and its treatment prompted discussions with Sir Alec Merrison, the vice-chancellor of Bristol University. In 1976 the university began the process to appoint a consultant senior lecturer in paediatric oncology but needed £140,000 to create the new post. The Leukaemia Research Fund agreed to sponsor £70,000 and, with half the money secured, it was up to Bob to find the rest. At this stage, with no experience of raising charitable funds, there seemed to be only one way forward: to give a personal covenant. By covenanting £4,000 per year the tax concession would increase the annual sum to £7,000. Bob signed for ten years with a personal commitment for the first five; if by then a viable charity had been founded, it would take over the commitment.

Bob received an invitation to sit on the eight-strong appointments board with a representative from the Leukaemia Research Fund. Being part of this selection process, which took place on 5 October, was daunting; Bob's knowledge in this field was limited because his experience came only from being the father of a child with cancer.

There were three applicants: Martin Mott, as was expected; Dr Peter Kearney, who stood in for Martin while he was in the States; and a radiologist, Dr Jane Bond, from the Institute of Child Health in London.

There was a division of opinion among the board members. While they all had a high regard for Martin Mott, some voiced their concerns at the level of travelling he undertook. Although Bob's instinct told him that Martin was the right man for the job, he wondered if his heart was ruling his head. Was he swaying towards Martin because of Robert? Was he taking the easy option by siding with the chair, Neville Butler, now a close friend, who also favoured Martin? Was he being fair?

Then something was said to one of the applicants that horrified him. 'How do you feel about pumping enough drugs into a child that would kill a horse?'

That question sickened Bob. What sort of people were they? Should he be giving money for this post? He was aware that cancer drugs were toxic poisons but the cold-bloodedness of the question made him even more fearful for his son. His immediate thoughts were to stop Robert's treatment.

By the end of the interviews, it was clear there were those in favour of Martin Mott and those who preferred Peter Kearney. Deadlock.

'Neville suggested that normal standing orders allowed the chairman to have the casting vote. But the others argued that as it had not been agreed at the outset, it would be quite wrong for Neville to have the casting vote, so it was suggested that the vote should be offered to the Leukaemia Research Fund's representative as he had a medical background and because he also represented one of the sponsors.

'Neville replied, "I take the point that he should have the casting vote and I am sure he will be fair and use it wisely; however, we must not overlook our other sponsor who is part-funding this post. So, if anybody is entitled to a casting vote, I feel it should be the personal sponsor." So, it fell to muggins,' said Bob.

This responsibility gave Bob his biggest dilemma. Which way should he vote? With no one to advise him otherwise, he stayed true to his gut feeling and the post went to Martin.

Bob considered the whole process an ordeal. 'I could not understand why there were so many knives out and that uncomfortable feeling stayed with me. One person on that panel didn't speak to me for about three years and another never spoke to me again. It was an enormous decision and one that I did not take lightly. I wasn't sure, I shall never be sure, that I did the right thing.'

The National Health Service did not fund this post; it was the first appointment of its kind in Bristol and there were only one or two others in the whole of the country. While the post was based in the children's hospital, it was a university appointment and some of the consultant's time would be taken up with research.

The new appointment brought other benefits. With a consultant in place, it became easier for Neville Butler to put pressure on the hospital to open a children's cancer unit; at that time, young cancer patients were mixed in with everyone else.

'It was a mega, mega step forward,' said Bob.

Martin Mott knew exactly where his new daybed unit should be but before this area could be allocated, it would have to be passed by the hospital's space committee, who were well aware of this need, as Bob had been pressing its case for some time. On a visit to a member of the space committee to finalise details, Bob was told that permission would only be granted if there was a proper set of plans drawn up for the new daybeds centre, the plans were available for a meeting at two o'clock that same day, and the plans were acceptable.

Bob was taken aback by this; he felt that this information had been deliberately withheld from him and now there was little time left to satisfy these demands. Moreover, action had to be taken that same day because the space committee would not meet again for several months.

After Bob told Robert that he had something important to do, he drove to Redland to see his architect, Richard Kingscott. He told Richard's PA that he needed to see Richard urgently because he had a dire emergency on his hands. Bob was immediately shown into the architect's office. 'I'm going to ask you the biggest favour that I am ever likely to ask you, Richard. Could you and one of your colleagues come with me—right now—down to the children's hospital? I need full-scale plans before half past one this afternoon to take to a meeting.'

Remarkably, Kingscott and his colleague downed tools, grabbed what they needed and followed him to the children's hospital. It took them about an hour to draw up the plans.

At half past one, Bob waited outside the committee door and, as the members arrived, he handed out the express delivered plans. 'There you are ... the drawings for daybeds,' he said with some satisfaction. Another rabbit pulled out of the hat at a moment's notice.

The hospital had a desperate need for disease-detecting incubators and Downend Round Table donated a sum of £4,500 to CLIC to buy them. When Bob tried to take an interest in their use, he was unable to locate them. Someone suggested that he should look in the lecture theatre where he found the boxes, still unwrapped and tucked away in a corner. Disillusioned, he kept an eye on them to see what developed. A month passed and the unopened boxes continued to gather dust. Frustrated by the delay in the utilisation of this expensive new resource, Bob took action.

'You've asked CLIC for these incubators and I want to know when are they going to be used and an assurance that their usage will be tied in with children's cancers,' he said.

'I'm not sure when we will be able to put them into action,' Bob was told and the matter remained unresolved. Another month passed by and Bob insisted that immediate attention be given to, what he considered, a major laxity. He demanded CLIC's money back within fourteen days or he would go public with the story; the cheque was swiftly forth-coming.

'The incubators were destined for another department and were not going to be used for childhood cancer at all,' said Bob. 'They couldn't get the funding so they asked CLIC because they thought that we would be able to raise it.'

There was also good news for the fledgling charity. The Chew Valley Round Table, alerted to childhood cancer by Bob Thompson who lost his son Matthew, raised more than £7,000 from a sponsored bed-push and decided to give it to CLIC; an encouraging indication that the name of the new charity and what it stood for were welcomed by the Bristol public.

Within weeks of setting up CLIC, Bob met a seasoned fund-raiser from Henbury: Marjorie Dawson. Speaking on Radio Bristol, Marjorie told listeners how she loved to knit outfits for dolls and then raffle them for charity. Bob called the station and asked them to put him in touch with her. They met soon after and Bob asked for her support. Marjorie became one of the charity's first fund-raisers; at Bob's suggestion, she wrote to a local football club to ask them to donate an autographed ball; then she took it upon herself to write to every football club she could think of—footballs bounced in from all over the country, sometimes raising as much as £100 for each ball. Over fifteen or so years with CLIC, Marjorie knitted yards and yards of wool. Bob was honoured to speak at Fred Dawson's funeral (Marjorie's husband) and later at Marjorie's funeral as well.

There were others just like Marjorie: Judy's sister, Margaret, was also among the first to start fund-raising—so many others, too many to mention by name. Through their hard work, the charity took off. Word spread—enthusiasm and generosity grew. Whole communities took CLIC to their hearts.

Soon, the concept of a 'Branch Canopy' for CLIC took shape. It was largely the inspiration of Dr Noel Meeke from Whiteshill, Stroud, who came up with the idea of CLIC forming a branch structure when his two-year-old daughter Suzie was diagnosed with cancer. The Gloucestershire branch, CLIC's first, was launched at the health centre in Stroud in April 1979. At the launch was Stella Elston, who had lost her four-year-old son Jonathan to cancer. Stella worked at Bristol Children's Hospital in the daybed unit and she suggested setting up a Bristol branch, which opened in October later that same year. Noel and his family worked tirelessly for the Gloucestershire branch of CLIC, and were there at the 25th anniversary of the Gloucestershire branch—together with their now grown-up daughter Suzie.

'Both Noel and Stella gave the most outstanding service to CLIC over many years,' said Bob.

In this way, CLIC's branch network grew in leaps and bounds. 'Branches just seemed to happen,' said Bob. 'Someone knows someone else, gets an introduction and suddenly, there's a new branch. It was quite wonderful really, the way it happened.'

Two years after the foundation of the Gloucestershire branch, CLIC was surprised to receive a large amount of money from fund-raising efforts in the small Devon village of South Brent. Jamie Halliday, son of the local GP, had died of his illness in 1980 and the villagers, wanting to show support to Jamie's parents, John and Anne, made generous contributions towards the work of CLIC. Later, John Halliday was approached about setting up a branch in his area, which became the Plymouth branch, with John as its chairman. In time, he became a CLIC trustee.

In Weston-super-Mare Pat Dain, who had lost her granddaughter Lucy to the same devastating illness as Robert, called a meeting in the Mayor's Parlour for those who might be interested in establishing a branch of CLIC locally. It was well attended and another group of CLIC friends and supporters emerged.

Bob's bank manager asked Dr Gwyn Llewellin, a friend who lived in Jersey, if he would like to set up a branch there and Bob went over to see him. The Jersey branch was born shortly afterwards and a branch soon followed in Guernsey, founded by Nigel Cann. The Channel Island branches received a boost when Dr Jan Kohler, a consultant from Southampton Hospital, visited them both to whip up enthusiasm among the new fund-raisers.

Branches popped up all over the South West and so many of them had personal reasons for being established. At one stage, there were more than 30 branches and support groups. The CLIC family continued to multiply. Then CLIC set up their research unit, headed by Keith Brown, in the Medical School of the University of Bristol in 1985 to concentrate on genetics. This research led to a greater understanding of solid cancerous tumours and Wilm's tumour in particular.

'CLIC grew so quickly and people came along with donations,' said Professor Neville Butler, CLIC's first chair. 'It wouldn't have happened without Bob—couldn't have happened without Bob—he is an exceptional man.'

19

My Name is Woodward, Bob Woodward

Bang in the middle of an already crowded life, Bob had to find time for what he and Robert dubbed a 'James Bond experience'.

'When I think about it now, I can't believe that I ever did it.'

Because Casa Spruce, their Spanish home on the Costa Blanca—built before Robert's illness—was now lying unused, Bob and Judy soon came to realise that it locked up funds for which they could find a more worthwhile use. After bringing the contents home to England to furnish the first Home from Home in Frenchay, the villa was sold and the proceeds deposited into the Bank of Bilbao in Calpe. But when Bob tried to arrange the transfer of this money to England, he was surprised when the Spanish bank told him that he could not do it: something was amiss.

As Robert was reasonably stable, Bob felt he could take a hasty trip to Spain to sort out the problem. However, when he picked up the cheque in Calpe, he was told that, to cash it, he would have to take it to the bank's headquarters, some 300 miles north in Madrid. Bob, already missing Robert, had not planned to be away too long and this extra travel began to worry him. He went straight to the bank in Madrid, where the manager was pleasant, helpful and spoke good English; another cheque was issued that was cashable at their London branch. Problem solved, Bob flew home with a smile on his face and the cheque in his pocket.

Accompanied by his bank manager, Norman Watkins, Bob presented the cheque at the Bank of Bilbao in London where the cashier told him that it was not possible to convert the peseta cheque into sterling. Until then, Bob had been unaware that his money had been paid into the wrong type of account; it should have been paid into a convertible account. He was, therefore, unable to change the Spanish currency back into sterling, which meant that he would also be unable to reclaim the dollar premium.

At that time, to discourage sterling leaving the country, a fluctuating dollar premium was imposed on the purchase of foreign property; the percentage depended on the prevailing monetary conditions of the day and was refundable on repatriation of the funds. In Bob's case, it proved to be a sizeable levy because the dollar premium, which had been relatively low on the purchase, ended up high on the sale; it was too much to lose. He sought advice and went first to the Bank of England, who were unable to help him. The Bank of Bilbao in Madrid told him that should he decide to cash the cheque into pesetas in Spain, he should be aware that—on the threat of a two-year jail sentence—it was strictly forbidden to take pesetas out of the country.

Time moved on and although there were other priorities uppermost in his mind, decisive action needed to be taken before the cheque became invalid. Bob telephoned the Bank of England and asked what might happen if he brought a large quantity of pesetas back to the UK. They told him, informally, that it was not the Bank's concern and whatever he wanted to do was entirely up to him; should he decide to bring the money to them in a suitcase, they would accept it. Bob's interpretation of this exchange was that he should go to Spain and bring the pesetas home.

Gauging the demands of Robert's treatment for a second time, Bob hatched a plan but decided it would be better not to discuss it with Judy because he knew that she would 'have kittens'. Although Robert sensed his father was up to something, Bob did not tell him either, as he did not wish to over-excite him.

'There was this threat of a jail sentence. Whatever happened, I couldn't be separated from my family but somehow or other I had to try to get my money back,' he said.

He approached Bill, a resident of Parklands, who had recently sold his business and had time on his hands. Bob made him a proposition.

'Would you like three days away in Spain?' he asked.

'Why?' Bill said. 'What's happening?'

'Well, you can earn yourself £500 cash in three days if you would do the following,' said Bob and explained his plan. Bill was intrigued and, after consideration, agreed to become Bob's associate—a decision he later regretted.

Bob visited a local printer called Alan Gunn and together they worked out the number of large denomination peseta notes to the value of £18,000. After Alan had cut an appropriate number of pieces of paper to the exact size to judge the volume and weight of that amount of Spanish money, it was easy for Bob to select a suitable suitcase to carry the money through customs.

A few days later, Bob and Bill drove to Heathrow to catch their flight to Madrid. Bob gave his companion a spare set of car keys just in case things did not go according to plan and, in order to avoid any suspicion linking the two men, Bill took an early flight and Bob flew out later in the day. They stayed in separate hotels and had an arrangement to rendezvous the same evening, when they enjoyed a meal together and ran over the details of the plan once more.

'Our first job was to find the bank where I intended to pick up the money early next morning. The plan was that I would carry a holdall with a black bin liner inside it; Bill would be stationed on the opposite side of the street, pretending to look into a shop window. I would be wearing my black mac and he would see my reflection as I left the bank. If I took it off and placed it over my arm, he'd know that there was something wrong; however, assuming all was well, he'd walk down his side of the street and I'd walk down mine. We'd meet up at the subway where I would pass him the black bin liner filled with the money to put in his holdall. After that, we would part company and from then on we'd be on our own; Bill would take the first flight home. To be on the safe side, I'd continue walking for a couple of miles before returning to my hotel just in case someone was following me. If there was, they'd find nothing on me and then I could fly home.'

The next morning, Bill was in place, looking into the shop window as arranged. Bob felt nervous, excited and guilty and had to reassure himself that he was not doing anything wrong: all he was doing was collecting his own money, no more, no less. With adrenalin levels mounting, he entered the bank and presented his cheque to the cashier.

'What do you want to do?' the cashier asked.

'I want to cash it, please.'

'You want all of this ... in cash ... now?'

'Yes, please, now.' The girl went off to seek advice and before long, a young man appeared.

'Do you want to cash this cheque now?' he asked.

'Yes.'

'All of it?'

'Yes.'

'One moment please,' said the young man before moving off to speak with his superior. Bob waited in anticipation. The male cashier returned and immediately started to count out the money into large bundles. Looking around, Bob spotted two swarthy-skinned men taking a great interest in what was going on. This bothered him as he would soon be out on the street carrying wads of cash and these two men would know about it.

'Excuse me, but could we do this in a private room?' asked Bob. The cashier stopped counting, tucked the money beneath the counter and went off again. This time he returned with a different man in tow.

'Is there a problem?' this new man asked.

'I just wondered whether we could have a little privacy and do this in an anteroom,' said Bob.

'Let me see the cheque,' said the man. His eyes scanned the cheque several times. 'It's an awful lot of money, isn't it? Why have you not cashed this before?' he said. 'Your holding bank is in Calpe, is it not?'

'Yes, that's right,' said Bob.

When the man disappeared again, Bob became agitated.

On his return, the man asked whether Bob had signed the cheque that morning.

'Yes,' he said. 'I signed it here.'

'We shall have to authenticate your signature again,' said the man. 'This young lady will show you the way.' She led Bob out of the bank as, apparently, the authentication could only be carried out at an adjacent office.

Meanwhile, Bill watched fretfully from his position on the other side of the street. Bob took off his mac, placed it over his arm and hoped that Bill would recognise the signal. (It was fortunate that it was not raining, as this would certainly have looked most eccentric and might even have brought unwanted attention.) Further down the street, Bob was ushered into another office, where, after another inexplicable delay, he signed more documents to conclude the formalities.

Bill stood resolutely at his post watching and wondering what was going on as Bob returned to the main bank premises. Inside the bank, there was yet more waiting to do when the bank official disappeared yet again. When he returned, he brought only bad news.

'I am sorry. We cannot help you. This cheque can only be cashed in your holding bank in Calpe,' he said.

Bob felt frustrated but knew it might make it worse if he made a scene; he left the bank in a daze. He blamed himself; had he not delayed the payout, he would be walking down the street with the money in his holdall. As it was, he was walking down the street with nothing save the obstinate, un-cashed cheque.

Bill darted across the road to meet him. 'We've got a big problem,' Bob told him. 'We have to leave Madrid right now and fly to Calpe.'

'Why?' asked Bill. Bob explained why on the way to the airport where, instead of flying home to Bristol, they changed their tickets and took the next flight to Alicante. On arrival, they hired a car and drove straight to Calpe where Bob contacted Arthur Gardner, one of his friends in the area.

'I don't suppose there's any chance that your basement flat is empty for us to stay in tonight?' asked Bob. 'We have to go to the bank tomorrow to collect the money from the sale of my property.'

Arthur had no objection. That evening, when they all went out for a drink, Bob was tense but his main concern was for Bill who was obviously worried and beginning to look a little unwell but there could be no turning back.

Early next morning, they assembled outside the bank. When the doors opened, Bill followed Bob inside but stayed close to the entrance. Arthur remained outside in his car; it was difficult for Bob to tell exactly how Arthur felt about the situation but he was grateful for his support.

Bob presented the cheque, passed over his passport for identification and signed his name.

'How would you like the money?' asked the cashier.

'Now! As fast as you can,' Bob wanted to shout out but instead, he said, 'In high denomination notes, please.'

As the cashier counted it out, Bob dropped the bundles straight into his holdall. He thanked the cashier but when he turned to leave, a voice halted him in his tracks.

'Señor, Señor.'

With a sense of foreboding, Bob turned around. What could have gone wrong now? The cashier smiled and pointed to a number of coins sitting on the counter. Bob thanked him again, tossed the small change in with the rest of the money and made for the door; he could hardly get out fast enough. When he was almost there, the cashier called again.

'Señor, Señor Woodward.'

What should he do now? Should he make a bolt for it? He could get to the door before anyone could get anywhere near him, jump in the car and take his chance. Time froze. What would James Bond do? This ludicrous thought saved him and his friends from possible catastrophe. Coolly, he turned and looked into the face of the advancing cashier.

'Señor,' the man said, 'su pasaporte.'

Bob smiled.

'I'd forgotten my passport. Had I bolted then, I'd have blown the whole flippin' thing.'

They piled into the car and Arthur took the precaution of driving around the block several times to ensure that they were not being followed. Satisfied that there was no one on their tail, they returned to the flat to prepare for the journey home.

Bill's language degenerated as he packed. 'Where am I going to hide all this?' he said, as he transferred the cash from the holdall into his suitcase. He pushed the money into his packed clothes: into his trouser pockets, down the trouser legs and inside the arms of his shirts. 'There's money coming out of everywhere,' he moaned. (Readers should note that Bill's degenerating language has been expunged from this text.)

'Don't worry about it, Bill,' said Bob. 'Just get on with it and shut the flippin' case.' (Bob's degenerating language, on the other hand, has been reported in full.)

They locked their cases, took them to the car and, after bidding farewell to Arthur, set off for Alicante. Minutes later, a few miles along the road, their car was flagged down and a bright light shone into their alarmed faces.

'They've got us ... they've got us ... they've got us,' squeaked Bill in his high state of anxiety.

'Hang on,' said Bob. 'It's probably something trivial.' And it was: the light-shining, flag-waving Spaniards were warning all drivers to be careful of a large rock from a recent landslide that was still obstructing the road ahead; with nerves jangling the two men continued on their way.

At Alicante airport Bill checked in first with the valuable cargo and when Bob followed a few minutes later he was just in time to watch a conveyor belt trundle a small fortune into the waiting hands of Spanish baggage handlers. He hoped he had not seen it for the last time.

They moved into the departure lounge and waited to board. All seemed well except that Bill was sweating so profusely that it dripped off the end of his nose. When they boarded the plane, as per plan, they sat apart; however, the next incident was unplanned. Trepidation mounted when the captain informed them they were to make an unscheduled stop in Barcelona. Bob's imagination slipped into overdrive. Why are we going to Barcelona? Will there be tighter security there? Even worse, do they know that we're carrying all this blessed money?

At Barcelona airport handlers removed the luggage from the hold and laid it out on the tarmac after which passengers were asked to disembark and identify their belongings. The planeload of travellers searched for their own pieces of luggage with varying degrees of enthusiasm. Although Bill looked ready to keel over at any moment he managed to stay upright. When at last the ground staff were satisfied that the passengers and their baggage had been reunited, the frustrated travellers were told to leave their luggage on the tarmac and reboard the aeroplane. A resounding silence was the only explanation for the delay.

Breaking the rules of the plan, Bill moved up the aisle and sat down in the spare seat beside Bob.

'I just can't stand this any more,' he said. 'Don't ask me to go back to my seat. I'm staying here. Blow the security.'

'Don't worry,' soothed Bob. 'In a minute, we shall be looking down at the sea and we'll be on our way home.'

This seemed to satisfy Bill—but only for a brief moment.

'What if the case doesn't turn up at the other end?' he asked.

'We'll just have to face that when we get there.'

The plane took off and the seat belt and no smoking warning lights went out. With a sigh of relief, Bill withdrew a slim panatela from his inside pocket and was about to light it when Bob burst out laughing. Bill removed the cigar from his lips; it was still in its cellophane wrapping.

'You're a bugger,' he said. 'You were going to let me light that.'

'Well, if that's what you want to do, it's up to you really,' laughed Bob.

Bill did not find it at all funny; he remained on edge and his anxiety had not improved by the time they landed. 'What's going to happen if they stop me in customs?' he said.

'Don't worry. I shall be right behind you,' Bob reassured him. 'And don't forget there's no problem about bringing foreign currency into the country. If they take it away, we'll get it back again because the Bank of England knows it's mine. My biggest worry is that when we open the case, we'll find a concrete block with a note from an about-to-retire Alicante baggage handler that says, "Gracias Señor, you have made me very happy."'

The two men passed through customs unchallenged. Putting this fleeting anti-climax behind them, they lost no time in scooting back to the car where they did their best to compose themselves.

'For goodness sake, open that bloody suitcase,' said Bill.

Bob unlocked it, lifted the lid and the two men peered in. Tentatively, Bob lifted a shirtsleeve; a quantity of pesetas peered back at him. It was all there.

Two jubilant men enjoyed the worry-free drive to Bob's office in Wotton, where Bob phoned his bank manager. Norman came round immediately and surveyed the mounds of cash stacked high on the desk; his eyes widened as Bob described the trials and tribulations of the last few days. Bill drove home while Bob and Norman took the money down to the bank to deposit it into the night safe.

When Bob told his family what had happened, his story produced mixed reactions.

'Rob was absolutely over the moon—what a tale. Judy wasn't so thrilled. She asked me why I hadn't told her what I was going to do. For obvious reasons, I told her. Just look at you. How would you have felt if you'd known what was happening?' said Bob. 'So, after that, I got in touch with the Bank of England and they were happy to repay the dollar premium. For weeks and weeks afterwards, Rob would say to me, "Tell me the James Bond story again, Dad."'

20

Thinking of Heaven

The impact of Robert's illness took its toll on Rachel and James because their friends were afraid of disturbing Robert while he was still in treatment and they stopped coming round as often. Although it seemed unfair, they meant only good by their actions. This state of affairs concerned Bob: it was something else that needed a solution. He talked it over with Jim Panes and they came up with an idea of finding a gypsy caravan for the garden. The caravan was an instant hit.

Robert's diagnosis and treatment, coupled with the extra burdens of setting up CLIC and research into the mosaic, all took their toll and for the first time in Bob's adult life his health began to suffer and he was unable to sleep. His doctor prescribed Mogadon, a short-term treatment for insomnia. Like so many others, Bob soon felt he could not manage without it. This lasted for four or five years before he cut down on the dosage. When he tried to wean himself off the drug he suffered muscle spasms and had to take pethidine, yet another powerful drug, for the relief of severe pain. It took a long time for him to feel really well again.

In 1976 Robert was getting so much pain in his legs that the doctors had to sever the nerves to remove his pain.

'This course of action was one of the most harrowing things for me to deal with. My faith was being challenged. I still felt that God would heal Robert but, if I believed that, how could I let them sever the nerves in his legs?' said Bob.

Robert managed enormously well throughout all of his problems and suffering. When he was at home Pat Dickson cared for him every day and Robert never once had a bedsore. His confinement to the house must have been heartbreaking for a sporting, active young boy, especially when at times he was unable to move from one room to another. It was then that Humphrey made an appearance. Humphrey the electric wheelchair enabled him to move around the house and to venture down the road to playing fields where he watched the other children. The sight of their son in a wheelchair was grimly painful to Bob and Judy, knowing what he had been capable of just a few short years earlier.

During the precious hours Bob spent with his son, they discussed many subjects including life, heaven and pain. One day, Robert complained of a particular pain in his chest.

'Well, that's a bit like the pain you had before,' said Bob.

'What do you mean,' asked Robert, 'like the pain I had before?'

'Well, is it like the pain you had before?'

'I don't know,' said Robert. 'That pain has gone, hasn't it?'

'Well, you had a pain just like that in your chest yesterday,' said Bob.

'That was yesterday's pain. Yesterday has gone.'

'I think that was so profound,' said Bob. 'This is today. This is the moment. This is now. I wish I could think like that sometimes.'

Another conversation centred on heaven.

'How would you define heaven, Dad?'

'I can't really define heaven, Rob,' said Bob, 'because no one who has been there has come back, so we don't know. We can only conjure up a picture of what it must be like.'

'How would you describe it?' asked Robert.

'I suppose the only thing I can say is, look back over your life and think of the most happy time that you've ever had: a time when you thought, that was wonderful. Well, just imagine if you could multiply that wonderful time a trillion times. I think it would be like that.'

This simple explanation seemed to satisfy Robert, who once described his love for his father as bigger than a trillion times a trillion, and Bob's use of the same number struck a familiar chord.

'We never expected to be thinking of heaven before I was twelve,' said Robert.

Bob was speechless; they had not spelt out to Robert that he would never get better. Now, it was almost as if there was no need to.

'There is nothing that tears your heart more than when you find yourself on your knees pleading with God to spare the life of your son and then, in what seemed to be such a short space of time, you find yourself on your knees again, pleading with God to take him,' said Bob. 'There were times when Robert was almost angelic, as if he'd been specially sent to us. These youngsters have special qualities. They become resilient to their dreadful problems and take on a depth of understanding that you only seem to find in a much older person. I learnt so much from Robert.'

Robert's sister Rachel said, 'Robert's illness had been very up and down; you'd keep thinking he'd gone into remission and then it would come back again. It was that, which was so very wearing. It seemed everything was good and his hair was growing back and then suddenly it would start all over again. I can remember Dad crying once, that was quite shocking for me: he'd just had a phone call saying that Robert's illness had come back again and he said, "How am I going to tell him that it's back and that he's going to have to start his treatment again?'''

Towards the end, Bob and Judy hardly left Robert's bedside.

'Just a few days before he died, Robert put his arms around Judy and thanked her for all she had done for him—and then he did the same to me. I guessed he already knew that it wasn't going to be very long.'

Robert died at home in the early hours of 1 July 1977 but, according to his father, it was as if his spirit left him the evening before.

'It was a strange experience; Robert took a huge breath in and then all his breath seemed to go just as if his spirit had been released. How could God's love for Robert be greater than mine?'

Torn in every conceivable way, Bob and Judy had to face up to telling Rachel and James and the rest of the family.

Rachel had recently completed her baptismal classes alongside Robert's closest friend Simon Curtis, Simon's sister Sally, and another friend, Mandy French. The service, scheduled for the Sunday night, fell between Robert's death and burial—in the normal order of things, Robert too would have been baptised that evening. In spite of the minister's offer to suspend the service, Bob and Judy felt that it should take place as planned and would be all the more special for doing so.

'It was quite wonderful. I don't think there has ever been a baptismal service like it. The courage of those youngsters, Rachel, Simon, Sally and Mandy; I have never seen anything like it. Then, within 48 hours, we were back in church again—for Robert's funeral,' said Bob.

'I remembered Gordon Glover saying he'd walked into Bob and Judy's home not long before Robert died and heard what sounded like an angel singing *Guide Me O Thou Great Jehov*ah. It was Robert singing, sat at the top of the stairs,' said Diane, Bob's sister.

'That was his favourite hymn,' said Bob, 'which he dearly loved to sing on Sunday nights. He would get his hymnbook and sing along with his favourite programme, *Songs of Praise*. He just loved doing that. After Robert died, Judy told me when she'd listened to him singing the line, *When I tread the verge of Jordan*, she thought it wouldn't be too long before he would be doing just that.

'Then there was the realisation of the finality of it all ... the separation. I wondered if we would completely lose our sanity. The pain was unbelievable. Rachel was fifteen and James just six. When I look back, I wonder how we all survived this terrible thing; but we did; we were given the strength.'

A week later Bob took James out for a walk over Frenchay Hill. Little James kept asking his father about all the things that Robert did and Bob listed them for him: Robert loved to play football; he loved to sing hymns aloud. To every one of Bob's memories, James came up with the same hopeful response. 'I can do that,' he said.

There were constant reminders of Robert. The car from Colston School, returning youngsters to their homes after Saturday sports, no longer stopped at their door but it still stopped further up the road; they could not help but watch as other people's children, dressed in their familiar striped blazers, got out. Bob said that Judy found it hit her hardest when she removed the nametags from Robert's school uniform.

All through this difficult time, while they were grieving, Bob continued to work for CLIC, providing support to others in similar situations. It proved good therapy to generate a spark to help others; he likened it to turning over their engines from his own 'flat battery'.

Robert's miniature footballers, whole teams—all with little numbers on their backs—were stored away; cine-films of holidays in Spain were placed in the attic, too painful to watch but still precious.

'We did a big clear-out recently, up in the roof,' said Rachel. 'They've still got some of his old toys and paintings; they kept a lot of his stuff but they won't really look at it.'

Bob did not disturb those storage boxes for a long time, not until the mid-90s, and then they were opened only once. CLIC was in the midst of launching new offices in London and Bob gave some of Robert's mementos—John Pullin's England rugby shirt and Bobby Campbell's Scotland football shirt—to decorate a wall.

'I hovered over that box,' said Bob. 'I took out letters from Bobby Charlton, from Gordon Banks and Bob Paisley and I looked at the photographs taken when we met them. It was very painful.

'It's nearly thirty years since Robert died, more than a quarter of a century. You think there's no way that you're ever going to be able to go on—no way. You ask yourself, how will we get through tomorrow? Tomorrow ... not next year. Even if we get through tomorrow, how are we going to get through the next day? Yet here we are, nearly thirty years on. It is a most incredible thing. It just shows how God enables you to survive.

'When a child dies, what is the right thing to do? Should you do this? Should you do that? Should you sit around the coffin? Should you talk about him every day or should you not talk about him at all. I still don't know. I have been alongside people when their child is dying, or when the child has died, or soon after. I couldn't advise any of them what to do next. I sometimes stop and think—did we do the right things? Should we have talked about him more often? Should we have talked with Rachel and James more than we did? I don't know, I just don't know. I think that there is something inherent in a parent to be as protective as you can possibly be to your children. You tend to go on and not dwell on the pain and anguish of what you're going through. All I could think was, if anybody feels one hundredth of what I'm feeling, I don't want to make it any worse for them by talking about it.

'I've knelt by the side of the bed and pleaded to God for Robert to live. I could not believe that He was not going to answer my prayers. Then, later on, for more than three months, I prayed just as fervently for him to die. None of it makes sense. It just doesn't make any sense at all. Yet, it is so incredible when you look at life and you see the many wonderful things that have come from the suffering of others. My faith helped me. This is only part of the journey; it's not the whole journey at all. If I believed that we were just here for a short trip along the road of life and there was nothing afterwards, I don't think I could cope. There must be more. Life is just so wonderful and the world is such a fantastic place: to spend so little time here and then disappear? No, I cannot believe that. Without question, I believe that God is there and that Robert is with Him.'

'When we discovered that Robert had been diagnosed with cancer, we were horrified,' said Derek Rowles, Bob's brother-in-law. 'We'd watched him grow up and I got really low and angry about what was happening to him but I couldn't do anything. My wife, Diane, a committed Christian, told me I could do something *very* important and that was to pray for him.

'For many years, I'd been an atheist and, as a scientist, the whole thing seemed ludicrous. But, without anyone knowing, I began to talk to God. I'm afraid my prayers often started, "Now, *You* listen to me ..."'

Soon after Robert died, Derek made a life-changing appraisal: so moved was he by Robert's suffering and conviction, he gave up his secure job and studied for several years, after which he became an ordained minister of Umberleigh Free Church in North Devon.

During Bob's time on the executive council of the Bristol and District Association of Baptist Churches they acquired a very fine church on an attractive lease in Stockwood, which featured a beautiful timbered ceiling. While the ceiling looked aesthetically attractive, there was a problem: it sagged. When the executive council asked Bob to suggest a solution, he had new timber bearers fitted to counter the droop. The work brought him into contact with the church owners, the City Mission; they were looking for a buyer. The church stood in a sizeable piece of land with room to extend the car park on one side and a potential building plot for one or two houses on the other. It would have been a good acquisition for the Baptists but, sadly, they could not afford it so, after some negotiation, the price came down and Bob bought it for them.

'There is a plaque at the back of the church, only a tiny little plaque, quite unobtrusive, which says that it was purchased in memory of Robert—which is rather nice. It is still there and it is still a thriving church.'

21

To Judy and Bob a Third Son, Hugh

Bob and Judy tried to be strong for each other but there remained a great void in the family; they felt that the only way to overcome the emptiness was to have another child. Judy became pregnant and, as an older mother, went for a routine test to make sure that there were no problems; the test failed and dark clouds gathered overhead once more.

'It was better that we didn't know,' said Bob, 'although, even if we had, we would not have wanted to terminate the pregnancy. We would have been guilty for the rest of our lives. I have thanked God a hundred times, no, a thousand times that the test failed.'

Hugh, their third son, was born on 24 August 1978. Bob received a telephone call telling him he had a son but, strangely, no congratulations were offered. Bob was frightened. He grabbed the awaiting bouquet of roses and charged over to the hospital. As he drove up St Michael's Hill, he glanced at the children's hospital on the opposite side of the road.

When he arrived at Bristol Maternity Hospital, two consultants stopped him from going into the maternity ward and ushered him into an anteroom.

'We're very sorry. Your son has Down's syndrome and major heart problems,' said one of the doctors. 'Your wife doesn't know yet. Would you like us to tell her or will you tell her yourself?'

Bob would really have preferred them to tell Judy but he knew that he could not let them. 'I just couldn't believe what we were going through again. To have to tell my wife that our new baby boy was Down's syndrome—just after her giving birth within a year of losing a son.'

He walked into Judy's room.

'There you are,' she said. 'You have another son.'

And then he told her. The joy that should have been shared between them was cruelly displaced.

Bob could hardly bear to think of what Judy was going through and no words could describe the way he felt at that moment. It was too much for him to cope with. He felt that they both needed some time to come to terms with this latest blow; the consultant agreed and arranged for Judy and Hugh to stay in hospital for a couple of extra days.

'Afterwards, I felt so guilty about doing that. So terribly guilty,' said Bob.

'Mum just sort of … got on with it really,' said Rachel. 'It must have been terribly difficult, particularly after Hugh was born, after going through all that with Robert and then the shock of Hugh having Down's syndrome but there was no question of her being depressed, having sleeping tablets or anything like that, she just … was. She just got on with it; she still kept going to church and doing the church stuff as well; it was business as usual, which is quite incredible.'

'Judy's faith supported her throughout it all,' said Bob. 'People have remarked about my faith but hers is different. It is simple and straightforward; her faith doesn't ask questions. Whatever comes, she accepts it as part of God's plan.'

Hugh was very special, with a lovely disposition, and Rachel and James absolutely adored him. When James came home from school, he would put his beanbag in front of the TV and share his crisps with his little brother while explaining the programmes to him.

'I thank God repeatedly for the privilege of being the father of four beautiful children each with their very own special qualities,' said Bob.

Apart from her natural mother's love, Hugh benefited enormously from Judy's expertise and skill as a trained nursery nurse as Robert had done before him.

Hugh suffered with poor health and there were frequent trips to the Bristol Children's Hospital. He needed an operation, subsequently carried out by heart surgeon, James Wisheart. Some years later, Wisheart was the subject of the Bristol children's heart scandal and, following investigations, was struck off.

'When Hugh was his patient, I got to know James Wisheart well,' said Bob. 'He was one of the most charming gentlemen I have ever met. Nothing was too much trouble for him. He spent a lot of time sitting with us and explaining things before Hugh's operation and then more time with us afterwards. I thought he was truly, a lovely man. I didn't know the details of James Wisheart's problems but when he was on the receiving end of such terrible press coverage I rang to tell him how sorry I was and that I would still have wanted him to do Hugh's operation in spite of what was written about him. I don't know whether it helped or not but, with my hand on my heart, that is how I felt … and I still feel the same way now. He prolonged Hugh's life.'

Between 1980 and 1985, while building the mosaic, running CLIC as well as what was left of Woodward Bros, Bob also found time to serve on the magistrates' court and the juvenile court for North Avon—to fill in quiet moments. He enjoyed certain aspects of his work as a justice of the peace but not all of them suited his nature. Some may accuse him of being soft but on many occasions he considered the defendants genuine and the courts too harsh. A young mother, in court for not paying her TV licence, pleaded and cried in the dock. She was very sorry but her other expenses—taking her children on an occasional day out, buying ice creams etc.—had taken priority. Bob felt sorry for her because she had put her children first. The hard and fast rules left little leeway for people of differing circumstances and, because he did not enjoy being part of the process that brought further hardship, Bob noted her name and address, bought postal orders to the value of a TV licence and posted them to her.

Occasionally, Bob was reprimanded for defying the clerk of the court's direction; he did not deliberately set out to offend, he just wanted to do what his heart was telling him. 'After all, it was a magistrates' court, not a clerks' court, and there were occasions when we didn't need to be as hard as we were.'

There were days when Bob had attended a distressing funeral of a child in the morning and later, still feeling the pain of the broken-hearted parents, presided over the juvenile court where there were healthy youngsters under threat of sentence whose parents showed little interest in what might become of them. The irony was hard to reconcile and became his reason for retirement from the court. 'I sometimes found that being involved in the juvenile court was terribly difficult. It tore me to bits to think of these kiddies who seemed to be unwanted by their parents when there were those of us who loved our kiddies so much but ended up losing them. One day I just said, I've had enough.'

22

Top Hat and Skateboard

As more children were treated in the growing oncology unit, the demand for places at the Frenchay bungalow increased and Bob looked for another property closer to the children's hospital. The South West Children's Heart Circle was also looking for a property, so the two charities got together and shared a hospital-owned house in Horfield Road; it became the first CLIC House. Demand for accommodation still exceeded supply, however, and even the availability of the property next door did not solve the problem. Some parents, after working tirelessly for CLIC, became upset when they needed accommodation in CLIC House and found there was no room for them. One parent suggested a hotel-style booking system but this was not adopted because, in so many cases, accommodation was often needed at a moment's notice.

These difficulties could only be resolved by CLIC buying its own property. Bob viewed countless houses on offer but never found one he liked. With help from supporters, he walked the streets pushing letters through doors of suitable premises asking owners if they were interested in selling. It turned out to be a winning idea when Pembroke House, in Fremantle Square, became available. The house, a large, three-storey Georgian family home, owned by BBC wildlife film-maker, Chris Parsons, was ideally located close to Bristol Children's Hospital.

It was not long, however, before CLIC outgrew even this property; then, opportunely, Bob heard a whisper about the house next door, which was owned by the Co-op. He paid the manager a visit but it was already too late: the house now belonged to someone from Chepstow. He rang the new owner, Mr White, but try as he might, Bob could not persuade him to sell. Where he failed, squatters succeeded: in they went—fifteen of them. 'The neighbours were intimidated by them, worried that rave-ups and glue sniffing in the garden could become the order of the day.'

Bob called Mr White again. 'You have a terrible problem, Mr White. I think you should come to Bristol to see it for yourself.'

Mr White was horrified. 'We can't even get inside the house to have a look at it,' he said.

'Of course we can,' said Bob.

'We can't. They won't let us in.'

'If we can get them to open the door, I'll make sure they don't shut it again. Then you follow me in,' Bob told him.

They marched round and hammered at the door; it opened immediately—but only a little. Bob shoved his foot in the gap and pushed his shoulder against the door to stop the squatters slamming it shut. It yielded; both men charged in, only to find themselves surrounded.

Bob did the talking: he told them that he and the owner wished to check the property over. Amazingly, the squatters concurred. Bob and Mr White inspected the house; each room had been painted in psychedelic colours: bright yellows, brilliant greens and vivid purples. After their tour, they left unhindered, both of the opinion that the state of the property left something to be desired.

'That was terrible,' said Mr White. 'Do you still want to buy it?'

'Yes, we do,' said Bob.

'Well, you won't want it with those people in it, will you?'

'We'll get an order to get them out.'

'Could you do that?'

'We'll have a go at it,' said Bob.

After they parted company, Bob started work on the business in hand and being a JP gave him access to expert advice.

In due course, the court hearing took place. The squatters' representative was well educated, nicely spoken and clued-up, but non-conventional: 'I shall never forget that boy speeding down over Nine Tree Hill, dressed in jeans, sweater and a top hat. He arrived at court on his skateboard,' said Bob.

The judge ruled in the plaintiff's favour and granted an eviction order. The morning after the eviction, Bob called round to the house and found a girl still there. 'Are you leaving?' he asked.

'Yes, I'm the last one to go,' she said, 'my boyfriend is on his way back with the van to pick up our fridge.'

The boyfriend arrived soon after and parked his white van messily, half on the road and half on the pavement. Bob watched them struggle with the fridge but when it became jammed in the house doorway, eager to see the back of them, he helped them carry it through the door, down the steps, along the path and out to the van. Finally, the last of the squatters slammed the van door shut and drove away forever. Bob watched it disappear into the distance; at last, it was over.

He phoned Mr White with the news. 'They've gone. I've just seen the last of them off,' he said.

'That's fantastic,' replied Mr White. 'Will you be up there this afternoon?'

'Yes.'

'I'd just like to pop over to collect my fridge; it's the only thing of mine in there. It's almost brand new.'

'Oh blimey,' said Bob. 'I think I've just loaded it into the back of their van.'

'Why did you do that?'

'I thought it was theirs.'

'Do you remember the van's number?'

'No,' said Bob. 'All I can tell you, it was white. I'm sorry; I think you've just made a donation to CLIC.'

Now, with two adjoining houses in Fremantle Square, CLIC applied for planning permission to turn them into single premises to be used as both the charity's administrative headquarters and as a Home from Home.

The planners' response was more than surprising. They advised CLIC that it had been running its Home from Home without the correct permissions and suggested that it submit a retrospective application for both houses to put matters right. This course of action seemed reasonable but later CLIC was rocked by the news that permission had been refused and it was given six months to vacate.

'What a bombshell that was,' said Bob. 'They didn't want the property used for parents and children to stay there. They wanted to put it back to a residential house but I refused to do that.'

The Georgian Society and the Kingsdown Preservation Society had opposed CLIC's application and lobbied the planning committee. Bob set about fighting CLIC's corner and appealed against the decision. When an emergency planning meeting was arranged to hear the appeal, he contacted the BBC, HTV, local radio and the press. They all turned up.

A coach transported the planning committee to Fremantle Square. Reporters surrounded the chief planning officer and he refused to enter CLIC House until they backed off.

Bob led the committee on a tour of the two houses while the trailing press, now at a more respectful distance, took photographs. The committee returned to the coach for the formal meeting accompanied by the media and representatives from CLIC. Bob held his breath in fear of losing the appeal, knowing the critical impact it would have on sick children and their parents. The meeting opened; one by one, the planners revisited every point on the agenda and, one by one, the committee reversed each finding that had been discussed and decided upon only a week earlier. CLIC had won. Bob feels sure that the presence of the media turned the tide in CLIC's favour.

CLIC decided to expand its holding of properties by introducing a crisis-break flat to provide a holiday-style haven for families suffering any one of a number of devastating circumstances: the newly diagnosed child;

relapse of an illness; and for bereaved parents and their families. The name 'crisis-break' says it all.

Bob proposed a front-line location with sea-views, within easy driving distance of a hospital children's unit in case of emergency. He favoured Sidmouth but was told that there was no point in even looking as so few suitable properties were in private hands. He looked anyway and, sure enough, the first thing he saw on Sidmouth seafront was a 'For Sale' sign outside a ground floor flat. He viewed the property there and then; although it needed some refurbishment to bring it up to CLIC's standards, it was too good to miss—a first class, sizeable sea front flat in the most glorious position on Sidmouth's Esplanade. It was not long before families were enjoying a welcome respite.

23

Being Brave for Each Other

Family life carried on. Judy, in her role as a Sunday school teacher, continued teaching at the Hillfields Baptist church Sunday school and went on to give six years service at Headway, the brain injury association in Frenchay Hospital, while Rachel began a four-year degree course in Ancient Hebrew and Biblical Studies at St Andrew's University. Bob thoroughly enjoyed his treks to Scotland to visit his daughter and sometimes took his mother-in-law Gwen, Judy, James and Hugh along with him. When he travelled alone, Judy, who loved to tend the garden, her pride and joy, stayed home to look after the boys.

In October 1982, on one of the return journeys from St Andrew's, Bob stopped off for the night in a small village where he phoned home from a call box; he was alarmed at Judy's distress: Hugh had suffered a cardiac arrest and had been rushed to Bristol Children's Hospital. Hugh was still in a coma a week later and, as Bob and Judy were preparing to visit him, the hospital rang.

'They asked us what time we were we coming in,' said Bob. 'It sounded ominous.'

Hugh died before they could get there. He was just four years old.

When Bob and Judy returned home from the hospital, they found James playing in the hall with his friend, Jonathan Thomas. James took one look into Bob's face; he knew instantly that Hugh had died and he screamed. James was uncontrollable and remained in trauma for three days and nights; his distress shocked and frightened them.

'When Hugh died it wasn't very nice,' said James. 'Mum and Dad had gone to the hospital to see him and my cousin was looking after us. Just as my friend was leaving, I heard him burst into tears on the front doorstep as Mum and Dad walked in and then I twigged what had happened.

'Two or three weeks before, Hugh had been really ill with a bad cold and when I came home from school, Mum wasn't there. I found out that he'd been rushed to hospital. I asked, he's going to be all right, isn't he? Oh, yes. But he wasn't. He was pretty ill, he had a hole in his heart and a massive scar from his operation. Then afterwards you hear, "It's for the best, really," but at the time you don't really think that.'

Rachel took the news of Hugh's death just as badly: she immediately caught a flight to Heathrow where a friend picked her up and brought her home.

'I used to play with Hugh a lot until I went to university. I spent a lot of time with him; it came as a shock when he died,' she said.

Gwen was devastated by the loss of another grandson: she had loved Hugh as she had loved Robert; she nursed him and had spent four wonderful years with him.

Much too soon after Robert's untimely death, the family was faced with another tragedy and forced to cope with the same consequences. It was too awful for words.

Following another sorrowful funeral in Fishponds Baptist church, Hugh was interred with Robert at Frenchay church; a new headstone, inscribed with both Robert's and Hugh's names, was erected and Robert's original headstone laid flat over the grave.

The problem with James continued. He would start crying at night and did everything in his power to delay going to bed; when at last Bob and Judy finally got him into bed, he did everything he could to stay awake. Bob sat in James's room for hours trying to coax him into releasing his fears. In the end, James told him what was troubling him: he had worked out that all the boys in the Woodward family were going to die and he was afraid that, if he fell asleep, he would die too. Bob told James that there was no way he was going to die—it was not going to happen. Slowly, James began to believe his father and he became more settled: no longer afraid to close his eyes, he slept peacefully again.

Emotionally spent, it seemed a good idea to get away from home so they all took Rachel back to St Andrew's. The family took a couple of days to return to Bristol, arriving home late one evening. Around 11 p.m., the telephone rang and a woman with a Scottish accent introduced herself as the theatre sister at Dundee Infirmary. Rachel was being prepared for an operation following a road accident; the surgeon would be operating within the hour. Rachel had been riding pillion on her friend Jean's motorbike when it tipped over and they both fell off. Jean hung on tightly to the handlebars but Rachel rolled across to the other side of the road and a car ran straight into her. She suffered a broken femur, lacerations and bruises but, luckily, nothing more serious.

'It was hard to take in,' said Bob.

The next day, Bob got back into his car and returned to Scotland, this time to Dundee, where he stayed for a week to help look after Rachel in the infirmary.

Looking back on Hugh's short life, Bob and Judy tried to make some sense of it. People said it was hard to believe that it could happen again, especially so soon after losing Robert, but Bob believes that God sent

Hugh to keep the family together and, in doing so, it would help them cope with their grief for Robert. 'Being Down's syndrome, Hugh had a special quality and I think God knew that we would all come to realise that Hugh would die young. God chose this way to give us strength to cope. That is my belief.'

One effect of the absolute sorrow of losing one child and then losing another was the family being brave for each other. Judy was brave for Bob and the children; Bob was brave for Judy and the children; the children, in turn, were brave for each other. This united front embraced the wider family but Bob's heartbreak played on him and almost formed a wedge between them. In his extreme anxiety, he became irrational over what might happen to his children and their friends. 'I worried about where they were going and whether they were in danger. It was sheer hell thinking that something might happen to them as well.'

Bob has the utmost love and respect for Rachel and James because they have had to play supporting roles so many times in their young lives. 'For years, Robert and Hugh had been the focus of attention and it is all credit to Rachel and James in the way they coped with that.'

How did they all get through it? Bob knows how: their certain faith. Even with this strength, it was never easy and never less than the worst possible nightmare. People commented on how the family coped and remarked, 'You've come through this ever so well.' Although Bob kept his thoughts to himself, he felt that these well-meaning people could not possibly understand and he thanked God they could not.

Although bereavement counselling was available for Bob and Judy, they were cautious of any such assistance. Bob questioned whether counselling could help them because he felt that, in spite of the best of intentions, some people's efforts could make things worse.

'They sent a young girl to see us after Hugh was born,' explained Bob. 'They didn't give us much notice of her visit. She plonked herself right in the middle of our three-seater settee and we sat in armchairs on either side of her.

'She said, "I understand you are wrestling with the shock of having Hugh and that he'll need a lot of hospitalisation—and so soon after the loss of your son with cancer. I know exactly how you feel."

'When she said that, I switched right off—I didn't listen to another word. How could she possible know exactly how we felt? That was our only experience of a counsellor; however, I would never underestimate the value of talking things over with someone as long as it was with the right person.'

Some time after Hugh's death, Bob met such a person: Sister Frances Dominica, who trained as a children's nurse at Great Ormond Street

Hospital for Sick Children. Sister Frances founded the world's first children's hospice in November 1982 after supporting the family of Helen, a two-year-old left helpless after a brain tumour operation. Sister Frances sensed the need for a small, homely house to provide care for children with terminal illness, and to this end, Helen House Children's Hospice was built in the grounds of All Saints' Convent in Oxford.

Bob found Sister Frances compassionate, loving and uplifting; he feels she possesses an extraordinary empathy for those who have lost their children. His friendship with Sister Frances presented a way forward through enlightenment and empowerment: he lost all sense of natural reservation; compared with the tragedy of sick children and their vulnerability, nothing else mattered. Where others feared to intrude, he was able to offer help and support in harrowing situations; he could approach anyone and talk to anyone, giving solace not only for distressed families but also his own. The pain was always there—would be there forever—but he determined that his children's suffering would not be in vain: Robert and Hugh would live on.

24

Tulip Trees

In the early 1980s two new building plots in Frenchay were added to the Woodward Bros holdings and both featured several rare old tulip trees, one in a state of decay. Bob sought advice from a tree surgeon but his only suggestion was to fell it.

It is reported that in the early eighteenth century William Penn, who married Hannah Callowhill, sent these tulip trees as a thank you present to his wife's family and other Quakers in Frenchay for putting up the money—several thousand pounds—as a mortgage on the state of Pennsylvania.

The tulip trees were of historic value and when the Woodwards applied for planning permission to build on the land there were objections. To ease the situation Bob placed notices in local newspapers inviting people to view the trees in the hope of receiving expert advice on how to save them. A number of people responded but no solution emerged. One visitor, the secretary of the Council for the Preservation of Rural England, told Bob that while she applauded his efforts to save the trees, she was surprised that he had not taken matters a little further.

'How nice it would be if you could get some more from Pennsylvania to keep the line going,' she said.

'Why didn't I think of that?' said Bob.

'Exactly,' she said.

After making enquires about importing tulip trees from Pennsylvania, in no time at all, Bob, Judy and James were taking lunch at the American Embassy in Grosvenor Square with Turner Oyloe, resident diplomat for agricultural affairs. Turner said that he would be delighted to arrange delivery of six trees from Harrisburg, to continue the line.

Bob told Turner of his silver wedding anniversary plans to fly Judy to the States and to drive from coast to coast and suggested that they might stop off at Harrisburg to thank the people for sending the tulip trees to England. Turner thought this an excellent idea.

When the trees arrived, determined that Frenchay should make something of the occasion, Bob asked members of the local council for their views. A civic reception in the nearby Crest Hotel was their response.

Bob approached George Carpenter, town crier of Wotton, to embellish the day in traditional style. In full bell-ringing regalia, George bellowed a welcome to the American guests of honour. He strode up and down and, in a tremendous ear-splitting voice, boomed that the trees were to be planted in separate sites. Six large circular excavations waited to receive the magnificent American specimens, *Liriodendron tulipiferas*, commonly known as tulip trees, but the enthusiastic gardener who dug the holes had somewhat overestimated the requirement as each young sapling measured no more than an inch and a half across.

After the planting ceremony, they all moved on to witness the felling of the ancient tree. Two pieces of tulipwood were set aside: one for carving and polishing into a goblet, the other to be left in its natural state as a keepsake. The ceremony brought a satisfying end to what could have been a botanical bloomer in the village of Frenchay.

During their 25th wedding anniversary journey across the States, Bob, Judy and James were entertained at the governor's house in Harrisburg where Bob presented him with the tulipwood goblet and a photograph album of the tree planting ceremony in Frenchay. Today, three of the six saplings are flourishing trees and can be expected to live for hundreds of years.

25

Pedro Gabriel

A week before his fourteenth birthday Pedro Gabriel was rushed into a Lisbon hospital with suspected appendicitis where, during surgery, the doctors discovered cancer. Facilities for treatment in Portugal in 1981 were not well advanced and children with cancer had only a slim chance of survival; luckily, Zita, Pedro's mother, worked in the hospital and was able to make inquiries into the possibilities of treatment elsewhere. She came to hear of a man who had visited Lisbon to present a paper on the treatment of children with cancer and that man was Martin Mott.

After hearing of Pedro's condition, Martin picked up the phone and rang Bob. If Pedro were to come to Bristol for treatment, could he stay at CLIC House? Bob's response was unequivocal.

'Yes, if we have space and if we haven't, we'll make space. It's his only chance,' said Bob. 'Let me know when to expect him.'

Two and a half hours later, Bob received another call, this time from Lisbon. Pedro was already on his way and would be arriving at Gatwick with his father that very afternoon. Bob wrote the name Pedro Gabriel on a large white card and set off for London.

White card at the ready, he waited at the airport arrivals gate. When a wheelchair, pushed by a British Airways attendant, came into view, there was no doubt it was Pedro.

'I had seen so many sick youngsters but never anyone who looked as sick as Pedro,' said Bob. 'I asked myself what would happen if he died on our way to Bristol. Then, almost immediately, I thought, no, he's not going to die. That's not going to happen.' Nevertheless, Bob was relieved when they reached the hospital. Pedro, already paralysed from the waist down, began treatment almost immediately and the horrors of chemotherapy took their course.

In time, when he was well enough, Pedro stayed overnight with his father at CLIC House, travelling to and from the hospital by wide-door taxi to accommodate the drip-bag perched on his shoulder like a parrot. Pedro had to wait until Christmas to be reunited with his mother.

Pedro and his family received love and support from the wider CLIC community and from other parents of children with cancer who took it in turns to look after them for short periods. In all, he stayed in Bristol for four and a half months until finally, he was well enough to return home where oral treatment continued in Lisbon.

Zita kept in touch and always telephoned Bob on Christmas Day. He could hear her excitement when she told him all the news about her son and what a fine swimmer he had become. Indeed, Pedro had amassed over 50 swimming trophies both before and after his illness. His speciality, the butterfly stroke, is one of the most demanding of swimming disciplines, drawing on extremes of strength and stamina; his success is all the more remarkable given his frailty during his life-threatening illness.

Unexpectedly, one year, Zita called during the summer; she garbled something down the phone. It was difficult to tell whether she was elated, terrified or grief stricken and Bob could not calm her.

'I can't understand you, Zita,' said Bob. 'Slow down.'

'It's Pedro. It's Pedro.'

'But what has Pedro done?' asked Bob. 'Please, what are you trying to tell me? What has Pedro done?'

'He is the BUTTERFLY SWIMMING CHAMPION of Portugal,' shouted Zita.

As Bob marvelled at her news, he remembered greeting the young, frail Portuguese boy, paralysed and wheelchair bound; he had doubted Pedro's strength to survive the journey from London to Bristol; and now, he was a champion swimmer of Portugal. 'What an outcome: butterfly swimming champion. Magic, really.'

When Pedro came to Bristol for CLIC's tenth anniversary celebrations, he would not hear of Bob picking him up at the airport and they arranged instead to meet at Bristol bus station.

'I stood by my car and watched the buses come in and the people get off. This young guy appeared with great big shoulders developed from powerful swimming. Pedro strode up the hill towards me. I just stood there, feasting my eyes. It was fantastic, absolutely fantastic,' said Bob.

The Woodwards and Gabriels are still friends and have visited each other over the years. Pedro married and has three daughters.

26

Mentors, Counsellors and Friends

A most extraordinary and influential man, Professor David Baum, came into Bob's life in 1985. Of small build but with striking looks and 'wonderful, dancing hair', he looked a bit like Harpo Marx—and was proud of it. David had been working in Oxford before accepting the post of professor of child health in Bristol.

'We hit it off from day one,' said Bob. 'I took him a CLIC tie as a gift but that was before I found out that Professor Baum always, always wore a bow tie, so that was a waste of time. Why we got on like a house on fire was a complete mystery: David was an absolute wizard—with a razor sharp mind. He specialised in diabetes, a brilliant man, not only a great medic but great in so many other ways.'

David had worked closely with Sister Frances Dominica during the setting up of the world's first children's hospice, Helen House in Oxford, and it was he who introduced Sister Frances to Bob.

'David got in touch with me and said I want you to meet the most incredible man,' said Sister Frances. 'You both have so many things in common you need to meet. When David brought Bob to Helen House, Bob was deeply, deeply grieving still. He didn't show it all that much but he was. As soon as you get to know Bob, you realise the immensity of his grief for his two sons. Our culture expects the man to support the rest of the family when tragedy occurs and, in common with so many fathers, Bob didn't have the opportunity to work through his grief. He told me about CLIC and we became very, very good friends.'

Sister Frances introduced Bob to the Duchess of Kent. As he had already approached St James's Palace to ask the duchess to be CLIC's patron—without success—this introduction was most opportune. Bob re-iterated his request and was invited to meet the duchess at St James's Palace, when she agreed to become patron.

'She became a wonderful friend and she always said how much she looked forward to my letters,' said Bob. 'She said they were full of news and kept her up with all the different things CLIC was doing; she said she felt she was part of the CLIC family.'

In 1986 the Duchess of Kent opened CLIC Annexe. Although CLIC House, which had already doubled in size, could accommodate up to 40 people, there was still too little room. CLIC acquired 3 Nugent Hill, which backed onto the garden of the existing CLIC House, to provide the further rooms needed. For the grand opening, the lord lieutenant and his assistant vetted everything that was to happen on the day. The pre-arranged instructions, which Bob describes as a military exercise, had a strict timetable of events: 'that will take three minutes ... five minutes here ... two minutes there ...'

'They stood behind the duchess and signalled to move us on a bit faster,' said Bob. 'When it came to who was to sit where, they placed the lord lieutenant's assistant opposite me for direct eye contact should we run a minute over. I told them that the duchess would be meeting fund-raisers from the branches. They said she would only shake hands with a maximum of twelve—and they must wait by the entrance to the marquee. During lunch, I told the duchess that I was getting nods from across the way and she asked why. We must be falling behind schedule, I said. "What are they going to do to you if we don't keep to time?" she asked. I said, I suppose I shall probably finish up in the Tower.'

After lunch, they walked out of the house, down the garden steps and into the marquee.

'How long do we have here?' asked the duchess.

'We have twelve minutes, Ma'am,' said Bob.

'Never mind about the programme. What would you like me to do here?' she said.

'I would like you to shake hands with *everyone*,' said Bob.

'Come on then, let's see if I can do it in the time.' The duchess shook hands with everyone in the marquee: 87 guests in all. She missed no one.

Before the event, Bob sent the duchess a copy of the book, *Children with Cancer, A Model of Care* by Don Carleton. In the book the author likens an order of monks in Iona to the CLIC *familia*, the aim of which is to 'change the world of the child with cancer, the world which all members of the child's family enter when they first hear the news of his illness.' Bob thought this would be of special interest to the duchess and he made a note on her copy to look at page 37. At the opening ceremony, Bob presented the duchess with another copy of the book and referred to page 37 again. 'Ma'am, I am sure you will take interest in reading page 37, which tells you about the CLIC *familia*,' he said.

'You asked me to read page 37 when you wrote to me and I did,' said the duchess, in front of everybody.

Bob burst out laughing. 'You're not supposed to say that,' he said.

One of his most treasured photographs shows them both roaring their heads off with laughter.

Helen House and CLIC shared many common aims and experiences. Bob and Sister Frances Dominica were eager to learn from each other, to develop their charities and help even more children and their families. They got along famously and became close friends. Bob invited Frances to CLIC House but on the day of her visit Bristol suffered a heavy fall of snow. Frances would not be put off by inclement weather and told Bob so when he rang her. 'The trains will still be running. Of course I will be there,' she said.

When her train arrived at Bristol Parkway, Bob and Jim Carbines, the CLIC treasurer, a man some nineteen years Bob's senior, were waiting to take her back to CLIC House. En route, the car hit ice and slid off the road. Frances took over: she and Jim would push while Bob steered. She paid no heed to the men's protests and told them she would rather push. Passers-by witnessed a well-known Bristol businessman being pushed in his executive car by a septuagenarian and a nun in full habit.

'It was so funny really but I felt safer pushing than steering,' said Sister Frances. 'In those conditions, I would rather not take the wheel.'

'It was awful to be the one steering while they pushed me along the road. I was inside in the warm and they were outside in the freezing cold,' said Bob. 'You could say I took my orders.'

In spite of the weather, they arrived safely at CLIC House.

'While I walked around CLIC House with him, I realised how deeply he felt for the families staying there,' said Sister Frances. 'But, at that stage, he almost dared not to get too involved. I think he became much more involved in later years but it must have been excruciating for him seeing other families experiencing what he had experienced.'

Some years later, during the formation of CLIC UK—a sister charity to help children in regions outside the South West—Bob sought the opinion of the BBC newsreader Martyn Lewis, a fellow CLIC trustee, in the selection of additional trustees. Bob suggested they both write down the name of their first choice; when they compared notes, they had written the same name, Sister Frances Dominica.

'I have really treasured my friendship with Frances,' said Bob. 'She has been mentor, counsellor and friend.'

27

What On Earth Is It All About?

In the meantime Bob's brother David and his wife May returned to the UK from New Zealand. For the next ten years David sold seed potatoes to farmers but in the late 1980s his customers faced hard times: in one week alone, three farmers committed suicide.

'I went into a farm in Bridgwater,' David said, 'and this lady came to the door crying. The kids were crying too. I asked if I could help. I couldn't make head or tail of what was going on, so I went next door and they said to me, "I was trying to catch you before you went in there. They found him hanging in the shed last night." That farmer was only in his early thirties.'

Another farmer told David he was unable to pay his bill as he had just two months to live. 'I was told to get the money out of him or sell his potatoes elsewhere. I thought what on earth is it all about? I just lost it completely.'

David became seriously depressed.

On Friday 13 February 1987 Bob returned home from a CLIC cheque presentation at Aztec West, north of Bristol. As he pulled into the drive Judy came running out of the house towards him: something was terribly wrong. She broke the news before he could get out of his car: his brother David had fallen 150 feet over the edge of the quarry near the old observatory at Weston-super-Mare; there was no information about his condition or even his chances of survival. John was already on his way to Bob's home so that they could travel down to Weston Hospital together.

Bob would not go into the house. He paced up and down outside and Judy brought him a cup of tea. When John arrived the two brothers sped to Weston unconcerned by the speed limit. May was already there in a most distressed state. She had yet to see her husband and had no idea as to his condition. They all waited and worried together. Then, unexpectedly, David was transferred to a specialist unit at Frenchay Hospital, which was just over Bob's garden wall.

They all dashed back to Frenchay where it took some time for them to find the neurosurgery ward. Just ten minutes later, they were told that David, having undergone a brain scan, had been returned to Weston. They were advised not to rush back again as there were a number of procedures to be completed before they would be allowed to see him.

At Spruce House the kettle went on again. In Weston Hospital later that evening, still completely in the dark as to the extent of David's injuries, the family was allowed in to see him.

'I could not believe that I was seeing my brother in this awful state,' said Bob.

May remarked sadly, 'He's cracked his front tooth and his watch has stopped.'

'If that's all that's wrong, I shouldn't worry too much about it,' said Alan, the youngest brother, who had just arrived from Bournemouth.

'Alan is worse than I am for making humour out of everything,' said Bob. 'But even in situations as worrying as this, there is humour. I think there is a fine line between distress and its reflex response. It's a bit like a seesaw; it tips one way and then the other. There was poor David, attached to a ventilator and heaven knows what else, and of all the things that May could have seen, all she noticed was the crack in his front tooth and that his watch had stopped.'

Later, when David was undergoing kidney dialysis in the intensive care unit, the ward sister told the waiting family that David was 'floating' in a semi-conscious state but they should be aware that he could probably hear everything that was going on around him. She suggested that they involve him in their conversation but advised them not to mention his fall, which he had only survived by a miracle through falling into a pile of loose gravel next to two men digging in the quarry. The effect on those men has not been recorded.

The family talked quietly to David, hoping against hope that he would pull through.

Suddenly, the peace in the ward was shattered. Bells rang out, the door crashed open and a trolley burst in bearing the large supine figure of an overdose victim. Urgent, almost violent, activity took place. The peace at David's bedside dissolved in an eruption of organised medical chaos.

'We've got to bring him round,' shouted the ward sister. 'Does anyone know his name?' She dashed out, doors swinging, only to return seconds later. 'Cliff, Cliff,' she bellowed in the man's ear.

'There we were, sitting round the bed not saying anything at all about David's fall, trying to do everything we could to help and she's calling out, "Cliff, Cliff." Of all the names that man could have had, it had to be Cliff,' said Bob.

The seesaw tipped again. There was the most appalling news: David's back was broken in two places and neurosurgeons confirmed that he would never walk again.

He spent a year in the spinal unit at Salisbury. 'How David survived it, I don't know, said Bob. 'My heart bled for him and May.'

'It was the hardest time I've ever had in my life,' said David. 'When I looked at my legs, I thought what am I going to do and then all I thought about was how can I do away with myself. Then, one day, I was looking out of the window and these little blue-tits landed on the sill; that day, Bob brought me in a tape player with Pavarotti singing and when I started listening to that I thought there's no way I can leave this world when there's beautiful music like that to listen to. It brought me round. My wife, May, has looked after me in my wheelchair for nineteen years; she is my absolute saviour, as is the Lord.'

The family rallied and visited David regularly. It was said that he had broken every bone in his body but, all things considered, his recovery was incredibly good.

28

Degree of Doctor of Laws, Honoris Causa

When Bristol University awarded Bob an honorary doctorate (the highest award that a university can confer) for services to children with cancer it took him completely by surprise. It was 9 July 1987. David Baum gave the citation, 'Bob Woodward, the Builder'. David was the second of the three inspirational speakers that Bob so greatly admired. Billy Graham had been the first and Sister Frances the second.

'It was one of my proudest moments and even more special and memorable because David gave the oration,' said Bob.

Before the ceremony Bob signed the university visitors' book and was overwhelmed that his signature followed many famous and illustrious names including that of the Queen. Sir John Kingman, the vice-chancellor, complimented Bob on his writing and said it was the best signature he had ever seen.

When Bob was ushered into an anteroom to change into academic dress, there were two robes displayed before him, both with tasselled headgear.

'There are two robes and two hats,' he said to David Baum, looking for enlightenment.

'Yes, that's right,' replied David. 'That's part of the ritual. You wear both.'

He marched out before Bob could see the mischievous smile on his face.

Left on his own to puzzle over the best course of action, Bob felt dismayed by his friend's lack of guidance. 'How the Dickens am I going to wear two robes and two hats?' he thought. 'Perhaps there's a place in the procedure where one is taken off.'

Then he overheard David talking outside, trying to hoodwink his secretary into thinking that the oration would be in Latin. Only then did Bob realise that David was enjoying winding up as many people as he could find. His suspicions were confirmed when the secretary came in to help him don the immense and heavy robe.

'Two robes! When I realised how big one robe was, there was no way I was going to say anything about a second; he would have thought I was a right flippin' Wally.'

The ceremony took place in the Great Hall of the Wills Memorial Building. David Baum, public orator, stood to honour his friend: he

142

painted a broad picture of the man, of his family, of small builder to mosaicist and of the gargantuan task of constructing the replica of the Great Orpheus pavement, and of his continuing work with CLIC.

' ... the scaffolding is up but the workers will be hard-pressed if the Trust is to keep pace with Mr Woodward's imagination, compassion, energy and commitment. Vice-chancellor, this University does well to recognise Bob Woodward, a great builder and a great Bristolian, with the degree of Doctor of Laws, Honoris Causa.'

Recipients of honorary degrees may invite a small number of guests to the ceremony. Bob invited 24. 'They were ever so good about it. They realised that I didn't know the procedure and they actually accommodated everyone, which was rather nice. I'd love to have got hold of Mr Cook, my old headmaster, and taken him there.'

David also organised the post-ceremony party and offered Bob a number of options to consider. Bob eschewed a formal, Grand Hotel type of event in favour of a barbecue in David's garden. The small 'house band' featured Hugh Coakham, professor of neurological surgery at Frenchay Hospital, on the clarinet. The happy party concluded with a game of rounders on Brandon Hill.

'It was fantastic, so typically David,' said Bob.

In that summer's *CLIC News*, Bob wrote:

'I must confess to have been completely dumbfounded to have been invited to receive such an honour and I am conscious of the enormous amount of work done by so many through the years to ensure the success of the CLIC Trust. Whilst it does seem to me to be somewhat unfair to be singled out amongst such an army of workers, I accept on behalf of all those who have served and, on behalf of my own family and, by no means least, on behalf of all the sick children who have set standards of courage, trust and fortitude that few of us could ever hope to emulate.

The number of CLIC supporters grew ever larger and it was decided to stage a variety show at the Bristol Hippodrome as a way of saying thank you. There was no admission charged: people were invited to make donations. The show was such a success both financially and with its audience that it became an annual event, although later shows raised less money after it was decided to pay performers and charge for admission. At one of the shows Bob was introduced to Roger Cook, the songwriter who lived in Fishponds, who with his colleague Roger Greenaway wrote 'I'd Like to Teach the World to Sing' among many others. He went on to write a song for Bob called 'All My Friends Are Children'.

Money was raised for CLIC in numerous ways. For a while Bob owned a 1965 black and yellow Rolls Royce, which he made available for weddings. He never charged for its use, instead preferring to invite donations. The Rolls Royce hit the road on as many Saturdays as there were weddings and he really enjoyed chauffeuring the bride and groom on the happiest day of their lives.

'Disappointing thing was … Judy never even sat in it. She would not go out in a Rolls Royce. She just never would.'

One of the highlights of the CLIC calendar was its Christmas party held in the festooned restaurant of the Bristol Maternity Hospital, directly opposite the former site of the children's hospital on St Michael's Hill. The parents and siblings of children currently undergoing treatment joined in CLIC's festive celebrations and doctors and nurses played their part in making these annual parties a roaring success. Puppeteers and comics such as the Norfolk Mountain Rescue Team and their friend, Tosser the rabbit, provided entertainment. The children screamed with laughter (as did the parents). Every year, the party was host to a very special guest … Father Christmas.

'When they asked me to do it, I shied away from it at first,' said Bob. 'I felt no way on earth could I meet these children knowing that, for some, it would be their last Christmas but when the person who was to play Father Christmas dropped out, I had to step in at the last minute.'

In the event, playing Father Christmas turned out to be a Christmas present for Bob. 'It was just wonderful. The only thing I didn't like was the grotty outfit. The beard resembled a dishcloth,' he said.

The costume was quite inadequate and, clearly, not good enough. The importance of an authentic, well turned out Father Christmas was paramount; and, determined 'not to spoil the ship for a ha'p'orth o' tar', Bob decided that a new outfit was the order of the day and he knew just the person who could make it. He asked Mrs Tranter, who had dressed a collection of dolls to depict the ages from Roman times to the present day that had been displayed alongside the mosaic to illustrate the changing fashions over 1,500 years. She readily agreed and together she and Bob shopped in the drapery department of Bright's of Bristol for the fabric to make a Victorian-style Father Christmas outfit. Weighed down by a quantity of luxurious red velvet, white fur edging and numerous other items from the haberdashery counter, she caught the afternoon bus back to the Somerset countryside where she lived.

Some months later, to the amusement of passers-by who might have caught sight of Father Christmas in full regalia in midsummer, a final fitting took place in the front room of Mrs Tranter's tiny cottage. The impressive outfit, complete with splendid beard and wig made by a London theatrical costumier, was a credit to them all.

As not all of the little patients were well enough to attend the Christmas party, Bob played Father Christmas again in the wards on Christmas Day. The importance of these visits was brought home to him during a conversation he had in Axbridge, where he had been invited to receive a cheque for CLIC. He noticed a young woman who was obviously extremely upset and he asked Alison McManus, the chairman of the CLIC Mendip branch, about her.

'She lost her little boy around Christmas time last year,' she said. Bob spoke with the young woman, who told him about her son.

'We have this wonderful memory of when he was in hospital on Christmas Day,' she said. 'He'd asked for a special kind of tractor for Christmas but when he woke up on Christmas morning, he was disappointed when it was not on his bed. After lunch Father Christmas came into the ward; such a lovely Father Christmas, beautifully dressed, it was just like a fairy tale. He came up to the bed, sat down, talked to my little boy and gave him the very tractor he'd wanted. It was absolutely wonderful.'

Her son died just two hours later.

The success of the parties and Father Christmas's visits to the wards was not just down to Bob's efforts but also to the team of CLIC play therapists, Helen Beswetherick, Elaine Eastman and Jane Nelson-Smith. So much of the children's delight, and their parents' wonder, was simply because Father Christmas knew exactly what each child wanted for Christmas. 'The time and effort the play therapists put in to finding out exactly what each child wanted for Christmas—to find just the right gift—was quite remarkable. It made Christmas for those kids.'

Unfortunately, the time came when the CLIC Christmas party could no longer accommodate all the children and it became necessary to restrict it to those who were still in treatment or had received treatment over that year. One little boy's conversation revealed the importance he attached to the CLIC parties and his absolute belief in Father Christmas. Snuggled comfortably into Father Christmas's lap, the little boy whispered how unhappy he was now that his treatment was over and asked, 'Could I have some more?'

'But finishing your treatment is wonderful news,' said Father Christmas.

'No it isn't,' said the boy.

'Why do you feel like that?'

'Because I won't be able to come to the CLIC Christmas party ever again,' he said.

The older children thought it great fun to play Bob up but were always careful not to give the game away to the youngsters. Their conspiratorial whispers gladdened his heart and some, after thanking Father Christmas for their presents, thanked him personally for everything CLIC had done for them.

These were special times for everyone in the family: the patients and their brothers and sisters each received a gift before being photographed with Father Christmas. Sometimes, well over a hundred presents were given away.

The duties of Father Christmas did not end there. Considerable planning went into making Christmas a magical time for the children isolated inside the Bone Marrow Unit where patients' immune systems were reduced to zero; stringent precautions prevented even Father Christmas from entering. Outside, a bright beam of light illuminated Father Christmas passing presents through the wall of the unit—or so it seemed to the excited young patients within. The real presents, sterilised, free from germs and identically wrapped, were already inside the unit, waiting to be distributed.

Of the many celebrities who offered their support to CLIC, it was the film star Jane Seymour who wanted to be directly involved with the children. Jane opened her home, the ancient and stunning St Catherine's Court near Bath, for a Christmas party for children suffering with cancer where, for nearly four hours, spellbound children and their parents enjoyed her hospitality.

The children's excitement mounted the moment they saw the twinkling Christmas lights, candles, beautiful decorations and the magnificent Christmas tree in the oak-panelled Great Hall.

Jane took the happy children to the top of the house to play in the nursery. 'All the toys here are not just for my own children,' she said, 'but are for our guests to play with as well.'

Later, everyone gathered to watch Marcel Steiner's Smallest Theatre in the World present Jack and the Beanstalk. Jane and her family, along with the invited audience, laughed out loud as Marcel, playing the Giant, roared, 'FE FI FO FUM!' as he lumbered around the Great Hall.

Next, the children tucked into a Christmas feast completely unaware that the chairs on which they sat may well have dated back to the reign of King Henry VIII.

After carols and a raucous rendition of 'Rudolph the Red-nosed Reindeer', a knock on the window announced the guest of honour, Father Christmas, with his sack of presents for the eager partygoers. Before it was finally time to go home, an announcement was made that Jane was to become a CLIC trustee—to the delight of the parents and organisers.

29

King of the Jumble

Another area of development within CLIC was the setting up of a chain of charity shops, of which the first opened in Bedford Street, Exeter, on 27 January 1989. The five-year plan was to open a shop in every town in the South West. Bob and the trustees were introduced to an ex-Barnardo's man called John Nickolls. John had been responsible for Barnardo's retail operation and for nearly ten years he brought his considerable expertise to CLIC.

'I joined CLIC on 1 September 1989 and at that stage there was just one CLIC shop open,' said John. 'It was going through terrible times and its sales were awful. Two others had been acquired but not opened: one in Wells, the other, a lovely little shop, in Straits Parade, Fishponds, which was actually the first Bristol shop.

'I opened three shops in a week once: Saltash in Cornwall, then, three days later in Clevedon and two days after that, in Tiverton. It was the busiest week of my charity life: finding volunteers, recruiting managers, training, opening ceremonies. It was very demanding but you just got your inspiration from Bob to keep going; he was that sort of man; you felt you had to achieve.'

Many of those who staffed the CLIC shops had their personal reasons for supporting CLIC.

'My son Lee had bone cancer and my teenage daughter Biddy went to stay with a friend in Weymouth in Dorset so she could have some fun,' said Ruth Cummins. 'Lee was having a double lung operation and we knew it was going to get a bit hairy. Lee had his operation on the Tuesday and I'd spoken to Biddy at 6 that night to find out whether she was OK and to tell her that her brother had come out of his operation.

'We were staying at CLIC House and at about four o'clock in the morning we were woken up by a heavy knocking at the door, which is strange because people don't do that at CLIC House. It was the police. They told us that Biddy and her friend Kerry had been killed in a car accident. Lee's dad, Bren, was staying close by with relatives and we went to see him.'

'That was one of the worst, worst, times when Lee was in hospital and then the news came through about Biddy,' said CLIC's housekeeper, Jo Harding. 'Bob completely dropped everything and took Ruth, her partner Simon, and Lee's dad Bren, down to the mortuary in Dorchester.

Bob was with them all the time. His compassion was always that he could just drop everything and do what he felt he had to do.'

'We had to tell Lee about his sister,' said Ruth, 'and we also had to identify Biddy's body. Although we'd heard about Bob Woodward, we had never met him but he came to the rescue and took us in his car to Dorchester.'

As if this was not enough, it was made worse by the manner of a member of staff at the mortuary.

'I was scared and he seemed very loud,' said Ruth. 'When I tried to explain that I'd never seen anyone dead before, his attitude was, in you go and get it over with.'

There appeared to be no facilities and the family found themselves speaking to the member of staff in his car. They were not even offered a cup of tea.

'Later, a senior police officer came to our house,' said Ruth. 'He promised us it would never ever happen again to other parents; training would be given and there would always be someone there to do it tactfully. Apparently, Bob had made a complaint to the police force, so without us even knowing he had done that for us.'

Bob continued to visit the family and he gave Lee the Kevin Keegan shirt that had been given to Robert.

'You can imagine how moved we were when he did that,' said Ruth. 'Bob seemed to call in every time he was down this way. Other people would cross the street because they couldn't handle what our family was going through, they didn't know what to say. Bob didn't ever turn his back on us. He supported us, talked to us and became a very special person in our lives.'

Only a few short months after the death of her daughter, Ruth Cummins lost her son Lee to cancer. Over the months that followed Ruth clung to the edge of an emotional precipice as she put her life on hold. One day, late in 1990, she received a message from John Nickolls asking if she would be interested in working for CLIC in the Saltash shop.

'I was extremely angry because I thought, how dare somebody think I am capable of doing anything with my life now,' said Ruth. 'Nevertheless, I rang John Nickolls and thought what a lovely man he sounded. Apparently, Bob had put my name forward. God sends angels in many disguises. Then I thought it would give me a reason to get up, wash and actually go somewhere. When I met John he listened to my story and said, "Do you think you could do this job?" Just before Christmas, the first without the children, John rang me and told me that I had the job, if I wanted it. It was the first time for a long time that I absolutely howled. I needed a new baby in my life and that's what the shop was.

'Simon, my partner, although a qualified architect, gave up work and we started up the shop together with John's help. Bob was there at the opening, which was wonderful. We had a wonderful team of volunteers who stayed with me right up until I left fourteen years later.'

When John Nickolls joined CLIC, he was not in his first flush.

'I was 54 years of age and it was the best job in my life,' he said. 'I looked after 23 shops altogether—I opened 22 and there've been a couple more since. The shop empire created a whole new image throughout the South West; it gave people knowledge of CLIC and what it did.'

'When we opened the Shirehampton shop with a cheese and wine party, I got up, said a bit about CLIC and welcomed the volunteers,' said Bob. 'Then, I said, I'm just a tiny bit worried about two or three of you in the front row. I trust that I am not going to sound personal when I say that I wonder whether you may perhaps have had one or two many glasses of wine because your faces are very blurred. One woman replied, "Mine's not," and she took her handkerchief out and wiped her face. I thought that was brilliant. Then someone came up with a joke about cheese in mousetraps: it's always the second mouse that gets the cheese. There was always such a good atmosphere in the shops.'

'There were over 400 volunteers and some of the shops were opened by people such as David Essex,' said John. 'Police stopped the traffic. What a memory that was in Staple Hill; I had a big speech ready to say at the shop door but it was so noisy I didn't say a word. David had to shout at the crowd. People like Eddie Large, Lady Bader, Bruce Hockin and Michelle Collins from *Eastenders* opened other shops.

'It was great fun behind the scenes. What we found in those bags—some unmentionables. Things were left in pockets: valuable jewellery, money, which was always declared to the police.

'One funny thing happened when a lady came running in and said, "My husband brought in some black bags yesterday. Could I have one of them back?" Well, it was too late by then. It had already been sorted. "Oh dear," she said. "One of them was for the launderette."'

30

Money Raised for Charity is on a Different Level

In the main, it was left to Bob to find suitable properties for CLIC's Homes from Home and he looked for 'For Sale' signs in the streets adjacent to hospitals. In Southampton he discovered two old houses owned by the health authority in a poor state of repair; CLIC bought them, knocked them into one and renovated them.

One potential property, under construction in Jack Straw's Lane, Oxford, was spotted by another Bob: Bob Thorndale, a parent of a child with cancer and a member of the Gloucester branch. He spoke to the builder and explained CLIC's special needs. The builder, John Cooper, was most sympathetic, as his business partner, John Chaundy, had lost his son to cancer some years earlier. John Cooper immediately understood the huge benefits that a Home from Home would bring to families in crisis. After further discussions, he offered to make all the alterations himself as his contribution for the new Home from Home. The trustees were bowled over by his generous response.

Almost immediately, the neighbours raised several objections to the idea. Most people rise to an occasion—their help and generosity can be relied upon—but some take an alternative view, especially when their status quo is challenged.

'People living in the street got wind that CLIC was going to buy this house,' said Bob. 'We had a battle on our hands, an absolute battle.'

Before the planning application was heard, he was invited to attend a meeting with the residents where they presented him with a number of alternative sites for the Home from Home, all with the same thing in common: 'not in our back yard.'

'One of the residents was absolutely livid,' said Bob. 'He told me that he would stop CLIC whatever else happened; his wife had suffered from cancer and he felt that the last thing she would want to see was bald-headed kids walking past their house, reminding her of what she had been through.'

At the planning meeting, Bob listened to the residents' objections before he was called to support CLIC's application. Afterwards, as he was leaving, he bumped into the protester from the street.

'We both went bananas,' said Bob. 'I left him in absolutely no doubt about the way I felt about him. We never spoke again but he did send a message to say that if planning permission were granted, he would rent his house to the most obnoxious characters he could find to make our lives hell. Well, he didn't have to look very far from home, did he?'

Planning was granted, work was completed and, after all that hassle, CLIC's families experienced no problems with their new neighbours.

Over the years Bob befriended many people, mainly from the West Country. He was to be found with some side by side in battle, shedding tears, sharing their tragedies; with others rejoicing in laughter, hope and battles won. So committed was he in supporting needy families that his life no longer seemed to be his own.

'It was my life—always being ready,' said Bob. 'I always considered myself to be on 24-hour call. I shall never understand how Judy put up with it; not only just once or twice, it was a way of life. She was wonderful; she accepted it completely. Rachel and James have been so supportive as well. James would say, "Do you have to stay in the office all day, Dad? Do you have to work again as soon as you get home?" They were the ones who made sacrifices. Tremendous sacrifices.'

'He wasn't there that much and he came home very late in the evenings,' said James. 'But he'd always come in and say goodnight. He was always doing something to do with CLIC, speaking or raising money. As I got older, I realised just what he was doing and he was doing it 18 hours a day or more. But he always made time to take us on trips and he always helped me with whatever I needed doing: my BMX bike—doing it up—whatever. When I look back now, I think, poor man, having to go through all that when I'm sure he had much better things to do.'

'CLIC did take up masses of Dad's time,' said Rachel, 'but even before CLIC he was doing things for the church or just generally helping people; he was always doing things for people, he has always been involved. It's the way he is. But he was always very good at finding time for us. He didn't really have hobbies; he would never sit down and read a book, I can't ever remember Dad reading a book. In any free time, he did sport with Robert and we'd go on outings, visit places, whatever. He was really good when I was a teenager, picking me up from places; he was fantastic. He would also collect my friends at midnight as well.'

On the subject of her mother Rachel said, 'Mum has always been very good in terms of supporting Dad, all the behind the scenes stuff. Since I was young, she's been doing voluntary work as well and a lot of the things she's done are not particularly glamorous like working in the burns unit for years at Frenchay Hospital and with the head injured: the stuff that other people might not want to do. She has given a lot. When the first Iraq war happened in the early 1990s, they didn't quite know what was going to happen if lots of injured British soldiers were sent back to be looked after. She volunteered herself and Dad for work in Frenchay Hospital: herself for the chemical burns unit and she put Dad down for the mortuary. Dad said, "The mortuary! That was very nice of her."'

One Friday evening Bob received an urgent message from Helen Crease who lived in Exeter. Helen's husband had died of a heart attack when she was pregnant with their son Ray and then, in what seemed no time at all, Ray was diagnosed with leukaemia. Bob kept in touch with Helen and popped in to see Ray whenever he could.

Helen rang to tell Bob that Ray had taken a sudden and dramatic turn for the worse. Bob immediately drove to Exeter hospital where he stayed the night. At daybreak, with Ray's condition unchanged, Bob rang Martin Mott for help. Martin reacted swiftly and sent one of his team to Exeter to offer additional expertise.

'Helen always told me that it saved Ray's life,' said Bob. 'I shouldn't have phoned Martin, really. I shouldn't have interfered but it was life or death.'

Bob never hesitated from attending the funerals of children who had lost their battles: over the years, there were around 300 in all.

'A lot of people think I'm a tough guy but I can't watch a Lassie film. OK, so I can stand up to people but just don't put Lassie on. I am the world's worst and I can't bear to see other people cry. The second they do, I'm finished. I'm not much good with any of that—and yet, somehow, I've managed all those funerals. When they first started, I wondered just how I would cope because there would always be more. How would I do it? Then, someone asked me to speak at one. What a compliment to be given the last word as a precious soul leaves this earth.'

'I remember once going to a funeral at Appledore in North Devon,' said Jim Carbines. 'There were crowds of people there and the minister asked if Bob would speak. He did and it was quite amazing how he was able to do that on the spur of the moment. People thought so much of him.'

There was one occasion when Bob's secretary told him that there was a call from Devon on the line. Young Matthew from Westward Ho! had died and his funeral was to take place at midday, in Barnstaple. Bob told his secretary he would not be available that day and drove immediately to North Devon. He arrived with just three minutes to spare.

'It makes such a difference when there are people in the congregation who have been through what the family is going through. It gives them that bit of added strength when they know that others have survived it and they can too. I think that is vitally important.'

It was remarkable that Bob could still take comfort from the fullness of life and, from that, gained strength to build—not with bricks and mortar but with faith and compassion—a support structure for others. 'I know I was called to do it,' he said. 'Both Judy and I feel it was a calling from above.'

CLIC's practice was to send flowers as soon as distressing news reached them, but one employee approached Bob to question this procedure.

'I'm not sure that I can continue to support CLIC. I don't like the policy that you have adopted here.'

'What policy is that?' asked Bob.

'The sending of flowers to parents. I don't think that is the correct use of CLIC's money.'

'There may be those who might agree with you,' said Bob. 'That has to be a matter of opinion but I very strongly disagree with you.'

'I think it's a terrible waste of money,' the employee argued. 'After losing a child, the last thing on earth they want is to answer the door and take flowers into the house.'

'That's one way of looking at it. But, as someone who has been in that position, twice, I can tell you that I loved answering the door to receive flowers from those who wanted to show us how much they cared. Unless there is a consensus of opinion that tells me it is wrong, CLIC will continue to send flowers,' said Bob.

Later, he set up what he called 'a flower run' at Christmastime, which he funds personally and continues to this day—a direct consequence of his realisation that Judy was the only new mother in the maternity ward without flowers on her bedside cabinet. If he hears of any family who loses a child during the year, they go on his list. Two or three days before Christmas, Bob makes between 25 and 50 deliveries.

Another incident and another dissenting voice took Bob completely by surprise. A successful gathering of branch committee supporters from all over the West Country took place in the Riviera Hotel in Sidmouth, which included an escorted tour of the crisis-break flat next door. Bob took great care to ensure that staff, branch members and shop volunteers had the opportunity to hear about what was happening in the trust, as well as share in the planning for its future. At these get-togethers, Bob's inspiring talks rallied the troops and rekindled their zest for fund-raising for CLIC; with their batteries recharged, they were ready to take on the world. His passionate approach rarely failed and Bob felt that this meeting was a particular success, until one long-standing fund-raiser approached him.

'I'm sorry, Bob,' the fund-raiser began, 'but I've got to give in my resignation.'

It had been a fantastic day and this came from a man who worked so hard for his branch. 'I'm very sorry about that,' said Bob. 'But why on earth do you want to do that?'

'I made up my mind today,' he said. 'I told my wife we have both got to pack it in.'

'Pack it in? Why, what has happened?'

'Now we've seen the flat, we can't support it. People are coming down here and are having a better holiday than we do. What the devil are we doing, working our insides out, raising money so they can do that? No, we can't support it.'

'I'm sorry to hear it,' said Bob. 'Will you reconsider?'

'No. I'm not prepared to discuss it with you. That's the end of it.'

True to his word, Bob never saw him or his wife again; nevertheless, he wrote to thank them both for all their efforts.

When anyone questioned the excellence of CLIC's accommodation for families by saying it was too good for the purpose, Bob always replied, 'When parents are faced with a life threatening condition to their child; when they are wrestling with what they've just been told, their next problem is where are they going to stay? They're in a pit of despair and when they step over the threshold of CLIC House, they're lifted. That's what CLIC House is there to do. When those parents walk through that door, it is essential for them to realise that there are people there who love them and are waiting to express compassion to them and to their families. That's the tonic of actually lifting them and holding them in the caring hands of CLIC. That is what we have to achieve and that is why the accommodation is as it is. There are children who cry when they leave CLIC House. If it has to be changed, then I'll have to go because I cannot be party to anything else.'

CLIC's housekeeper, Jo Harding, said, 'Wonderful friendships have been made between people thrown together by the misfortune of having a sick child who, in turn, were inspired by Bob to become firm supporters of CLIC.'

On this subject, Bob thinks that the Homes from Home are precious for another reason. He has been alongside parents and watched their marriages fall apart because of the pressure. He believes that the Homes from Home saved some marriages by taking some of that pressure away—keeping the family together as a unit. 'That's something that you'll never see on any set of CLIC accounts,' he said.

Spending the money raised for charity is a mammoth responsibility and one he never takes lightly. 'Perhaps I did get paranoid about it but it annoyed me so much when we took people on, paid them well and found that some were not as committed or gave as much effort as the unpaid volunteers. They were in the minority, of course, or CLIC would never have survived. CLIC could boast many dedicated, hard working employees. Money raised for charity is on a different level.'

Specialist treatment for burns, neurosurgery and plastic surgery were provided for children in Ward 8 at Frenchay Hospital. While young patients undergo surgery, their parents could stay close by in CLIC Cottage. It came as a shock when the Hospital Trust announced the closure of Ward 8 in order to save £25,000. The proposed closure meant that young post-operative patients would be nursed at Bristol Children's Hospital, six miles away from the neuro and plastic surgeons at Frenchay.

Bob was incensed. 'It's a place that I visited so many times, where I got to know so many people. CLIC funded the refurbishment at the end of Ward 8 where we put in overnight accommodation and new bathrooms for parents. We had also funded CLIC Cottage. We spent quite a bit over the years and now all that money was going to be wasted.'

Even though there were demonstrations and heated arguments, it seemed that nothing could stop the closure of Ward 8.

'We had a real ding dong over it,' said Bob.

He brought a mechanical digger on site to use as a protest if the collective minds of the trust could not be persuaded to rethink its plans. To generate publicity, he would have used it to block the entrance to the ward as a visible protest against the closure. Furthermore, to make them sit up and take notice, Bob presented the Hospital Trust with a bill for £80,000, CLIC's costs for the setting up of CLIC cottage and the refurbishment of Ward 8, making the point that should the trust save £25,000 by closing the ward, it would cost them £55,000 to do so. These efforts, the demonstrations and the effects of negative publicity were rewarded by the trust making a U-turn.

'Because we intervened, Ward 8 had an extra life.'

31

Beyond the South West

Increasingly Bob found that CLIC took up more and more of his time; this led to him buying Chipping Manor from the Woodward Bros partnership to provide him with a regular rental income. Although this freed him to concentrate on the charity he and John still needed to make other financial decisions. The maintenance costs of Market Street in Wotton were slowly eroding their rental income, and so they sold the properties and selected a financial adviser to help them invest the proceeds. He promised to do wonders and the first year was a great success, turning in an increase of over 14 per cent.

'We thought this is pretty good. It was just like giving a donkey strawberries,' said Bob, using a favourite saying. But the excellent returns were short-lived and in the second year the yield was more than disappointing.

'It was in 1988—the investment crash, our investment crash—when we ran into difficulties,' he said. 'We were in trouble. The stock market crashed and took most of our income with it.'

Bob's financial predicament forced him to consider giving less time to CLIC. From the outset, he had worked full time for the charity but had never drawn a salary and so he suggested to the trustees that he take a year off to sell the Woodchester pavement replica. His suggestion coincided with a report on CLIC by the Charity Effectiveness Review Trust (CERT), which had been consulted for advice on the rapidly growing charity.

CERT recommended that Bob should take on a paid role as a chief executive but this proposal went against the grain: Bob felt that he could not accept payment for running his own charity. Years later, when storm clouds gathered over his horizon, his decision was criticised.

Faced with losing their founder, leader and figurehead for a year, the trustees met to consider the options. What if it took Bob longer than a year to sell the Woodchester pavement—what would happen then? What if he should not return? What could they do to keep him? One of the trustees, John Halliday, proposed measures to allow Bob to reclaim his out of pocket expenses and to be paid for his travelling costs. Then it was pointed out that Bob not only spent time on CLIC but he also gave a lot of time to the Institute of Child Health, and so the solution to the problem would be to find a sponsor to fund Bob's work for the institute.

Professor David Baum spoke to the vice-chancellor of the university who agreed to give Bob a contract for a new, non-medical consultancy, providing a sponsor could be found. This would cover Bob's input and expertise in a variety of ways by extending the work of the Institute and, more pertinently, the exploration of new fund-raising opportunities. Sponsorship came from a private family trust, the Needham Cooper Trust, in 1990: this satisfied all parties, as the funding would not come out of public donations and meant that Bob could continue working in an unpaid capacity for CLIC.

Even with the Needham Cooper Trust sponsorship, it was still necessary for Bob either to sell or find somewhere to exhibit the mosaic. While he was looking for a buyer a promising new opening presented itself. His fame as a mosaicist had spread far and wide and, in his capacity as a member of the Society for the Preservation of Roman Mosaics, Bob was invited to give a talk at the Paul Getty Museum in Malibu. Accompanied by his good friend, Don Reed, they mingled with a group of academics from American universities at their hotel, who hardly gave them the time of day. Later, when they registered at the Getty Museum, the atmosphere remained frosty although it was obvious that they were taking part in the conference.

'Very few of them spoke to us,' said Bob. 'At the reception, we did get to speak to some but they were in a different league: eggheads really.'

The seminar was scheduled to run over two and a half days. The format of the presentations was steadfastly rigid throughout. One after the other, the academics got up with their sheaf of papers in hand, pressed a button to illuminate their slides, read their scripts (which might vary from 35 to 45 minutes) and, at the close, waited for questions from the floor. For the run-of-the-mill speaker there was likely to be just one question; the above average speaker was rewarded with two. All speakers returned to their seats amid dispassionate applause of equal measure and made way for the next.

Bob's slot was scheduled for the final day and he was to be the last presenter. The penultimate speaker approached him the evening before. She appeared anxious. 'I believe you are speaking last,' she said.

'Yes, I am,' said Bob.

'I'm concerned that my presentation is not going to be long enough. I shall be hard pushed to make it last for more than a quarter of an hour. Will that be an embarrassment for you?'

'No,' said Bob confidently, 'some extra time will be a bonus. That will give me just over an hour.'

That evening, Bob considered his presentation; as was his custom, he had come all this way without a script. He stayed up well into the night, making notes, thought twice about them and ditched them. Eventually, he decided to take a practical approach. He would arrange the slides of the Great Orpheus pavement in alternate order, showing the original first followed by the replica, and then make comparisons; having made up his mind, he fell into an easy asleep.

The following morning everything went to plan; the penultimate speaker, true to her word, sat down to the customary detached response after just ten minutes. Bob stood up, walked to the podium, looked into the eyes of academia and, in a rare moment of doubt, thought, 'How are they going to receive me?'

He need not have worried. Once into his stride, Bob gave an authoritative performance to a captivated audience. His talk was the showstopper of the day. Unsurprisingly, such was his enthusiasm, he overran his extended time and it took a knock on the door to interrupt his flow.

'I'm sorry, sir, but we have to close the building—you have about fifteen minutes left,' said the security officer.

Clearly disappointed, the audience requested additional time. 'I'm sorry,' repeated the officer, 'you might have 20 or 25 minutes but that'll be all.'

There were requests for Bob to complete his presentation back at the hotel but there was a problem: he and Don had checked out earlier that morning and their luggage was sitting outside in the car. They intended to leave that evening but the delegates, eager to hear more, implored them to stay.

Bob could not help thinking, 'Just listen to them, the same academics who could hardly pass the time of day with us only two days ago.'

Itineraries were adjusted and Bob and Don returned to the hotel with the others. Discussions continued for a further three hours in the hotel restaurant and Bob enjoyed every second.

Sadly, as much as the Woodwards' replica of the Great Orpheus pavement had been admired, the Getty Museum only exhibited genuine antiquities but, as a direct consequence of the colloquium, Bob received a letter from the American Universities' Organization of Roman Studies inviting him on a lecture tour of American universities.

'What a fantastic thing that would have been,' said Bob. 'I would've loved to have done it but CLIC would have suffered.' He just could not consider it and, regretfully, declined.

Still hoping to find somewhere to exhibit the mosaic Bob and Don drove inland, across the Nevada Desert, to Las Vegas: Bob had identified Caesar's Palace as a potential venue.

After breakfast the next day, the two men walked along the Las Vegas Boulevard to Caesar's Palace where Bob asked to see the manager.

'Gerry Gordon's the man here,' he was told. 'He's the vice-president.'

'Is there a possibility of seeing him?' Bob asked.

'No possibility at all. He's too busy. What do you want with him?'

Bob spoke briefly about the mosaic.

'Mr Gordon wouldn't be interested,' was the instant response.

Disappointed, Bob and Don left Caesar's Palace and retraced their steps along the Las Vegas strip. An enormous sparkling display above the MGM Hotel caught their attention: Tom Jones was in concert.

Bob told Don that he had been led to believe that, in search of work, his grandfather, with other relatives, left Gloucestershire and ended up in South Wales. It was Bob's Aunt May who took it upon herself to research the possibility of a family connection to Tom Jones because Tom's real surname was Woodward and, after comparing notes with the star's relations, she was adamant that Tom Jones and Bob were second cousins.

'There may be a way of getting to see Gerry Gordon after all,' said Bob. With this in mind, Bob and Don strolled into the MGM and asked to speak to Tom Jones. The response was predictable.

'Is his manager in then?' asked Bob. 'His son, Mark Woodward.'

'Who shall I say is calling?' said the receptionist.

'Tell Mark that it's Bob Woodward,' said Bob, hoping that Mark would take it for granted that they were related.

The receptionist made the call and passed the phone to Bob.

'Hello, Mark, thank you for speaking to me. My name is Bob Woodward and I'm from Bristol. I understand that your father's grandfather and my grandfather were brothers, so we must be distant relatives. But, not too distant I hope,' he added.

Mark seemed unimpressed: 'We've got ever so many relatives,' he said.

Bob went on: 'I was really hoping that you might be able to help me. I need to discuss the possibility of bringing a copy of a Roman mosaic to Vegas and I would like to speak to Gerry Gordon over at Caesar's Palace about it.'

'That won't be a problem,' said Mark. 'By the time you walk over there, I will have rung him and he'll see you.'

'Thank you,' said Bob. 'Please give my best regards to your father.'

This time Caesar's Palace was expecting them and they were immediately ushered into the elusive Mr Gordon's office. Never happier than when he was expounding a passion, Bob eagerly showed Gerry the

Samuel Lysons book. The exquisite plates of engravings and illustrations of the original Woodchester pavement mesmerised Gerry and soon they were discussing the Woodward replica. Unhappily, his interest was short-lived: having to store the mosaic when it was not being exhibited was not a viable proposition for Caesar's Palace at that time.

Bob and Don returned to England; disappointingly, the search for a suitable venue to exhibit the replica of the Great Orpheus pavement would have to go on.

The mosaic was eventually sold to a local businessman, Alec Lawless, who with Bob's help made it possible for the pavement to be displayed in a converted pottery at Prinknash Abbey in Gloucestershire.

Discussions took place at CLIC over some years regarding the setting up of a chair in Paediatric Oncology at Bristol University but competition for the charity's finances had so far excluded this possibility. By 1990 the subject was brought into sharp focus when a donation of £2 million from an anonymous benefactor for the setting up of the first such chair at St Bartholomew's Hospital (Bart's) in London caused considerable unrest at Bristol Children's Hospital. Dr Martin Mott could well be a contender.

Although it was suggested by a number of medics that Martin would never leave Bristol and therefore there was nothing to worry about, Bob believed that leaving it to fate represented an enormous risk. He remembered how he had felt some fifteen years earlier when Martin had taken up a contract in America and now he considered the feelings of the parents whose children were under Martin's care. He fully understood the loyalty and reliance they placed on the doctor overseeing their child's health and future, and felt that CLIC needed to retain continuity. In Bob's opinion this could only be provided by Martin Mott, the man who had been there from the start.

In the event Martin did apply for the position at Bart's; his application was successful and this created a huge dilemma for Bob. In a move that later caused some controversy, he visited the vice-chancellor to ask about the cost of setting up a chair in Bristol. The university's finance department calculated a package of £1.6 million. Well experienced at dealing with the university, Bob pushed for a better deal. Negotiations continued until the cost was reduced to £1 million. This was still a considerable sum, but Bob felt that the chair was now a viable proposition, especially as it would include a professor, a full-time researcher, a part-time secretary and accommodation. The £1 million was to be paid in five equal annual instalments. CLIC's trustees backed the idea.

There were funds available for the first instalment and the trustees committed themselves to the subsequent payments, plus interest on the outstanding balance at one per cent under the market rate.

The deal was to cause absolute chaos. While Bob was not alone in supporting a chair in paediatric oncology in Bristol, many disagreed: there was opposition from diverse quarters who were unhappy with the financing arrangements, the lack of procedure in making the appointment and even the need for the chair itself. Objections came from some branch committee members, the Vote Committee ('Voice Of The Experts' made up of consultants, surgeons, nurses, social workers and others) and from within Bristol Children's Hospital. Others voiced similar disagreement and CLIC lost several influential members and fund-raisers. Some were scathing in their criticism of CLIC, calling it 'Martin Mott's chequebook'.

Despite the considerable opposition, the appointment went ahead and CLIC's trustees made it a condition of financing the chair that Martin should be the first incumbent, without advertising the post or interviewing other candidates. Bob defended CLIC's controversial decision. 'Had the position been advertised, it would have made nonsense of our funding it. We set up the chair to keep Martin in Bristol. If we hadn't done that, we would have lost him.'

During its review of CLIC the Charity Effectiveness Review Trust recommended that a full-time general secretary should be appointed to take over day-to-day administration. They also suggested that a new charity should be set up with its own deeds and trustees to provide CLIC's model of care in response to the growing demand from other regions. The new charity should be called CLIC UK while the original trust should be renamed CLIC South West. In the winter 1990 edition of *CLIC News*, journalist James Belsey wrote, 'The aim of CLIC has remained constant—to change the world, the world of the child with cancer and that world must now extend beyond the South West of England.' The trustees appointed to serve alongside Bob were Martyn Lewis, the BBC broadcaster, Lady Bader, Martin Mott, David Baum, Professor Michael Preece, Sir Jeremy Morse, Sir Richard Gaskell, Sister Frances Dominica and Jack Lyes.

CLIC UK was launched on 29 November 1990. Bob had reservations about the plan to replicate CLIC's model of care to the rest of the UK in this way; he would have preferred CLIC to remain a single charity, extending itself gradually. However, those who lived in the South West welcomed the news that all of the money they raised would now remain in their region; they felt strongly that other charities in the rest of the UK should raise their own funds.

Bob commented: 'I felt that the extra time and effort required to run separate charities was an unnecessary burden on the hub of the organisation and, in time, this proved to be the case.'

Nevertheless, he wrote in the winter edition of *CLIC News*:

> There is no other charity in the country which has the objectives of CLIC. We are unique and we have to accept the demands that are coming from all over Britain ... The better our service, the more calls we get from other regions and some of them are desperate pleas for help. I'm very saddened when I hear of situations which remind me of what we endured as parents all those years ago. We cannot ignore these pleas for help. It is time for a national organisation to help with the fight to save young lives.

An important donation from CLIC went to help establish a children's hospice near Barnstaple in Devon. The children's hospice was the inspiration of Jill and Eddie Farwell: two of their three children were suffering from an obscure degenerative disease. In their exhausting situation they relied on respite by staying at Helen House Hospice in Oxford but, living in Barnstaple, it still meant a long and tiring journey for the whole family. They could see a desperate need for a children's hospice closer to home in the South West. They called the Institute of Child Health and discussed their idea with David Baum of whom they had heard so much when they stayed at Helen House. David asked Bob to attend the meeting.

'Jill and Eddie Farwell expressed concerns that we might feel they were poaching on CLIC's territory and vying for the same funds. I told them that while we may be competing for the same cake, together, we shall just have to bake a bigger one,' said Bob.

He backed up his sentiments by suggesting to CLIC trustees that they make the first donation—which they did: £10,000. The delighted Farwells invited Bob to chair a meeting to launch their appeal. Together with David Baum, Sister Frances, Martyn Lewis and the Bishop of Exeter, Bob also became a patron of the appeal.

The fund flourished; with the help of the local church, the appeal fund purchased a parcel of land at an excellent price in Fremington near Barnstaple. Building began using warm, golden-coloured Ham stone from local quarries. 'Little Bridge House is a stunning place and it was a wonderful project to be involved in.'

There is often a price to pay for an ever-busy life and in 1992 Bob's health gave some cause for concern. One evening, he went to bed feeling unwell with a pain in his chest and it slowly got worse. His arms felt like lead and sweat poured from him. The increasing pain alarmed him and he called for Judy. One look sent her immediately to the telephone to dial 999. Within minutes paramedics were on the scene and flattened Bob out on the bed. He heard someone say his heart had stopped and there was talk about using a defibrillator.

Bob was anxious for his son. 'James had already gone to bed. I heard him open his bedroom door and I could feel him watching me being carried out. I knew he would be remembering that when they took Robert away, he never came back.'

They rushed Bob into nearby Frenchay Hospital and took him straight to the cardiac ward. At first, it appeared that he had suffered a massive heart attack but next day, results showed that he had not. It was a warning: his over-stressed body had mimed a heart attack and this may well have been a precursor to what would follow within a few years.

The year ended in great style for the Woodwards. When the 40th anniversary of the Queen's accession to the throne coincided with the 25th anniversary of the accession of the Sultan of Brunei Darussalam, the Queen held a state banquet for over 170 guests at Buckingham Palace in honour of the Sultan and the Raja Isteri. One hundred of these were by invitation of the Queen and the others were guests of the Sultan. Dr Robert and Mrs Judith Woodward were honoured to be counted among the Sultan's guests on 3 November 1992.

The invitation caused much excitement in the Woodward household; a smart hotel in London was booked, where, dressed in best bib and tucker, they waited for the stretched limo to arrive (arranged by a friend of a friend) to take them to Buckingham Palace. When it failed to turn up, Bob swiftly ordered a taxi and the Woodwards arrived at the Palace on time. The limo arrived at the hotel ten minutes too late. It had been the driver's ambition to drive his stretched limo through the gates of the Palace and he was extremely disappointed at missing his opportunity.

The occasion was glitteringly impressive. Members of the Royal Family, the Sultan of Brunei and the Raja Isteri welcomed their guests, the procession moved forward and Bob and Judy were presented.

The long banqueting table, set with an endless array of gold cutlery, crystal, and the most beautiful flower arrangements looked magnificent beneath the pipers of the Second Battalion Scots Guards in the gallery.

Bob and Judy viewed the table plan with some concern when they saw that they were to be separated and would be sitting on opposite sides of the great hall. Bob sat between two strangers, while Judy found herself next to a naval officer who knocked over the gravy boat during the meal.

'Of all of the people to knock over a gravy boat, it had to be the blinking Admiral of the Fleet,' smiled Bob. 'Can you imagine the headlines? "Admiral of the Fleet in gravy boat drowning."'

Before mingling with other guests, Bob and Judy enjoyed a 'splendocious' four-course meal of Crème Dubarry, Filet de Saumon Medici, Carré d'Agneau Mozart and Bombe Glacée Vanille Grenadine; the wines were Sherry Fino La Ina, Wehlener Sonnenuhr Spätelese 1986, Château Léoville Las Cases 1979, Moët & Chandon 1985 and Croft 1970.

Bob confessed to taking a couple of souvenirs: several royal name-tags from the tables—a conservative choice of keepsakes by today's standards. Later, they met up with the Duchess of Kent who took them on an impromptu tour of parts of Buckingham Palace.

32

The Hole in the Wall Gang Camp

One grand plan considered by CLIC at this time was the idea of a special camp where sick youngsters could take a break away from home. It was the inspiration of Jonathan Fenton-Jones, a design consultant, who had been working on the idea since 1988, and he proposed it to the Institute of Child Health. Impressed by Jonathan's vision, his idea was adopted by the institute and taken forward by CLIC in 1990. The project gathered momentum and, after searching countrywide for a suitable site, Jonathan proposed Drake's Island, a property of the Crown Estate in Plymouth Sound. Although situated in splendid surroundings, like many good things, it was not perfect: the island was often shrouded in mist and was the adopted haunt of a teeming seagull population, which had become aggressive to visitors.

In spite of the problems of the location CLIC pursued the opportunity to develop what it called a Re-Creation Centre with the aim of providing a two-week holiday for up to sixty children with life-limiting disorders where they could form friendships while enjoying the freedom of the outdoors.

'And in a moment we will be interviewing a representative from film star Paul Newman's Hole in the Wall Gang Camp. He is in the UK looking for a charity to set up a similar venture here — to help sick children,' said the presenter on the radio.

Bob pricked up his ears; it was the first time he had come across the Hole in the Wall Gang Camp and wanted to know more about it. He made contact with its representative, a man by the name of Hotchner, a director on the Hole in the Wall Gang Camp board. Hotch, as he was known, invited Bob and Professor David Baum to meet him at an office in Westminster where he extended a further invitation to visit the camp in Connecticut.

Paul Newman founded the Hole in the Wall Gang Camp, designed as a Wild West hideout, in 1988. It is a non-profit making residential summer camp where more than 1,000 children between the ages of seven and fifteen, suffering from cancer and other life-threatening illnesses, attend each year, free of charge.

The entrance sign into this children's fantasy adventure playground declares, in blue and yellow letters: Yippee, you're here! There are totem poles, teepees and wigwams, a lake and a boathouse. The tree-lined dirt road runs past stables and barns, through fields and woods to the main complex. There is an Olympic-sized swimming pool, log cabins circling a wide green, and a theatre; there are craft-making facilities designed as Western-style shops and the camp has its own infirmary, the OK Corral. In this wonderland, children find a renewed sense of 'being a kid' and they get to do some of the things that no one knew they were capable of doing. Also, there are organised retreats for the children's parents at resorts around the United States, which offer respite, counselling and mutual support, free of charge; the Hole in the Wall Gang Camp fund helps other camps with missions similar to its own.

As Bob and David's trip to Connecticut was sponsored by CLIC and the Institute of Child Health respectively, the two men searched for cheap flights until they found a good deal with Air India. At the airport they noticed that some of their fellow passengers were travelling suitcase-free while attempting to check-in a bizarre collection of furniture. 'I thought we were flying Air Pickfords,' said Bob.

Their flight was delayed for ten hours because the plane had not yet left Mumbai. When at last they boarded and took their seats, they watched in disbelief as a number of primus stoves were set up in the aisle. Bob, who is not a lover of spicy food, likened the flight to seven hours locked in an Indian restaurant.

On arrival in New York they waited at the carousel for their luggage: only Bob's case appeared. David looked worried; his case contained everything he needed for a ten o'clock lecture the next morning at Yale University; it also contained a wedding deed, written in Hebrew, for a ceremony in Chicago at the end of the week. The deed was imperative … the marriage could not take place without it … and it was in the missing suitcase. Moreover, for the journey David had travelled in a check shirt and jeans, not quite the attire for his lecture the next morning. In desperation he clambered on to the carousel and strode forward against the oncoming flow right up to the delivery hatch before disappearing through it. He reappeared moments later, hair dancing and case-less.

'I am very sorry but your case is still in London,' was the unwelcome news.

Bob placed his arm around his friend's shoulders and gave him the only bit of comfort he could think of. 'It's terrible news but it could have been much worse, David,' he said. 'It could have been *my* case.'

After dumping Bob's luggage at the hotel in Newhaven, they went straight into town where, luckily for them, they spotted a men's outfitters, still open for business. 'Off the peg' tailoring never fitted

David and although he found a mushroom-coloured gabardine suit, it needed a few alterations. To have it ready for collection by 9.30 the next morning was a tall order but after hearing David's tale of woe, the obliging assistant agreed. To complete the ensemble, David added a selection of shirts and inevitable bow ties (he always wore a bow tie). Happily, his case turned up three days later just in time for the wedding.

After meeting at the Hole in the Wall Gang Camp's offices, Bob and David travelled the 70 or so miles to the camp; they both marvelled at the camp's location, tucked away in the heart of the Connecticut countryside, almost undetectable amid the rising hills and dense woods.

'The camp is mind-boggling and I wrote a piece on it for *CLIC News*. I tried to conjure up the feelings of a youngster going there for the first time. Where is it? Is it up on the hill? Is it near the sea? Are we there yet? Just to see the countryside in Connecticut is quite beautiful: acres of green, a touch of England, really. Then suddenly we went up this road and saw this big wooden archway with "Hole in the Wall Gang Camp" written across the arch in pieces of log: the hideout for Butch Cassidy and the Sundance Kid. It was just how you would imagine a big ranch would look in the Wild West.'

Just like a cowboy film, they went through a boulder-lined pass where it opened out on to a track road. After a mile or so, they came across an enormous lake.

'I think the lake is 40 acres and brimful of fish; they take the kids out in boats on fishing expeditions: it is magnificent. A bit farther on, there's a huge equestrian centre with horses and donkeys; experienced people help the children mount, take them round the circuit and in to the fields. There's a stockade, just like the Alamo, where the giant gates are always open and inside there are log cabins set in a huge circle. David and I slept in bunks in one of the log cabins: it was fantastic. The camp is a little Wild West town with a saloon, a barber's, and there are craft shops, everything you can think of. Even the administration office has been built in Wild West style. Right up at the top, the huge dining hall seats 120 kids and we had lunch with them: the atmosphere was electric. They're spending another £1 million on Rosie O'Grady's, the music hall where, twice a year, a host of stars come down from Broadway, mix with the kiddies, and involve them in the show. While we were there, Joanne Woodward and Jason Robards joined in. Paul Newman, complete in stripes and straw hat was giving out popcorn; he really looked the part; it was great.'

They all met up that evening at Hotch's home—white, with columns at the end of a long drive—before going on to dinner at a restaurant with Paul Newman, who admits to having become 'a major fan of Bob'.

During the evening, Bob tried to persuade him that his wife, Joanne Woodward, was a long lost cousin of his.

'Do you know, Bob,' said Paul. 'I think she might buy that.'

'He was very nice and easy to get on with,' said Bob. 'We had a long meeting with him about Drake's Island; he was absolutely sold on the idea, especially after seeing Jonathon's drawings, so we got an undertaking from him that he would put up the equivalent of £1 million to kick it off.'

An excellent start but they needed to find more—an awful lot more. Henry Hector, who renovated the nautical school at Portishead near Bristol into luxury accommodation, became involved with the cost estimates. Initial figures of £3–4 million had already persuaded some in CLIC that this was a project too far and the final figures of £7–8 million became an impossible dream.

Bob admitted to having doubts when he realised the enormity of the funds involved. 'We eventually backed off,' he said. 'It was an interesting project but in the end it didn't come to anything. I was disappointed but, on the other hand, I would have hated for it to have gone ahead only to find that we had chosen the wrong site. There's something always a bit magical about an island and I think we got carried away with the idea.'

33

Lesley and Kate

Huw Griffiths, a neurosurgeon from Frenchay Hospital, held a number of clinics in Uganda where he came across little four-year-old Lesley Gesa, who suffered from headaches and difficulties with her sight. At that time in Uganda many children were misdiagnosed and written off as Aids victims but Griffiths felt sure that Lesley had a brain tumour and he wanted to bring her to Frenchay for an operation to give her a chance of life.

Lesley's parents, Aggrey and Margaret, brought her to the UK but had to leave their other children Apollo, Jean and Vivienne, at home. The Ugandan bank where Aggrey worked in middle management helped fund their trip to England. The family stayed free of charge in CLIC Cottage, situated in the grounds of Frenchay Hospital.

Bob first met the Gesa family when he was walking the dog. He could see a light on in the cottage and he tapped on the front door to say hello. If they ever needed anything, he told them to call him; Judy would rustle something up and he would bring it over.

The operation, sadly, did not save Lesley's sight; it was a savage blow to the family and while Aggrey was trying to come to terms with this, he was recalled to Uganda, leaving Margaret behind to take care of Lesley. Bob introduced Margaret and Lesley to members of Fishponds Baptist church and it was there that they found comfort and friendship while Lesley was recovering.

When at last they returned to Uganda, their home-coming turned to anguish: in Margaret's absence, Aggrey had married someone else. Although he was still looking after their three other children, there was no room in his home for Margaret and Lesley and they had no option other than to take up residence in a nearby hovel—with neither power nor running water.

When Bob heard about this, he rallied support. 'We formed what we called the Lesley Support Group and rounded up about forty supporters from a number of churches and playgroups that Lesley had attended. They gave whatever they felt they could give and, in the end, we had nearly £2,500 a year coming in.'

Their generosity allowed Margaret and Lesley to move out of the hovel and into a rented house. For a short while, all seemed well until Margaret called Bob to tell him that there were difficulties with Lesley's treatment. It seemed that the local medical consultants did not have the expertise to deal with her problem, so Bob arranged conference calls between the Ugandan consultant and Frenchay-based neurosurgeon, Hugh Coakham. It soon became obvious that, if they were to save her life, Lesley needed further treatment back in England.

Flights were booked with a reluctant British Airways. 'I had to fight them tooth and nail. They didn't want to carry someone who might die during the flight. I persuaded them by telling them I was Doctor Woodward—I didn't explain doctor of what.'

Over the next twelve months Lesley's treatment continued successfully but there were those who questioned the prolonged use of CLIC Cottage and it became necessary to find other accommodation for Lesley and her mother. The support group was quick to act: it rented a small house in Frenchay for close on a year, and continued to help them even after they returned to Uganda.

From time to time Lesley returned to Bristol for treatment and she and her mother enjoyed shopping in charity shops, choosing clothes for themselves and for Apollo, Jean and Vivienne.

Earlier on, when Lesley had stayed in CLIC Cottage, she took part in a walk from the cottage to the West Lodge, now Frenchay Village Museum; the story was covered by local television.

'I walked with her—very slowly, of course—she was not very mobile. I expect she did half a mile there and back; she raised about £1,200 for CLIC. She loved doing it,' said Bob.

Margaret has been reunited with her three other children and they are all living together again. Lesley and Margaret remain a part of Bob's life, as the methods for keeping in touch have grown more sophisticated. Nowadays, Margaret texts Bob, which is her cheapest way to make contact, and then he calls her back. 'She's a very bright lady, very switched on and a nice person. There is nothing that she would not do for Lesley.'

'We first met Bob in 1989 when our daughter Kate was diagnosed with a brain tumour,' said Kathy Jeffery.

Five-year-old Kate was taken to Plymouth for treatment and the family stayed at CLIC Lodge. When Kathy mentioned they had to carry Kate up and down the steep stairs and it would be helpful to have a handrail on both sides, just a day later, two workmen arrived to measure up for the extra handrail.

'They were just very ordinary, very nice, unassuming people, who had a bit of fun with Kate and got on with what they were doing,' said Kathy. 'It wasn't until later when we were reading the CLIC magazine we recognised that one of them was Bob Woodward. He didn't say, "This is who I am," or anything like that, he just came in and we took him to be a workman.'

Through the following years, the families became friends.

Then, in 1998, when Kate was rushed by air ambulance from Treliske in Cornwall to Frenchay Hospital in Bristol, she and her mother were parted for the first time.

'When Kate took off in the helicopter, I just burst into tears,' said Kathy. 'My husband Tony said, "Don't worry, I'm going to ring Bob."'

Bob promised to meet the air ambulance and suggested that he keep in touch by mobile while Kathy and Tony made the three and a half hour journey by car. 'I'll tell you everything that's happening, as it's happening,' he said.

'I was so worried because Kate was delirious when she left and I thought she's not going to know him,' said Kathy. She need not have worried. Kate recognised Bob straightaway. 'I felt so reassured because he went into the emergency room with Kate and he acted on our behalf because they were asking lots of questions about Kate's history.'

Bob liaised by going outside to phone Tony and Kathy and returning inside to relay the answers to the medics; by the time Tony and Kathy got to Frenchay, their daughter was already in theatre.

Kate was in hospital for nearly nine months and Bob and Judy visited the family on most days.

'Judy's been wonderful too,' said Kathy. 'She's very down to earth. They're a very special couple.'

On weekdays Tony held the fort at home in Cornwall to look after their son Edward and drove up to Frenchay at weekends.

'On several occasions when Kate was rushed into theatre, Bob would be there for us,' said Kathy. 'There were times when he sat throughout the night with me; he would just sit there and nine times out of ten we'd start laughing about something and the time would fly by because he's just got the knack of making you laugh.'

Should Kate's condition suddenly change during the working week, Tony was an agonising three and a half hours away. 'Knowing that Bob was with me helped Tony as well because he knew I was all right,' said Kathy.

It was World Cup year and Bob was really looking forward to watching the matches but on the day of the final Kate fell ill again and Bob sat with Kathy all afternoon.

'Then, someone said France had won the World Cup,' said Kathy. 'I said, oh no, Bob, it was World Cup Final Day. He said, "It doesn't matter, it's only another four years before I can see it again."'

Kate calls Bob 'the daft ha'p'orth' because he larks about to make her laugh and when he completed the London marathon she upgraded his title to 'The CDA—the champion daft ha'p'orth'. When she is unwell, Bob's humour does not always go down quite so well and she tells him to 'put a sock in it.' One evening, he was ready for her: he took a black sock from his right pocket and a white sock from his left pocket.

'Kate, which sock shall I put in? The clean one or the dirty one,' he asked.

34

Chernobyl: Nuclear Energy, Out of Control

Anna Melnychenko was born in Kiev in 1979. She was seven when the nuclear reactor at Chernobyl exploded, just 60 miles away. It was late April 1986.

At first the Soviet government withheld information and, locally, nobody knew of the severe and immediate danger to their health; however, the Melnychenko family was given an early warning. Their neighbours had contacts outside the Ukraine, in Western Europe, and they heard the news from them. Before leaving the area, the good neighbours told the Melnychenkos what had happened and that they should leave their home. Their warning went unheeded: Anna's family did not believe the story.

The official government news came four days after the disaster and only after high levels of radiation had been detected in Scandinavia. Soviet President, Mikhail Gorbachev, made the following statement in a broadcast to his country: 'Good evening, comrades. All of you will know that there has been an incredible misfortune—the accident at the Chernobyl plant. It has painfully affected the Soviet people, and shocked the international community. For the first time, we confront the real force of nuclear energy, out of control.'

American satellite pictures showed that some sort of explosion had blown the top off the number 4 reactor. The other three reactors had been closed down. The pictures suggested that the core had been exposed, meaning that the levels of escaping radioactivity would be substantial. Containment buildings are normal in the West but there were no containment buildings in the Soviet Union to prevent the release of radioactivity following an accident. Local reports told of thousands of people being evacuated from nearby Pripyat. While there was no immediate danger to Western Europe, the report stated, radiation from fall-out in the long term could cause cancers.

Panic hit the region as the population tried to evacuate. Transport and tickets were scarce. Residents noticed there were no buses: they had all been used to evacuate people from the immediate locality around the power station. Frightened parents put their unaccompanied children onto trains just to get them safely out of the area.

Anna's grandmother had heard of a remedy for radiation: she smeared iodine on her family's skin. The seven-year-old Anna can still remember

173

empty streets and being told to stay indoors. How did she feel? Was she frightened? 'All I can remember was there was no queue for ice-cream.'

Eventually, the family made their escape and moved to Krasnodar, a town deeper inland, in Russia.

The Chernobyl nuclear disaster, caused by an experiment that went wrong, was responsible for the deaths of 31 people immediately after the accident. Several thousand more deaths have been attributed to it since. In May 1986 Soviet television pictures showed the deserted city of Chernobyl and the report suggested the situation was under control.

Although Kiev and the surrounding cities and region were badly affected by the radiation, due to prevailing weather conditions the wind pushed toxic poisoning towards the city of Minsk in the neighbouring province of Belarus. And then came the aftermath.

Five years after the Chernobyl nuclear disaster, Dr Hugh Carpenter, the medical first secretary at the British Embassy in Moscow, brought a deputation from the Filatov Children's Hospital to Bristol University to observe some of the work carried out at the institute and to see something of the charity work that supported it. The Filatov, celebrating its 150th anniversary, placed special emphasis on the care of children with cancer following the Chernobyl disaster. When the deputation heard about CLIC, which was among the charitable forerunners in funding paediatric oncology, they expressed a wish to visit CLIC House.

Afterwards, to strengthen this newly established link, Dr Carpenter offered to reciprocate, specifically asking that a place be reserved for CLIC's founder who had been out of town during their tour in Bristol.

Moscow was Bob's first major official trip abroad; he was accompanied by Professor David Baum and they both enjoyed a wonderful, interesting but harrowing experience that forged lasting friendships.

David gave Bob some impromptu speaking opportunities, one in the Filatov Children's Hospital and another at the British Embassy. It was Bob's first experience of speaking through an interpreter and he appreciated the time this gave him to consider his next topic.

'You always hope that the interpretation is exactly what you're saying,' said Bob. 'But there's no way of knowing that until the audience start throwing things at you.'

On their first night in Moscow, the Bristol delegation attended a reception hosted by the British Council, where they grew better acquainted with Hugh Carpenter. There was mention of the Gorbachev Foundation and its work relating to children with leukaemia and cancer. Bob asked if there was a possibility of visiting the foundation and Hugh promised to see what he could do.

'Tremendous character, Hugh,' said Bob. 'Present him with a challenge and there is nothing on earth he will not do to rise to it. The next day, David and I were told that we could visit the Gorbachev Foundation in the afternoon and there was a good chance that we might see Mr Gorbachev himself. And that is exactly what happened.'

Accompanied by a BBC cameraman and reporter, they arrived at the imposing home of the Foundation bearing gifts—a CLIC book and tie—where they met the former Soviet leader, Mikhail Gorbachev, for an all-too-brief few minutes.

Aspects both unfamiliar and foreboding tempered the exhilaration Bob felt in this foreign and strange new world of Russia.

The Bristol delegation stayed in a colossal hotel of innumerable floors. Bob admitted to feeling intimidated when he shared the lift with several bolt-upright, granite-faced Russians. 'Some of them didn't look as if they'd been born, so much as quarried,' he said. 'I think the Russians were going through a very difficult time and they were a sad, downcast sort of people. They looked like that most of the time.'

As he was about to climb into bed, there was a most unholy commotion outside his room in the corridor of the eighth floor but, although he was tempted to see what was going on, he thought better of it.

In the morning, the absence of the landing window told all: a brawling guest had been on the receiving end of a violent blow, which threw him through the window to the concrete pavement below. Security men, dressed in combat gear, their dogs keeping Slavic rubberneckers at a distance, guarded the tarpaulin-covered body.

Later, during a filming sequence in busy, bustling Red Square—where the sense of history is almost tangible—a man carrying a rolled umbrella approached them. In one short, sharp sentence, he ordered them to cease filming immediately. They tried to remonstrate with him; when he did not respond, Bob pleaded with a passer-by to interpret on their behalf. The passer-by's cautionary advice was to do exactly as the man with the rolled umbrella ordered and leave while they had the chance; they should not speak to the man again; he was a member of the secret police.

Soon after, the party returned to Red Square to soak up the atmosphere of the Kremlin against the night sky. 'It was an incredible sight.'

Bob and David witnessed some frightening medical practices in the Moscow Bone Marrow Transplant Unit, a truly magnificent facility but for the lack of specialist staff and equipment. They were astonished when, ignoring obvious health risks, doctors performed a bone marrow transplant in front of them and the BBC television cameras. 'I could not believe it when they opened the doors and let everyone in,' Bob said.

They also visited a children's cancer unit where the pathetic sight of the children filled Bob's senses; he had stepped back in time. 'The children wore square cloths over their noses and mouths; the material hung down in front of their faces. They reckoned it would help keep the children free from germs. That didn't make any sense to me at all. Some of the face cloths didn't even look clean.'

As he walked round the ward, he met some of the families and gave the children what few, simple gifts he had with him: pens, pencils and balloons. To raise their spirits (and his own) he blew up the balloons then set them free; they zigzagged through the air, expelling splendidly vulgar raspberries before dropping to the ground.

Henry Hector marvelled at the way Bob created rapport so quickly with children. 'I can remember the first time I went into the Bristol Children's Hospital with Bob to visit a family whose child was terminally ill,' Henry said. 'I was terrified. We were both very tense and I felt that I would break down when I walked in. Bob was nervous too but when he got to the front door of the hospital, it was as if someone had turned on the lights. He brought such warmth and life to that room, his strength is unbelievable.'

Bob will always remember those Russian children but the memory of one little boy stands out; he had no toys at all apart from a pencil sharpener in the shape of a tiny red aeroplane. Bob spent some time playing with him and making him smile. 'I built up quite a thing with this little lad and we both had a lot of laughs.'

As Bob turned to go, the boy grabbed his tiny red pencil sharpener, the only toy he possessed in the whole world, and presented it to him.

'That's his only toy,' Bob said to the interpreter. 'There's no way I can take it.'

'You must take it,' the interpreter told him. 'He will be ever so upset if you don't. He will think you don't want it.'

Bob treasures that little red aeroplane and it sits on his desk at home.

He and an associate, Dr Fleming Carswell, became separated from the main party and accidentally ended up where they should not have been, where the authorities did not permit access.

'We found two lads tied to their beds. One kiddie, in his misery, had been crying for hours and hours. His face bulged and a fly crawled over his swollen cheek into his mouth. He just didn't have the strength to bother about it; he just let this fly carry on. We were told later that these children had behavioural problems and that is why they were tied to their beds.'

The nurses and doctors were dressed in turn-of-the-century workhouse uniforms: in greys and pale blues. A baby trapped in its cot, almost demented by its own distress, lay unattended.

'The whole place looked like a monstrous institution,' said Bob. 'Had I been there as a kiddie, I would have been frightened out of my life. Things were terribly backward; they were obviously poverty stricken but they are a very proud people; they would not have appreciated criticism.'

This whole episode was a jolt to Bob's system and he wondered what he could do—what anyone could do—to make a difference. He felt that this wretched experience had a purpose and he resolved to do whatever he could.

Following his instincts sometimes brought him into conflict with other CLIC trustees but never with David Baum and Sister Frances who were kindred spirits: they shared his attitude that no obstacle is too great to overcome but others proved not so understanding and this irked him.

'We have got more than enough to do here ... a challenge like that is so big you can't possibly make any difference ... we shall have to say no in case someone else asks on another day,' were some of the negative reactions.

'I suppose in a way, they were right,' said Bob. 'But with a bit more effort we just might make a difference. Until you try, you don't know, do you? There's no question that Pedro's life was saved because he came to Bristol; that didn't mean to say that we had to look after every sick child in Portugal. A child is a child, even if we only help a few, what a difference it will make to those few.'

In spite of trustees' concerns that they may be about to open the floodgates, Bob made up his mind that where CLIC could help, it would. 'If you can say yes, say it now; only say no when you've got to say no. If the floodgates open, we'll deal with it then. Let's deal with those in the water at the moment. Fish them out first. Defeatist attitude, I just can't bear it. Mind you, I do wonder what those hospitals are like now and how much progress, if any, they've made. I don't know that we really made a great difference at all; whether we might have done eventually—I'm still not sure.'

Later, at home in Bristol, Bob and David heard that there was a likelihood of Mikhail Gorbachev coming to England on a lecture tour and they discussed ways to nurture an alliance with him.

Every year, Fishponds Baptist church produces a motto card. The motto in January 1976 was 'With God all things are possible.' Given that this coincided with the launch of CLIC, the choice of motto made a huge impact on Bob and he hung the card on a wall at home.

'It's been on the wall ever since, except when I go out on a new project or to a meeting that's a bit different from usual—or it might be a time when I'm feeling a little nervous. On these occasions, I take the motto card with me and just put it inside my pocket: just a little reminder never to be afraid of anything. It was in my pocket when I went to Moscow.'

35

The $1 million Brick

CLIC received so many enquiries from overseas that thoughts turned to sharing its model of care further afield.

'There was a real sense in which Bob and David Baum had a vision for the globe; it was the world they saw; that is how CLIC International happened,' said Sister Frances of the genesis of the third CLIC charity. 'If I had a criticism, it might be that we were trying to run before we could walk, that we'd have done better to focus on CLIC UK; but David and Bob are people who, when they see suffering, have to do something about it because they can't bear it. And I share that. You can't bear to see suffering and not actually be involved in a practical way.'

Following in the footsteps of CLIC South West and CLIC UK, CLIC International was established with its own board of trustees. After receiving its first donation from an American family, in keeping with its name, the new charity was given free use of offices in New York.

Bob decided to ask Mr Gorbachev to become president of CLIC International, so he spoke to Mr Gorbachev's interpreter, Pavel Palachenko, who suggested that Bob write a personal letter to the former Soviet leader. There followed a speedy and positive result: Pavel invited Bob to meet Mr Gorbachev to discuss the presidency of CLIC International the next time Bob was in Moscow.

Airborne once again for Moscow, David Baum pondered on what Bob would say to Mr Gorbachev when they met. It was January 1993.

'We will be meeting a man who, until recently, was arguably the most powerful on earth,' said David, 'so what are you going to say to him? Mr Gorbachev, please would you be our president? What are you going to say?'

'I shall say something like, "It's an honour to meet you, Mr Gorbachev. I have enormous respect for you as I believe you are one of history's great humanitarians,"' said Bob.

'Stick with that,' said David. 'I think he'll like that.'

Before the meeting, they met Mr Gorbachev's bodyguard and Bob and David were delighted when, after several attempts, they managed to extract a smile from him. Then, the big moment arrived: the double doors opened and David and Bob, accompanied by Hugh Carpenter, entered the inner sanctum. Mr Gorbachev rose from his desk, walked straight over to Bob, and enveloped him in a warm bear hug.

'Mr Gorbachev welcomes you to Moscow,' Pavel said. 'Mr Gorbachev wants you to know that he believes that you are one of the world's great humanitarians and it is an honour to meet you.'

Bob started to laugh and David followed suit.

'Pavel,' Bob said, 'allow me to explain why we're laughing.'

Then he told Pavel of their conversation during the flight to Moscow in preparation for this meeting; when Pavel relayed it to Mr Gorbachev, he quickly joined in the fun. It was hard to absorb that they had only just met and yet, here they were, all laughing together.

The group sat down and Mr Gorbachev led the discussion, covering the troubles in Ireland, the Middle East and the Far East. He summed up by propounding that if only people looked out for their neighbours, if only people sat down together at the table to break bread, they would live peacefully side by side. Just those caring things would go a long way to sorting out global problems: family problems too. He believed the answers to these issues were as simple as that. After putting the world to rights, they moved on to the business of the day.

Bob said, 'It would be a wonderful honour, Mr Gorbachev, if you would consider becoming president of CLIC International.'

Gorbachev offered his hand. 'Yes, Robert,' he said. 'Yes, yes, yes.'

Bob smiled and reached into his briefcase. 'Pavel, will you please tell Mr Gorbachev that I have six certificates ready to be signed by the president of CLIC International.'

Bob laid the parchment documents out onto the table and Mr Gorbachev signed each one. They pushed the boat out by toasting the occasion with a round of soft drinks. Mikhail Gorbachev took his charity commitments very seriously and this was only the second time he had agreed to the use of his name in this way in spite of receiving hundreds of requests. It was a huge triumph for CLIC.

After enjoying a splendid evening together, Bob and David decided that, instead of taking a taxi back to their hotel, they would trudge through the tremendous amount of snow and ice on their way to the underground.

Emerging from the subway station, with several roads left to negotiate before reaching their hotel, it remained treacherous underfoot and Bob slipped.

'I thought that's funny, there's my shoes up there,' he said. 'My feet were up above my head. I'd gone down with an almighty bang and I thought I'd broken my back. David was very good: he knelt down by my side to check me over. "I'm sure it hurts terribly," he said, "but I don't think you've broken anything." So, I sat up and David put his arm around me and said, "It could have been worse, you know, Bob. It could have been me."'

The Duchess of Kent asked Bob about Mikhail Gorbachev's involvement with the new CLIC charity.

'Mr Gorbachev has agreed to become president of CLIC International,' answered Bob.

'That's wonderful,' the duchess said.

'Can I impose on you further and ask you to become a patron of CLIC International as well?' Bob asked.

'You weren't thinking of leaving me out, were you?' smiled the duchess.

On another trip to Russia the visiting party included Henry Hector who had worked on the abandoned Drake's Island project; he came along to give a second opinion on plans for building refurbishments. Together, Bob and Henry visited a ward in Moscow Neurosurgical Hospital for children with brain tumours where every one of the young patients had lost or was losing their sight. They walked down bleak, grey corridors, which seemed to go on for miles. The long, narrow ward, lit by single, low wattage light bulbs every few yards contained, nose to tail, army-type metal beds.

'There must have been 30 or 40 beds with a child in each,' said Henry. 'Sitting on the bottom of each bed was the mother of the child. Underneath the bed, there might be a sheet of polythene or a sheet of cardboard and, in the evening, the mother would pull it out to sleep on it. Next morning, she pushed the sheet back underneath and resumed her position sitting at the bottom of the child's bed all day.'

All of the children had bandaged heads and eyes. It seemed that there was no diagnostic treatment and it was only when they went blind that their problem was discovered.

'Six out of every hundred may have lived,' said Henry, 'but the hospital said, in reality, it was zero.'

One five-year-old boy waited quietly for his operation. His mother was convinced that the operation would give him back his sight. It was to be his birthday present. There were several teenagers who were taking it much harder than the younger ones; to be robbed of sight at their age was more than they could bear and their parents were doing all they could to pacify them.

During the tour, an alarming incident happened when, after being formally introduced as Dr Robert Woodward, Bob found himself in the midst of a group of gowned and rubber-gloved medics. A surgically masked person took Bob's arm and helped him into a gown before pushing him through some double doors where a prominent screen caught his eye and he witnessed the open skull of a child who was undergoing surgery for the removal of a brain tumour.

'It was a real spine-chiller,' Bob said, 'and I thought I might pass out. If there had not been other people there I'm sure I would have.' His thoughts turned to the child's parents whom he could imagine would be waiting anxiously for good news.

In spite of their desire to improve conditions at that particular institution, both he and Henry admitted to feelings of impotence.

It transpired that there was a second childhood cancer centre in Moscow and Bob arranged for a visit to be included in his itinerary. This hospital was immense but run down and sad; Bob thought it an awful place: broken concrete steps and, along the main corridor, corroding manhole covers decayed in crumbling cement. Nevertheless, the staff welcomed him and invited him to lunch.

'How I ever got through it,' said Bob, 'I don't know. I didn't recognise the food at all; it looked like an old-fashioned doughboy swimming in a bowl of grease; and it tasted like it looked; it was foul. I nibbled away at some of it to make it seem that I was enjoying it but, all the while, I was looking for somewhere to tip it. There were other delicacies on offer: strips of toast with bits of fish on, that sort of thing, but nothing tasted anything like it does at home. I drank water; how safe that was I shall never know.'

After lunch, they took him on the grand tour. His guide told of the cancer centre's wonderful results and proudly took him to see their new equipment: two wall-mounted soap dispensers. 'Their idea of new equipment for a cancer unit was something that delivered a dollop of soap into your hand. That was it.'

The relationship between this cancer centre and the previous one was non-existent. 'No,' Bob was told, 'we don't have anything to do with them because their performance is so poor.' The guide made it sound as if this cancer centre was a world leader and a star attraction.

Only a day later, through the Gorbachev Foundation, Bob met Professor Alexander Rumyantsev. 'Now, will you come to see my childhood cancer centre?' he asked.

Bob reacted with surprise—there was a third centre? He was even more surprised to find that it was located in the same hospital as the second one. When they arrived at the crumbling edifice of the same massive hospital, Rumyantsev led Bob upstairs to a floor just above the soap dispensers.

'I have been here before with a medic from downstairs,' said Bob.

'Never,' said the professor.

'Yes, I was. I was here yesterday.'

'You don't want to take any notice of him,' said Rumyantsev. 'We try to avoid any children going down there at all.'

Bob was astounded. 'It was a lottery into which of the three units a child would end up.'

What confronted him in this third centre distressed him enormously: so many children in cubicles lying in tattered linen on old broken beds. Some rooms boasted the luxury of a lavatory but with no air break between the lavatory and the room. The general standard of cleanliness was appalling. There were no books or games: mothers and children had nothing to do. Poorly equipped offices sported the latest fax machines, unused, as there was no paper to fill them. This encounter with the Russian health service was no better than the one he had experienced the day before.

Bob's visit coincided with the onset of a period of hyperinflation in Russia. The rouble exchange rate that had been around eight to the dollar only a few months earlier, had fallen to 256. Just two years later, when Bob visited Belarus, the value fell to 11,000 roubles to the dollar.

Professor Rumyantsev had attracted Dutch and German sponsorship for the bone marrow transplant unit that ran the whole length of the ward. The accommodation was magnificent but it was bare, just empty cubicles, no equipment.

'It was a beautiful unit but I can't see how anyone could possibly survive in there,' said Bob.

Having seen first hand the needs of children in Russia, Bob accepted a sponsored invitation to speak at a child health conference in Vancouver, where he met Erina Malikova, a paediatric oncologist from Minsk in Belarus, who was involved with the building of a new hospital. She needed help with some of the issues they were facing, specifically with the accommodation of parents of sick children. At the same time, Ian McGrath, a medical researcher from Washington, and a Canadian consultant were discussing setting up an international charity linking Washington, Canada and Minsk; its aim was to identify cases of children with cancer as a direct result of the nuclear incident at Chernobyl and they were seeking help to attract funding for it. Bob made arrangements to visit the area.

While changing flights at Moscow for Minsk, the Belarus-bound party, which included Bob Constantine and his cameraman from Bristol-based HTV, was highly amused by a vision of ancient aviation slouched on the tarmac before them.

'There was this rickety old thing with chewing gum on the wings and sticky tape, and we were laughing at it,' said Henry Hector.

It turned out to be their plane and Bob was relieved that Judy could not see it. Like so many intrepid travellers before and since, and in spite of their darkest concerns, the party resignedly climbed the steps into the belly of the primeval flying machine.

The dilapidated exterior of the aeroplane turned out to be in somewhat better condition than the cabin interior: the group was hard pushed to find decent seats in working order; seat belts were a forbidden luxury and they sat beneath gaping, broken overhead compartments. Farther along the aisle, a hound of donkey-sized dimensions had requisitioned a section of the cabin for itself.

'There was no stewardess. When the plane took off, some passengers had to stand and they hung on to the roof like they were travelling in the London underground,' said Henry.

The flight, mercifully, proved uneventful and when they touched down safely, their relief was ruined by the prospect of the return journey.

In stark contrast to Moscow, Bob was amazed at the quality of the new hospital in Minsk but wondered where the money for equipping it was coming from. It was intended that this hospital would treat many of Chernobyl's tragic victims and Bob saw an opportunity for CLIC to build an accommodation block, the 'Children's Inn', in the hospital's grounds to help the families of the ever-increasing children diagnosed with thyroid cancer.

'The crew filmed a pledge for $1 million, which I wrote on a brick. It was just a publicity stunt and the people there realised that there was no legal obligation but I was hopeful of raising the money,' said Bob.

Henry's business contacts with a telecommunications company offered a solution. The company, which aimed to supply mobile phones to a number of former Soviet states, needed a conduit to facilitate an introduction to the authorities in Belarus. Should this introduction lead to a contract, the company was prepared to pay a commission of $1 million, which Bob and Henry requested to be paid direct for the Children's Inn.

The success of this immense venture needed the assistance of others. Contact was made with members of the local parliament and Bob developed a relationship with the Belarus ambassador in London.

'He was a delightful character to deal with,' said Bob. 'When I needed to renew my visa, they did it for me there and then, while I enjoyed coffee and chocolate biscuits with the ambassador.'

Henry suggested that they invite the mobile phone executives, together with John Sunley, chairman of the Sunley Holdings Group, to a lunch at the Four Seasons Hotel in Park Lane to mark the 21st anniversary of the founding of CLIC. Belatedly, on the morning of the lunch, it struck Bob that it would have been a good idea to have invited the Belarus ambassador as well and he set off to rectify his oversight.

'What a chump I was not to have thought of it before,' he said.

Holding on to his belief that he would be no worse off should the ambassador refuse him, he rang the doorbell of the Belarus embassy. Fortunately, the ambassador was in and accepted the last-minute invitation.

His presence made the telecommunications executives realise how serious Bob and Henry were about the Minsk venture and the lunch was a great success; however, hard work, the best of intentions and just-in-time ideas do not always produce results, as regrettably resistance from the Minsk parliament prevented a successful conclusion.

While Bob was in Belarus, he became interested in Children in Trouble, a small charity in Minsk, which was run from a hostel by a handful of people, who themselves lived in poor accommodation.

'They apologised because there was no room for us to stay but I have to be honest and say I was pleased,' said Bob. 'The hostel was on the ground floor of a huge, grey, sombre-looking building, which went right up to the sky; it was sad, neglected and run down; it wasn't very good at all but it was all they had. To youngsters, it must have looked so intimidating.'

Although the hostel was close to the centre of Minsk, the condition of the road leading to it was extremely poor: broken tarmac; kerbstones pulled away from the pavement; and derelict cars parked on grass verges. Through the rickety old door, the interior space was ghastly: shabby, antiquated, metal-framed windows; odd rugs scattered over crumbling linoleum flooring; the whole place was grubby and had not seen a decorator for many years. Everything about it reeked of poverty and deprivation; however, all the people who stayed there, some for a very long time, were thrilled with it.

It would not have been easy for the charity to serve a meal to the foreign visitors but they managed to find something for their guests to eat. Bob and Henry sat down to a repast of indeterminate content and doggedly forced down what they could while studying the healthy cockroaches decorating the walls. After lunch, when Bob was offered a seat on the sofa in the chairman's office, he crashed down into it: the springs had completely collapsed. He felt so sorry for these people who barely smiled, these people who tried so hard but had the weight of the world upon their shoulders.

There was accommodation for up to eight families and in one of the rooms, Bob met a boy of around fourteen. Pictures, painted by the boy, covered the walls and he was working on a new canvas. It was his version of the text 'Suffer little children to come unto me' and depicted Jesus gathering the children to his side. The face of Jesus and the face of the first child, a girl, were complete and he had sketched empty boxes where the other faces would be. For Bob, this unfinished painting was an evocative reminder of the unfinished work of CLIC.

'This picture is fantastic,' Bob said. The boy's face lit up. 'I would love to take one of your paintings home with me. May I buy one?'

'No, I will give you one,' said the boy who could speak a little English. 'You choose.'

'I would dearly love the one you are painting now,' said Bob.

'I will send it to you when it is finished,' said the boy.

'I would like it just the way it is. Will you sign it for me, please?'

This painting has meant so much to Bob; it is a poignant symbol of CLIC's work and a reminder that there is still a long way to go.

'I felt absolutely thrilled to bring that picture home with me. I had it framed and it hangs in Robert's bedroom. At the time, I felt a little mean taking it, especially as it was unfinished. I think the boy understood what I was saying when I tried to get across to him that it would mean even more to me left unfinished. The sad thing is I don't know what happened to him and I would like to know.'

Bob and Henry expressed a wish to visit Chernobyl and were driven away from Minsk into woodland.

'We went through this beautiful pine forested area and suddenly we saw a sign with a skull and crossbones on it, which had been shot full of holes,' said Henry. 'Then there was nothing ... nothing, but nothing; it was just brown, dead earth. This was the area where the rain fell: the polluted rain, the fall-out. Everything in it was dead, no green at all and yet at the edges, there was grass and forest.'

When they spoke to the people in the hospital, Bob and Henry noticed that so many of them seemed to have warts, blisters and deformities.

'It was said that this was their heritage for the next 200 years,' said Henry. 'Their bodies would be polluted for 200 years.'

Back in Minsk, Children in Trouble was negotiating with a 92-year-old woman to buy her home, a timber-built dacha, situated in the forest; it was an ideal property to serve as a Belarusian equivalent of a CLIC crisis-break flat. The old woman, who lived alone, still managed to grow her own vegetables and fetch water from a well but her children felt that the time had come for their mother to take a rest and move into town with them.

The going rate for this type of home was £5,000 and Bob hoped that the dacha would be the first project funded by CLIC International, a new offshoot of the CLIC family, based in the United States.

'We sat on bare tree trunks,' said Henry. 'They laid a table for us on a plank of wood and they brought out food for us to eat: two little gherkins, three small tomatoes between maybe eight of us. There was a piece of white pork fat, no meat, just a piece of this white lard that a lot of eastern bloc countries tend to eat and a smallish loaf of black bread. To them, it was an absolute feast and they made it a special occasion because Bob was there. They treated us like royalty.

'We sat there under the stars and you could see forever; you could see two, three times around the galaxy, there were never as many stars. The language was a problem but then someone sang a song, a moving Russian song; we just sat there all together.'

Finally, the visiting party celebrated the 'purchase' of the old lady's dacha by drinking water from the well.

'I don't think we should have done that, being so close to Chernobyl,' said Bob.

At the inaugural meeting of CLIC International trustees, held in New York, it was agreed that the dacha was a suitable and worthwhile proposition to support but at a later meeting in the Belarus embassy in London they discovered that there was a 40 per cent levy on charitable donations brought into Belarus. Naturally, Bob did not want the money dissipated so he decided to take the law into his own hands. He advised the only trustees he could find at short notice, David Baum and Jack Lyes, of his plans to carry undeclared currency into Belarus to avoid throwing away valuable public contributions. They became anxious for him when they heard this.

Bob considered the possibilities of what might befall him should he be caught. One thing was certain—all of the money would be confiscated. But his uppermost thoughts were for the people in Minsk whose needs were so desperate; one way or another he was going to make sure that they would not lose out. Bob carried £5,000 of his own money, converted into US dollars, and presented it to Children in Trouble in Belarus; he was given a receipt, which he later produced for reimbursement from CLIC International.

After the anxiety and romance of buying the pretty little dacha, practical realities enforced another course of action on Children in Trouble. The Minsk charity possessed only one vehicle, a Mercedes truck, which broke down irreparably just before the purchase of the dacha, and the charity asked if they could use the money to buy a replacement vehicle instead. As this need was greater, CLIC International trustees granted permission for the charity to use the money to buy a Mercedes minivan.

'The dacha would have been a lovely little place for families to stay. I wished that I could have afforded to have bought it for them,' said Bob.

Although there were many positive aspects about CLIC's involvement with the former Soviet states, there were equally as many negative ones and, after a while, disillusionment set in.

CLIC International's original plans included funding improvements in Professor Rumyantsev's hospital, but when Bob heard of the experiences of another charity, there were second thoughts. This other charity had been so moved by the plight of the young patients that they donated a commercial washing machine so that the children could at least enjoy clean linen during their time in hospital. When the charity returned to the hospital three months later to review the result of their gift, the washing machine could not be found; it was eventually located, up and running in the home of the hospital manager.

On an earlier occasion, Bob and Fleming Carswell were shown a ward, empty of beds, but filled with unopened cardboard boxes and wooden crates, which contained medical equipment donated by the Hope Charity. The boxes had stood undisturbed for more than two years: lamentably, no one in the hospital knew how to use the contents. It was no wonder that CLIC International and others, before and since, became disheartened faced with indifference, inadequate resources and corruption.

Two decades after the disaster at Chernobyl, the surrounding area, covering some 30 square kilometres, is a prohibited zone. The nearby city of Pripyat, devoid of human inhabitants except for occasional military patrols, is home to a teeming wildlife. Kestrels nest in the city's abandoned apartment blocks while deer and moose roam the streets. The nuclear power station closed down for good in December 2000, nearly 15 years after the accident. In the Ukraine the incidence of childhood thyroid cancers has multiplied ten-fold in the years following the explosion. Residents in Belarus and the Ukraine say that they 'don't know what is in the air or in the water.' Anna Melnychenko, now in her twenties and living in Swindon, hears reports from friends and family that births are often complicated and most children seem to have allergies and other complaints; people still worry about long-term health effects for themselves and for future generations.

36

The Gorbachev Lectures

In 1993 Mikhail Gorbachev was invited to the UK for a lecture tour, which was sponsored by Astec Communications of Cheltenham.

Efforts to arrange this tour were considerable and a large host committee was established on which both Bob and David Baum served. Mikhail Gorbachev was president of only two charities: Green Cross, an environmental charity in Switzerland, and CLIC International. It was therefore highly significant that the Gorbachev Lectures were to conclude in Bristol at the invitation of Bob Woodward, where Mr Gorbachev would receive an honorary doctorate of Laws from the university.

When Mikhail Gorbachev arrived with his wife Raisa in Aberdeen, the first stop on their tour, Bob and David greeted them as members of the host committee. It was evening time and the reception was held in a local hotel. Bob and David had been advised that dinner jackets were the order of the day but, of the assembled group, they were the only two wearing them; they had been the victims of a prank. David handled the potentially embarrassing situation with aplomb.

In the reception line-up, Mr Gorbachev laughed aloud when he noticed the two of them, standing side by side, in dinner jackets.

'Mr Gorbachev wants to know why you are all dressed up,' said Pavel.

'We are dressed like this tonight because we have special roles to play,' said David. 'We are wine waiters: Bob is responsible for the red and I am responsible for the white.'

Pavel interpreted and Gorbachev laughed again. What could have been a humiliation turned out to be great fun because of David's quick thinking.

The Gorbachevs' itinerary took them to Edinburgh, London, Oxford and, finally, Bristol. On 10 December Bob welcomed his eminent guests to CLIC House and said, 'The only word I can think of to describe this occasion is Gorbellous.' He looked at Pavel and said, 'I should be interested to hear you translate that.'

After Mr Gorbachev's response, a giant cracker appeared. Bob took one end with Raisa, and Judy took the other with Mikhail. When they all pulled together, it split asunder to reveal three children dressed in traditional Russian costumes. It was a splendid moment.

Days before, it had been uncertain as to whether CLIC House could accommodate a party of such numbers as the garden was too small to hold a large enough marquee. It became possible, according to Bob, due to the efforts of one man, Roger Cole, a scaffolder whom he had known for some forty years. Level with the windows at the back of CLIC House and accessible through french doors, Roger constructed an enormous platform where he erected the marquee.

Later, at the university, David Baum gave the oration at Mikhail Gorbachev's honorary doctor of Laws ceremony in front of a packed audience at the Wills Memorial Building. The response—from an authentic world statesman—left everyone completely enthralled. As Mikhail Gorbachev left the stage there was one intimate moment of tenderness: he looked at Raisa, sitting in the front row, and smiled.

37

Budapest

Conditions in Hungary in the 1990s were still very different from those in the West. Although Hungary's 'market socialism' had made it more affluent than its neighbours by Eastern bloc standards, it suffered from rising unemployment and its economy was struggling. Hungary held its first democratic elections in 1990 but inevitably it took time for economic momentum to build up.

In 1994 an international conference for paediatric oncologists, SIOP (of which Martin Mott had been the secretary), took place in Visegrád, just outside Budapest. Martin invited Bob to talk about CLIC. When they met Professor Dezso Schuler, a paediatric oncologist and president of SIOP, Bob asked if he could visit the cancer centre for children in Budapest.

After the conference Bob spent two days at the children's cancer unit, where an inscription carved into the stone wall above the doors of the clinic, 'Suffer little children to come unto me', was said to have been left untouched by the erstwhile Communist authorities solely because there was no reference to Jesus.

Bob expressed a wish to meet as many parents as he could and the hospital arranged a get-together on the following day. Before meeting the parents he visited the hospital wards to speak to some of the children. The face of one little lad will stay with him forever; Bob guessed that the likelihood of the boy's survival was remote. The mother told him that her son needed a liver transplant. She was, however, optimistic about his chances because she had set up a fund to raise £47,000 to send him to London for specialist treatment. The fund had been running for some time and stood at £37.

'She was clinging to a straw,' said Bob. 'What can you say to comfort a mum in a situation like that?'

Another mother had been in the hospital looking after her child for three years. She remained at the cancer unit even when her child was not on treatment; she dared not go home because there was a chance she might not be able to afford to come back again for her child's next course of therapy. In three years she had seen her husband and her two other children only twice. These people's problems were so hopeless that just the knowledge of them, coupled with the huge medical and social divide, lent a different perspective to Bob's own experiences.

'How do you re-charge your batteries?' Bob asked them. 'Is there somewhere for you to stay at night that's comfortable enough to lift you and give you strength to get through the next day?'

It seemed that no one could tell him and he was determined to uncover why these parents were so reticent. The answer eventually came from two women who took Bob to a lift where they drew back the concertina metal gate and beckoned him inside. The ancient lift clanked its way down into the pit of the building where they stepped out and walked to a stone spiral staircase. Following the rusting iron handrail, they descended past the flaking, decaying walls until they reached an outside yard below.

'She wants you to know that this is the place she dreads most of all,' explained the woman who acted as interpreter. 'They all dread the darkness because this is a refuse dump and, at night, they have to walk through the rats to get to their beds.'

All three walked across the yard into a tunnel dimly lit by two naked light bulbs; ahead lay the dilapidated, padlocked door of a disused boiler house. The other woman produced a large key and opened the door to reveal a sea of mattresses in an airless, windowless room. A single light bulb hanging on a solitary length of flex presented stark illumination of the lime washed walls. The squalor confirmed it—these people desperately needed Home from Home facilities, which Bob hoped would be forthcoming with the support of CLIC International.

'There is one thing you can be sure of,' he told the parents. 'If there is ever a chance of finding some accommodation for you, CLIC International will come back and do something about it.'

With the disappointments of Russia behind him, Bob felt a closer affinity with the Hungarians; perhaps any efforts made here would be more likely to succeed; however, Professor Dezso Shuler said that finding suitable property near the hospital would be highly unlikely. The buildings in that area were so large they were unaffordable. Nevertheless, Bob believed it just might be possible and asked Dezso to keep it in mind.

Just eight weeks on, Bob received an excited telephone call from Dezso asking to meet at the Francis Hotel in Bath.

'I had to come, Bob,' said Dezso, 'to tell you face to face. Only last week, bulldozers pushed down the building next door to the hospital; they are going to build flats there. I have talked to the builders and we can buy six flats all together in one block for £150,000.'

'Right next door to the hospital,' said Bob. 'That's amazing—the chance of a lifetime.'

'Will you come over?' asked Dezso. 'Then you can meet the builders to see their other developments and gauge the standard of their work-manship.' Bob agreed to come.

He presented Dezso's report of the opportunity to buy six flats next door to the hospital in Budapest to his fellow CLIC International trustees but they were not quite as enthusiastic as he expected and reminded him that CLIC International funds amounted to only £25,000. Just what was the point of him going over there to see the builders, they asked?

'We can do what we do over here,' said Bob. 'We can put down a ten per cent deposit to secure it. The flats will take a year to fifteen months to build and in that time, I could raise the rest of the money. I want to do this. I desperately want to do it.'

The trustees said that if Bob believed he could pull it off, then it was up to him but they cautioned him: they were not fund-raisers and so the onus fell entirely upon his head.

Bob flew to Hungary where he visited one of the Budapest builders' existing developments. He was suitably impressed with the standard of work and a meeting was set up with lawyers to arrange the purchase of six new flats adjacent to the hospital. It turned out to be a somewhat unusual encounter as the weeping mothers of the sick children were also present. They told Bob that so many had promised to help them but he was the only one who had come back.

Roused by this heart-rending reception, Bob prepared to sign the documents when, suddenly, the euphoric moment was shattered.

'You do realise that you will be unable to renege on the deal,' said the lawyers. 'As a foreigner you must place 100 per cent of the purchase money into the builders' nominated bank account. It is not an unreason-able safeguard when you think about it.'

Bob did think about it and thought it extremely unreasonable, given the financial circumstances of CLIC International. What was he to do? How would he raise the money? The mothers watched expectantly. Their words echoed in his ears: he was the only person who had come back.

'I prayed silently,' said Bob. 'Lord, you brought me here, you showed me the problem, you set me the challenge and I have come back. I cannot let them down; surely, you don't want me to let them down?'

Then he lifted his pen and signed the purchase documents; everyone was in high spirits; they all shook hands and he caught the first flight home.

During breakfast the next morning, Judy asked how it had gone.

'Fine,' said Bob and he told Judy about the dilemma before he signed the contracts.

'How were you able to sign?' Judy asked. 'What was the answer to your prayer?'

'Well, Lloyds Bank is CLIC's bank as well as ours. The only unencumbered asset we have is our house and Lloyds holds the deeds. I shall raise a £150,000 loan on our deeds.'

'I hope you know what you're doing,' was all Judy said, in response to her husband's incontestable decision to mortgage the family home.

'That was *all* she said,' said Bob. '"I hope you know what you're doing."' He thinks that Judy's unshakeable support was nothing less than fantastic.

Unlike Judy, the manager at Lloyds Bank was not quite so supportive. Why risk your personal property, he asked, when CLIC had a considerable property portfolio.

'Because I don't want to go back on my word,' said Bob. 'I can't let them down.'

Others reiterated the bank manager's concern over the mortgaging of personal property for charity business.

'Trustees Ian Harvey, Vince Harral and Jack Lyes all said that they did not think I should put my home on the line,' said Bob. 'They expressed misgivings if something unexpected should happen to me during the fund-raising. Where would that leave Judy? It was very thoughtful of them. Even so I still took personal responsibility for the debt.'

Before securing the loan to pay for the flats in Budapest, there was another issue to be resolved. Was it right to use a property belonging to CLIC South West as collateral for a CLIC International project? Was it the right thing to do to bring about the aims of the infant charity? Although some were unhappy that funds were to be diverted not just away from the South West but also out of the country altogether, the trustees concluded that it was.

In spite of the continuing success of new ventures under Bob's stewardship, certain relationships within CLIC were slowly turning sour. Most things do not happen by chance and Bob had gained the reputation of being 'unstoppable'. It was regarded as one of his strengths: he could often get things done when others could not. The flipside, however, was Bob's refusal to be deflected even when some considered his course of action to be wrong and he became the target of increasing criticism.

Even a charity with the noblest of intentions can experience these problems, and CLIC proved no exception. It was to descend into a period of dissatisfaction, infighting, revolution and ultimately, evolution.

38

Le Walk

Chris Head, CLIC's director for fund-raising, advised that 120 members of various charities were to be offered the opportunity to walk the entire length of the soon-to-be opened Channel Tunnel to raise money for their respective causes, and CLIC had been offered one place.

Bob was very excited. 'Just the thought of walking from France to England ... I mean, there are not many people who have done that. The tunnel gradually descends for the first five miles and then levels out for 20 miles before it steadily inclines for the final six miles. That's 31 miles—it's a long time to hold your breath, isn't it?'

Should he be unable to do the walk for any reason, Bob thought it wise to recruit a stand-in and he knew the right man for the job—his good friend Roger Cook, the songwriter, who agreed to understudy on the day if necessary. On their first training session they walked along the cycle track from Fishponds to Bath; it was their intention to glean a few long-distance walking tips from the former cricketer Ian Botham, who was appearing in pantomime there, and to make the most of an opportunity to generate some publicity for CLIC.

They set off in good spirits ... but it took much longer than expected to reach their destination.

'It very nearly killed us,' said Bob. 'When we met Ian, the first thing he said was, "If you wear those shoes you'll never make it."'

With the condition their feet were in, it was easy to believe him and it was fortunate they had arranged transport back to Fishponds where they had left their car ... but Bob had other ideas.

'The real challenge,' he said to Roger, 'would be to walk back.'

'You must be out of your mind.'

'It's a challenge,' said Bob.

It may well have been a challenge but it was certainly a huge mistake. By the time they reached Keynsham, their legs had turned to jelly and they resembled two stumbling drunkards. As rural cycle tracks do not feature taxi ranks, they had no alternative but to limp on to the bitter end.

'We slipped into the pain barrier and never came out of it,' said Bob. 'I could feel blood swishing around in my shoes and when we got to the car, I could not bend to get inside. And poor old Roger ... I thought I was going to have to lay him in the boot. We almost screamed with pain, just trying to get into the car. When at last I managed to get in, I couldn't move my legs to put my feet onto the pedals. It was agony.'

Somehow, they got moving and after dropping Roger off at his home, Bob returned to Judy in need of tender loving care. It was not forthcoming.

'You know you're going to kill yourself, don't you?' said Judy, who thought the whole thing ridiculous.

'If I do, it definitely won't be as painful as this,' Bob really wanted to say but he said nothing as he did not want Judy to know just how much pain he was in. After running a bath, he stepped in wearing his blood-caked socks with hopes of gently soaking them off. 'When I looked at my feet, I didn't think they would ever heal but I couldn't let it take too long because I had to be out training again.' The need for suitable training shoes had not occurred to Bob, and it was G. B. Britton of Kingswood, the famous Bristol shoe manufacturer, which came to his rescue by supplying a sturdy pair of walking shoes for his training sessions.

Bob sought personal sponsorship for the Chunnel Walk and successfully trawled his friends and acquaintances to raise £18,000. John Sunley, the property developer, agreed to sponsor him for £1,000 but for one mile only—the last mile of the 31. A few days before the big event, there was more good news: a charity in London, the Lennox Children's Cancer Fund, made a hefty contribution of £50,000 and thereby almost quadrupled the total.

With this enormous amount of money riding on the successful completion of the Chunnel Walk, there was no backing out but there was still one more problem for Bob to face—his 'little bit of claustrophobia'.

'Somehow or other, I was going to have to conquer it,' said Bob. 'But how the dickens was I going to do that when I had to walk through a fifteen foot pipe and not be able to get out until the end? It would be like getting in at Bristol and getting out at Bridgwater.'

The day came and the valiant walkers checked into their hotel in France. Following a pleasant evening meal, Bob became increasingly aware of a familiar pain—sciatica—and sought the help of a local physiotherapist. He awoke the following morning, still in pain but he bit the bullet, pulled on his walking boots, which had been donated by Plus 50 Safety Products of Bristol, and went ahead with the walk.

Many celebrities took part on behalf of their chosen charities and Daley Thompson, the triathlon athlete, led the walk. Nigel Havers, TV's Green Goddess Diana Moran, and Nicholas Witchell the newsreader were among those who lined up ready to undertake the gruelling twelve-hour marathon.

'Le Walk' took place from Calais to Folkestone on 12 February 1994. The televised event began with the cast of the BBC comedy *'Allo, 'Allo* welcoming the 120 walkers at the entrance of the Chunnel. Because he could hardly walk, Bob was one of the last people to enter.

'I looked up at the strip lights in the tunnel,' he said. 'They seemed to go on forever.'

He gritted his teeth and thought of the pain that so many children suffer in cancer wards; he thought of Robert and all that he went through. His sciatica was temporary and held no comparison to the pain that they had suffered. Bob started to walk.

'I was delighted when I reached the first bend, which I thought was probably about three or four miles into the tunnel. Then, I saw the marker: it said one mile. I could hardly believe it.'

He became aware of a support vehicle, following him closely. 'You're way behind everyone else; you're going to have to jump on the cart with me,' a voice said.

Bob kept walking.

'Jump on,' said the driver. 'I have strict orders.'

'No, I'm not getting on,' Bob insisted, determined to increase his pace to make up time.

The driver, obviously not happy about Bob's intransigence, continued to follow, waiting for him to falter. He had a long wait. After a few miles, the pain eased and Bob began to catch up with the others.

'When I saw people in the distance, for a moment, I thought I had strayed into the wrong tunnel,' he said.

Doggedly trailing Bob, support-vehicle-man suddenly became distracted by two other walkers who offered less resistance to the allure of a comfortable ride. After that, Bob experienced his first high: there were a number of walkers trailing behind him. Then he came across former England captain, Graham Gooch, who encouraged the walkers into a friendly game of cricket.

An army of volunteers, selflessly giving their time to support this event, treated the walkers to drinks and chocolate bars along the way. Farther into the tunnel, the participants enjoyed a brief pit stop for a welcome lunch before pushing on.

Later in the afternoon, the officials waited for all the walkers to reach a specific place in the tunnel where they were confronted with an enormous bank-vault type door. After turning the locking mechanism wheel in the centre of the great door, it opened and everyone was ushered into an antechamber beyond, which barely measured six feet across. The door shut behind them with a whoosh and a resounding thud, sealing them in.

Struggling against his rising panic, Bob's 'little bit of claustrophobia' swept over him. 'I thought I was going to go bananas but I was determined not to make a fool of myself. Talk about being claustrophobic — there were more than 120 of us in there.'

His discomfort alleviated when the door opened at the far end of the antechamber; he could hear music. The group found themselves in a cavernous holding and exchange bay, one of several 'cross over' passages used to switch trains from one track to another. This unusual venue, 150 feet beneath the seabed of the English Channel, played host to an exclusive party. A steel band played and while the walkers enjoyed more food and drink, dancers entertained them. Some of the walkers joined in but Bob did not. Assembling the walkers in the train-holding bay was all part of the timing as they were to exit the tunnel at a pre-arranged time to coincide with the live TV show scheduled for that evening.

Nearing the end of the marathon, Bob felt drained, both emotionally and physically, not surprisingly as he had never walked 30 miles in his life before.

With the other triumphant participants, he emerged from the abyss to the sound of whirring cameras and welcoming voices: the first people to walk from France to England since the Ice Age over ten thousand years ago. Cosseted in foil wraps, they queued to receive their medals from Richard Branson but when it came to Bob's turn, there were none left. The embarrassed Mr Branson confessed that they were four short but promised that four additional medals would be cast within the week. Then it was discovered that four stewards had stood in line alongside the walkers and claimed them for themselves. The relinquished medals were eventually awarded to the rightful recipients later that week.

Judy, James and Bob's brother, Alan, were there to meet him. Bob chose not to stay long at the reception. He climbed into the car, reclined the passenger seat and lifted his weary feet up onto the dashboard. 'I thought I was going to die. But if ever the chance came to do it again, I would take it. It was wonderful — it was too good to miss. Whoever would have thought you could walk under the channel from France to England?'

39

Unrest Within

By the mid 1990s the unrest within CLIC could be clearly heard throughout the region and Bob's position was coming under increasing pressure from schismatics. Conversations ceased abruptly when Bob was nearby and he sensed instability. 'A handful of people were becoming uncooperative ... awkward ... difficult ... I felt that something was about to happen.'

The offer to finance the Budapest project by re-mortgaging a CLIC property had put pressure on CLIC to raise the necessary funds. On top of this was the issue of funds leaving the country, which was unpopular with those of a more parochial persuasion. It was said that Bob was spending CLIC's money before it had been raised, even though many long-term CLIC projects were financed in this way. At branch level, there were those who questioned whether their chairman should be concerned with helping children and their families overseas, further fuelling the unrest.

Rumours began to circulate that all was not well at CLIC HQ. Some said that Bob was difficult to work with, complaining he was unable to delegate. Sister Frances shed some light on this. 'His standards are of the highest and, in his reckoning, people didn't always achieve the standards he set. Employees, while they may give very generously, have other bits of life to live as well. You see, CLIC was like his child and they were threatening, as he saw it, the life of CLIC, so he retaliated ... he's a perfectionist.'

Gill Nickolls, CLIC's administrator for many years, agreed. 'He wanted perfection and it didn't always happen, but he was out there to try and make it happen.'

Notwithstanding the standards he set, Bob genuinely wanted to find others who would share the task of taking CLIC forward. 'He was always so full of hope when there was going to be a new senior appointment,' said Sister Frances. 'This was going to be the person who would help him to make it what it should be. But every time it failed.'

'Bob set high standards,' said John Nickolls. 'He wanted results and he paid well to get them. He always delegated to me. These days, they say, "Give him his head," and he did just that. There were never any problems of him not being right behind what I was doing. He was always there to support but he never intervened.

'He does not suffer fools lightly. He used to say to me, you won't improve the world of a child with cancer without, along the way, ruffling up a few feathers.'

So, what was it like, working for a man who felt that nothing was impossible, a man who felt that with maximum effort and with the help of God, it might be that children could be saved from the ravages of cancer?

Bob readily admitted to being demanding, and his commitment and drive are unquestioned. Could he have achieved all he had without these qualities? Given the all-encompassing importance of CLIC to its supporters and families of stricken children, his insistence on the highest of standards should have been expected. In the power struggle that ensued these criticisms were to play a significant part. How fair they were only those who worked with him can judge. It was a matter of record, however, that his personal style had worked with countless volunteers, supporters and staff within CLIC and in his own building business over the years. Recent years had seen Bob continue many happy and successful working relationships with other charities.

An anonymous donation of £50,000 was to cause further controversy. CLIC UK had been the recipient of an earlier donation of £200,000 from the same benefactor who always stipulated that overheads of his chosen charities must be kept within certain limits. Unfortunately, by this time, the overheads in CLIC UK were beyond these and, rather than lose the funds, Bob placed them into CLIC International, earmarking them for a Home from Home at the Royal Marsden Hospital, although that project was later shelved. While it may have seemed that Bob's actions were overriding, he disagreed: 'They said the money should have been put into CLIC UK,' said Bob. 'They said I had no right to do it but in the circumstances I had every right in the world.'

Where this money was placed was not the only problem: where it was to be spent also attracted disapproval. Although the strength of the relationship between Bob and Martin Mott was one of the cornerstones of the early years of CLIC, there were times when the two disagreed. 'Martin was opposed to the Home from Home concept and did not visit CLIC House when it was opened in 1981,' said Bob. 'He later opposed the purchase of the Plymouth property. Martin always considered that Homes from Home drained money from resources that could have been used for treatment. The weight of his opinion may have gone some way in shelving the Royal Marsden project.'

In spite of the growing criticism, root support for Bob in the branch network of CLIC remained high, although some wanted to restrain his enthusiasm for new projects outside of their own objectives. To those on the outside, all appeared to be running smoothly, so what was it that turned harmony into contention? What motivated some to keep their heads down and not get involved and who, even now, do not want to talk about it, referring to that period as being 'water under the bridge'? The events of the forthcoming months were to shock CLIC supporters and, to this day, they are unclear as to exactly who, or what, brought it about.

As Bob's personal stock fell within CLIC, a new relationship was to have a profound effect on his future. He first met Charlie and Mary Dobson in 1995.

Every year, the honour of starting the CLIC Fun Run at Oldbury-on-Severn fell to Bob. The annual run was organised by Pat and Roger Smith and held in memory of their son Tommy who lost his fight against leukaemia in the early 1980s. One year Bob received an excited phone call from Pat telling him that a company in Bristol, owned by Charlie and Mary Dobson, had donated £1,000 to that year's event. 'Would you thank him in one of your beautifully handwritten letters?' she asked.

Bob took the opportunity to enclose a book about CLIC with his letter to the Dobsons and an invitation to CLIC House. While they declined the invitation, they complimented Bob on his handwriting.

The following year the Dobsons donated a further £1,000 to the Fun Run; Bob sent another thank you letter and invited them once again to visit CLIC House. For the second time his invitation was declined but, some months later, a Christmas card arrived at CLIC International with a cheque tucked inside for £10,000.

'Mary was the one who eventually instigated our visit to Bob,' said Charlie. 'Mary was a believer in putting money into research.'

'I felt if they found a cure for something, you help so many more people and I was very interested in funding a research project for CLIC,' said Mary.

'Mary and I were always quite in awe of CLIC's achievements,' said Charlie. 'Virtually every shop, pub, take-away you went to there was a CLIC collection box to be seen. It was one of those charities where you would always put £1 in the tin. I was very impressed with how Bob had created such a high profile for CLIC and a great awareness with the public.'

They all met up in the New Year. 'We would like to come over to see you. How are you fixed right now?' asked Charlie on the phone.

'I'm just doing some correspondence,' said Bob.

'Put the kettle on,' said Charlie. 'We'll come over.'

Fifteen minutes later, over coffee, Charlie and Mary told Bob about their company, Spandex, which was established in 1976 (the same year as CLIC) from one small room in Portland Square, Bristol. Spandex, a wholesale supplier of materials to the sign industry, had done enormously well; it expanded into Europe and the United States and became the biggest company of its type in the world. Wanting to share the fruits of their success, the Dobsons set up the Spandex Foundation, giving one per cent of annual profits to help seriously ill and disabled people in the Bristol area.

Then Charlie came to the point of the meeting: 'Bob, if we were to make a substantial donation to CLIC, what would you do with it?'

'That would depend on the amount,' hedged Bob. 'My answer would be different if it was for £1,000, £5,000, £10,000, or more. If it was a "mega sum", I would use it to fund a research programme.'

'That was music to Mary's ears,' said Charlie. 'We had a figure in our minds of £200,000. Moreover, Bob said what he would love to see was a research project in Frenchay Hospital with a CLIC flag on it. I told him to put the kettle on again because Mary and I needed to chat about it.'

When Bob returned with the refills they had made their decision.

'We like the sound of funding a research project very much and we'd like to give you a cheque for £200,000. Will that get one up and running?'

'Yes,' Bob said gratefully.

'We shook hands and had another cup of coffee. He was on cloud nine,' said Charlie.

Bob took the good news back to CLIC's trustees.

To Charlie's annoyance a delegation from CLIC came to visit him and implied that all was not well at CLIC HQ. They advised him of the dissent within CLIC regarding Budapest and questioned the wisdom of having a CLIC research lab at Frenchay, arguing that if there was to be a research lab it would be better at the children's hospital.

'I didn't like their attitude or them questioning Bob's judgement,' said Charlie. The Dobsons were not put off and, conscious of the pressures and the controversy over the Budapest property, offered Bob and James, who was now working with his father, office accommodation at Spandex for CLIC International, away from the strained relationships at CLIC's headquarters.

'I said to Mary, Bob is in some difficulty here,' said Charlie. 'He's really gone from the heart and decided that CLIC International would fund a Home from Home in Budapest. Mary and I felt that we probably would have done the same in his shoes. He was willing to mortgage the very last thing he had left, his house. He'd seen these children in dire straits and he just couldn't stop himself, he had to do something and he did it. Now he was in hot water and we had the solution. So, we decided to help. We truly believe in Bob Woodward and nothing, absolutely nothing, will change our opinion of him.'

At a second meeting with Bob to arrange a time and date for the cheque presentation Charlie and Mary said their goodbyes and started for the door; Charlie hesitated, turned and walked back.

'By the way,' he said, 'we shan't be giving you £200,000; we'll be giving you £350,000 to cover the house in Budapest the dissenters keep on about—now you can tell them to get lost.'

'I knew, with every pore in my body, that God would honour all that had been achieved for those desperate mums,' said Bob. 'Yet I was astounded at the way in which the problem was solved with Charlie and Mary's incredible generosity.'

The postscript to this story is a happy one. After the triumphant opening of the CLIC flats at the hospital, both the mayor of Budapest and the president of Hungary wrote to Bob expressing their appreciation. At Christmas, Bob still receives thank you letters from parents and sometimes an enclosure from the children. He remembers this success warmly: a success born out of adversity so far away.

It was also the last major CLIC project in which Bob Woodward was involved.

Part 2

Demolition

1995–2006

'Facts do not cease to exist because they are ignored.'
Aldous Huxley

40

Million Dollar Smile

In March 1995 the BBC newsreader and CLIC trustee, Martyn Lewis, invited Bob to a special event in London, requesting a prompt arrival at 6 p.m. On this occasion, Judy was unusually assertive in hurrying Bob and his brother Alan through the front door, telling them that she had heard television reports of heavy traffic. Just moments after they left, Judy, accompanied by family and friends, followed closely behind. When Bob and Alan arrived at the BBC studios in London, Martyn ushered them into a reception area where about twenty people waited to present Bob with a large cheque for CLIC.

'When I stepped onto a platform and started to thank them for the cheque, the wall began to move, the platform swung round and I found myself being moved into another arena. Then I saw all these faces, one was Esther Rantzen, welcoming me. Only then did I realise that I was on the *Hearts of Gold* stage.'

BBC's *Hearts of Gold* ran for several series between 1988 and 1996 to celebrate the lives of ordinary people who had made their mark in a number of different ways. Bryony Daly, from Devon, who had suffered with bone cancer, was there to honour Bob. She had first met him at one of the CLIC shows at the Bristol Hippodrome. 'Bryony always smiled a million-dollar smile.'

The programme featured a number of pre-filmed tributes.

It was said that Bob had achieved the impossible by getting Mikhail Gorbachev to come to Bristol to accept the role of president of CLIC International. Professor David Baum said, '... how does one approach a Nobel Prize winner, a world leader, a person who has changed history, when we are coming from nowhere? But, in comparison with what he felt CLIC might bring to Russia and to the world, this became a trivial issue. With his particular approach, which is a combination of good judgement, good sense, charm and charisma unmatched and unstoppable energy and tenacity, put those together and the walls, like the Berlin wall, come tumbling down.'

The Duchess of Kent said, 'He loves people and he can't bear to see people suffer so he takes away the pain, he brings back the smile to a child's face—it's really basically as simple as that—that's what gives him happiness.'

'Although it was very nice of them all to have done this,' said Bob, 'the way that Martyn presented it made it sound as if there was only one person running CLIC. It sounded as if there was just this one person doing everything. It was terribly embarrassing, really.'

Just before the credits rolled, Bob said, 'I can see about five lifetimes' work out there. I wish I was 20, 30 years younger but I am very thankful that I have been given the stamina, energy and health to be involved and to be part of what is a great family, because CLIC is a very special family.'

The timing of *Hearts of Gold* with its unreserved accolades—which Bob had been the first to say had been a little over the top—did not go down at all well with some colleagues and aggravated the friction within CLIC, although there was genuine warmth from true friends and colleagues. David Baum was to the fore; he could not have been more delighted had he received such recognition himself. He turned the coach trip home into a party, with champagne for everyone, and he led the singing all the way back down the M4.

'It's wonderful to have a friend like that,' said Bob.

Bob first met Esther Rantzen when she came to the opening of CLIC's London office, and later, when she presented him with a Childline Award. 'I went to see her after *Hearts of Gold*. She said to come up one day and have egg and chips with her in the BBC canteen. So I did.'

Later, when Bob received letters criticising his stewardship of CLIC, he wryly remembered the fulsome praise showered upon him on television. How quickly those words had been forgotten.

41

Kangaroo Court

When the sheer pace of work took its toll on Bob's health, it was suggested that he take a three-month sabbatical from his role as chairman of CLIC SW and CLIC UK. In his absence, acting chairmen took over; nevertheless, his involvement with the families of sick children and his speaking commitments continued. Bob also decided that, in spite of a number of good trustees at the New York office including Mark French from Frenchay who was then an executive chef at the Marriott Marquis, he could no longer commit his time and energy to the expansion of CLIC International in America. Without Bob's influence and driving force, it seemed prudent to review the feasibility of the venture and, sadly, it looked as if there would be no future for CLIC in the USA. Having made this decision, CLIC needed to find a deserving home for the New York funds, which had been donated by an American family in appreciation of their child having undergone a bone-marrow transplant in England. Bob talked it over with Howard Pearson of Yale University who suggested that the money be given to Bob 'Woody' Wilkins who ran a programme called *Dances with Wood* for youngsters hospitalised for lengthy spells. The programme involved making kit-cars, then customising them, after which Woody set up races around the hospital wards, which were enormously popular with the young patients. A deserving cause had been found.

When Bob returned to work he went into training for the London Marathon.

'I did more and more walking to get my feet used to being pushed hard. I went training with David Fry, the Kingswood town crier, a guy who did an awful lot of walking. For this walk, I wanted to do something different, something distinctive, something that had not been done before, something that was most likely to be caught on camera to get some publicity for CLIC.'

He came up with the idea of carrying children on his shoulders. An extreme idea, perhaps, but Bob explained, 'I went to see John Swift who has a polystyrene company and I asked him whether he could make some polystyrene children for me to carry on my shoulders.'

Yes, he could, but John needed three children as models. Bob asked Frenchay C of E School if they could help. 'We placed a bench against a wall for me to sit on and got three lovely kiddies to sit on the wall behind me so that John could work out the proportions.'

From a single block of polystyrene, John made an impressive model of three children with arms extended, waving, all appropriately dressed in CLIC T-shirts and CLIC hats.

'Wherever you looked, it was important to see CLIC's logo,' Bob said.

On the day of the London Marathon, as Bob made his way to the group of walkers aged 60-plus, a TV crew swooped down on him. 'The moment they saw the children on my shoulders, they were there, which was the whole purpose of the exercise. It was a scorcher of a day and with that polystyrene model wrapped warmly around me, I think the water in my head boiled several times! I encountered another problem around Canary Wharf when the wind caught it, pulling me back. I was afraid it was going to break but, overall, it was enormous fun and attracted tremendous publicity for CLIC.'

Judy and James ran their own marathon jumping on and off tube trains on the London Underground, constantly surprising Bob by popping up in front of him as he made his way around the course.

'It was lovely seeing them so often. I was able to get a photo of us all, with "the kids" on my shoulders at London Bridge.'

As he reached the final stretch going down the Mall, a microphone was pushed into his hand for an impromptu interview. He had completed the course in 6 hours, 55 minutes and 16 seconds. 'I felt a bit downcast then because Judy and James weren't there to see me finish but it was a good job they weren't really. I had begun to feel a bit giddy and wobbly so I went round the corner, leant up against a wall and just slid down it. I did wonder if I was going to blinkin' die. I felt absolutely awful but I knew that somehow or other I had to recover before Judy saw me.'

While Bob took a few days off to recover, he delegated the task of interviews for a new London-based post within CLIC. When one applicant expressed an interest in a more senior position, it was suggested by members of the interview panel that he might be an ideal candidate for the pending role of CLIC chief executive officer. After a further interview and ratification by the trustees, the appointment was filled.

'It was some weeks later that I became anxious,' said Bob. 'Few in the CLIC branches or shops had seen or heard anything of the new CEO and I was considering calling a trustees' meeting to discuss my concerns when I was sidetracked. I was summoned to a meeting scheduled for the next day. There was an air of secrecy and I wanted to know what was going on.'

The following morning, a copy of the matter for discussion arrived at Bob's home. It was a dossier of 88 pages, attributed to the new CEO. The section headings were damning: Staff Morale, Financial Irregularities, Mismanagement ... The offender, the dossier stated, was Bob Woodward.

'I could not express my feelings upon reading it,' Bob said. It was, however, the final pages of the report, which really astonished him: they contained his already written letter of resignation.

30 August 1995
To: The Executive Council, Domiciliary Care Nurses, All funded posts, Branches and Staff.

LETTER FROM THE CHAIRMAN

Many of you may be aware that I recently travelled to Minsk in Russia to meet Dr Olga Alienikova who is a Paediatric Oncologist with whom I shared the Children's Cancer Sessions at the Global Health 2000 Conference in Vancouver. A new Children's Hospital has been partially built in a new site in the forest area on the outskirts of Minsk at a cost of US $20m. This has been funded by sources in Austria and Germany. A 60-roomed parents hotel has also been planned on the site and although no money has yet been found, an estimate of US $1m. dollars is required. Many of you may also be aware that whilst on this latest visit I signed a promissory note (written on a brick) to fund this exciting project known as the CLIC Inn. I hope to raise most of the funds by the 20 April 1996 to coincide with the 10th Anniversary of the Chernobyl disaster, which has affected 9 out of 10 children in Belarus. This region receiving the largest amount of contamination due to the accident.

As a consequence of this pledge I shall now have to devote most of my time and energies on this exciting, new and latest development to bear the CLIC name. Therefore, I have decided to step down as the Chairman of CLIC SW and CLIC UK in order to spend more time overseas and try and replicate our unique Model of Care of which we are all so very proud.

(Name withheld) will take over as Chairman of CLIC UK and (Name withheld) will take over CLIC South West. (Name withheld) will still remain as Chief Executive for both of these charities.

Having now made this decision, the pleasing aspect for me

personally is that after nearly 20 years of occupying just about every room in Spruce House with CLIC files I am going to finally set-up an independent office from which to operate. This means that I am at last able to try and return to some form of normality in my home life and would therefore appreciate any future phone calls about CLIC business be directed to the Chief Executive, at Head Office.

Please do not think I am abandoning you. As the Founder of CLIC, my new role will become more of an advisory one to both CLIC SW and CLIC UK and as such you will all see me from time to time.

Finally, I wish to take this opportunity to thank you all personally for your loyalty and dedication and above all your commitment to CLIC which I shall now be trying to emulate overseas. You can all be very proud of your achievements.

Robert N Woodward
August 1995

'When I started reading it, I thought I was having a mental breakdown. When did I write this? I couldn't remember writing it,' said Bob. It took a moment for the truth to dawn on him. 'Of course. Someone else had written it. I felt I was the victim of a conspiracy and found it hard to believe that anyone could behave in such a manner.'

Bob left home that day to attend a meeting that would consequently change the course of CLIC's future.

'It was a most humiliating experience and what could best be described as a kangaroo court. They said there were concerns about a number of things that were happening within the charity and wanted to bring these matters to the attention of the trustees. If that was the case, why hadn't they notified them of this meeting? What they really meant was, if I was prepared to sign the resignation letter, in exchange, the dossier would be destroyed and nobody would ever get sight of it. I was going to be let off! I said, "You can get lost. I am not signing that letter and I take umbrage that there are only three of you here and that you have not alerted all of the trustees." So I refused to sign and resolved not only to copy the "report" to each of the trustees of all CLIC charities, but also to take it to the Charity Commission.'

When Bob studied the report, he found that the most worrying item related to his travel claims: some paperwork was missing. He could not understand this because his travel files were always available for inspection at CLIC headquarters. He searched high and low without success.

The missing travel expense records remained a mystery for three years, when, quite by accident, they were found, along with other papers, in black bin-liners in an off-site container used to house unwanted office furniture.

In spite of the repeated concerns of those who thought it better that CLIC sort out its own problems, Bob decided to involve the Charity Commission and on 28 September 1995 took copies of the dossier along with him.

'I discussed the situation with two officers who told me that, by involving the Charity Commission, I was opening "Pandora's box". That didn't worry me because I believed that having opened "Pandora's box", the Commission would monitor the situation in a fair and efficient manner.'

Regarding the new CEO, it was discovered that, among other issues, references had not been taken up and, with the benefit of advice from the Charity Commission, Bob contacted him to secure his resignation.

The following day Bob received a letter from the CEO which stated that he wished to tender his resignation as chief executive of CLIC UK and CLIC SW with immediate effect. He expressed regret that matters had ended as they had, and confirmed that he had prepared the report, which he accepted was inaccurate, and Bob's proposed letter of resignation, on the specific instructions of another trustee. He concluded by wishing both Bob and CLIC well for the future.

The content of this letter said it all and should have been more than enough to clear Bob Woodward's name.

42

Political Manoeuvrings

After this unexpected sequence of events, when it was suggested that Bob 'draw back from the firing line and let somebody else take the strain and the flak', it sounded to him like good advice and he stood down. To accommodate this, a temporary independent chairman took over while Bob continued to serve as a trustee for all three CLIC charities. However, he stated that he was only prepared to stay with CLIC if the perpetrators of the report, which he felt had been designed to discredit him, resigned; nevertheless, no resignations were offered. The new chairman told Bob that now *he* was in charge, things would be done his way, although Bob had been assured that the resignations would be forthcoming if he stood down.

'As I drove home, I realised I had handed CLIC over on a plate,' said Bob.

Bob resigned as a trustee of CLIC SW and CLIC UK on 24 November 1995. 'My biggest dilemma was that I did not want to disillusion our supporters; above all, I wanted to safeguard CLIC's reputation. I was proposing to stand back from the day-to-day running of CLIC and to accept the position of life president, which had been mooted several times in the past, but only if a reliable team was in place to handle the management of CLIC.'

Sister Frances was also asked to resign and, believing it would help Bob, she resigned out of loyalty to him. She never received acknowledgment or acceptance of her resignation.

'I was incensed to learn that Frances, one of CLIC UK's first trustees and finest ambassadors, had been asked to resign,' said Bob. 'I felt that such political manoeuvrings were offensive and inappropriate within a charity.'

On 2 December 1995 Ian Harvey wrote to Bob to advise him that, by a majority decision of the joint trustees, his resignation from both CLIC South West and CLIC UK has been accepted. Bob found it difficult to believe that this short note represented the cessation of 22 years of his life with CLIC. He was also disappointed with the Charity Commission. 'They said they would monitor the way that CLIC was run. This did not happen. It was a shambles.'

Bob issued a press release a few weeks later to say that he had resigned in order to concentrate on the work of CLIC International outside the UK. However, it was later agreed by the trustees that Bob should remain a trustee of CLIC SW and CLIC UK after all, and he was reinstated.

Soon afterwards, as a direct result of his appearance on BBC *Hearts of Gold*, the North British Hotels Trust invited Bob to Edinburgh to discuss the possibility of setting up a Home from Home there. It was a tremendously exciting project and one that would cost CLIC very little because the property was being offered at a peppercorn rent. In addition, the Hotels Trust had agreed to sponsor the renovations, estimated at £350,000. This was too good to miss. When CLIC UK took no action, Bob asked the Hotels Trust if it would accept CLIC International to take on the responsibility for running the Edinburgh Home from Home. CLIC UK trustees later criticised Bob for this unilateral action, even though there had been no constructive suggestions as to how the project might otherwise have been saved.

'It would have been more appropriate for CLIC UK,' said Bob, 'but their lack of interest meant it was not going to happen.'

On 26 March 1996 Bob and David Baum, after obtaining advice from a leading charity lawyer, challenged the way the charity was being run and what they had been advised were breaches of the law. Within a few days half CLIC's trustees resigned; while some were rare attendees of meetings, others were major contributors of long standing. What had prompted such action, following so closely on the meeting of 26 March?

This disaffection seemed extraordinary considering the effusive praise which had been heaped upon Bob on *Hearts of Gold*, when an audience of millions was told that he was 'an amazing, a truly remarkable man.'

43

Charity Commission Suspension Orders

On 22 April 1996 Bob, Sister Frances Dominica, Professor David Baum and their solicitor attended a meeting at the Charity Commission's offices in Taunton. An official said that the problems CLIC had encountered were not uncommon. He hoped CLIC would come through this difficult stage so that it could continue to help children.

'We came away feeling that we had been given a mandate to continue and I made plans to appoint additional trustees from the branches,' said Bob.

When CLIC's executive council met, however, it passed a vote of no confidence in the trustee board for CLIC SW.

'I was soon to realise that even with an incredible number of supporters, it only needs a tiny group of individuals with their own agendas to erode the strongest foundations,' said Bob.

After the upsets of the previous months and the exodus of so many trustees, a series of press interviews were scheduled to present the good news about the presentation of the largest single donation that CLIC had received to date: £350,000 from Charlie and Mary Dobson of the Spandex Foundation. A new research project would receive £200,000 and the remaining £150,000 would pay for the Home from Home in Budapest. Unfortunately, the presentation was spoiled when a team from HTV's current affairs programme, *West Eye View*, interrupted a sequence of filmed interviews for BBC, HTV and Sky News by shoving a camera into Bob's face and pointedly asking about the recent trustee resignations. He lost his cool and shouted at the interviewer.

'It was my biggest let down of all when I lost my temper but I couldn't step anywhere without one of them being there right in my face,' he said. 'They didn't want to hear about Budapest, they didn't want to hear about the research, they didn't want to hear about Charlie and Mary Dobson's generosity, they didn't want to hear about the money at all.'

On 28 May 1996 *West Eye View* was broadcast. Its contents disgusted many of Bob's supporters. 'It was so damaging to Bob, just by the innuendoes,' said Sister Frances. 'That man would have given the shirt off his back for CLIC.'

Earlier that day Bob, Professor David Baum and Jim Carbines had

216

been called to a Charity Commission meeting to be told that, while it was to be hoped that CLIC's troubles would soon blow over, nevertheless, the commission was serving orders on all three of them, suspending them from all of CLIC's charities while the situation was being investigated.

While Jim Carbines was disgusted by his suspension and felt the commission overreacted, Bob was devastated. 'There are no words to describe my horror and humiliation at being suspended from the charity born out of the suffering of my own son, which had become my life.'

'Bob was judged by those who were completely out of touch with the feelings and values of ordinary people,' said Steve Dayman of Meningitis UK. 'Unfortunately, some people didn't treat him with the respect he deserved.'

The continuing stress affected Judy and she lost her voice for some weeks. But there was no let up: a number of rumours began to circulate, raising the question of possible financial irregularities.

'It was suggested that I was the subject of a National Insurance Contributions Agency inquiry and that the Inland Revenue was investigating me,' said Bob. In due course he received *refunds* from both agencies but these suggestions seemed to be the start of a one-sided campaign, which continued to hound him.

All this was happening to a man who, with colleagues and volunteers, achieved enormous heights in helping children with cancer and their families. Since the very first days, back in the mid 1970s, CLIC had made great efforts to change the world of the child with cancer—through treatment, welfare and research.

Some of CLIC's achievements under Bob's stewardship include:

- Britain's first-ever Home from Home;
- the paediatric oncology unit at the Bristol Royal Hospital for Sick Children;
- crisis break accommodation for families;
- the first team of domiciliary care nurses to service an entire region;
- the best 'Shared Care' service with oncology clinics held in every major hospital throughout the South West;
- clinical sessions across an entire region in district hospitals;
- CLIC's own 'ambulance' service with specially converted vehicles to ferry children to and from treatments;
- a team of play therapists for children during visits to hospitals;
- the first chair in paediatric oncology in the UK;
- the CLIC Model of Care which is available in whole or part

throughout the UK;
- a research unit and research programmes;
- a branch network;
- and a chain of charity shops.

From such small beginnings, Bob had presided over a charity that became so well known. On ITV's Charity Telethon in 1988, when the actor Patrick Malahide appealed on behalf of CLIC, his closing words left a powerful imprint, 'CLIC—easy to remember—impossible to forget.'

Bob later made a complaint to the Broadcasting Standards Commission about *West Eye View,* which by that time had screened a follow-up programme. In its findings, the Broadcasting Standards Commission made several criticisms of the handling of queries relating to financial issues and stated that 'The Commission considers that the programme oversimplified matters ... Moreover, HTV could have made it clearer that in no way was Mr Woodward trying to use CLIC for his own personal gain ...'. But it went on, 'While there were occasions in which the programme might have portrayed Mr Woodward more sympathetically, particularly with regard to financial matters, the Commission finds that overall there was no unfairness ... Accordingly, the complaints are not upheld.'

The journalist and HTV board director Bruce Hockin later reflected:

> There was a problem in the CLIC organisation and everyone was fighting their own corner. As a journalist, if I had been in *West Eye View's* position, I would probably have seen it the same way. The sad thing is, however, they weren't aware of the full facts, and this was the weakness in the programme ... .

Of the commission's judgment, he commented: 'That was a travesty of justice. How on earth the Broadcasting Standards Commission could come out with a judgment which finds, in three cases, the programme was at fault and then says, "Well, it didn't actually damage Mr Woodward at all," is a nonsense.'

The Charity Commission's inquiry finally concluded on 13 December 1996, a long eight months after it had begun. The commission made a press statement to the effect that they had found no evidence of any deliberate wrongdoing. Bob received a call from BBC West TV presenter, Chris Vacher, inviting him to give an interview that same afternoon. On Bob's arrival at the studios, he was greeted with the words, 'Isn't it great? You've been vindicated.' But Bob felt anything but triumphant: 'I didn't feel anything. I was just numb. My mind focused on the fact that I had been "in the dock" for almost a year; that I had been found "not guilty" was almost an irrelevance. All I could think was that I should never have been in the dock at all.'

After a short interview with BBC TV *Points West*, Bob moved on to the BBC Radio Bristol studio for another interview, this time with Keith Warmington and Mark Seymour from the Charity Commission.

'It wasn't an easy interview,' Bob said afterwards, 'but above all I wanted to be positive and I wanted everyone to see that I was fully supportive of the new board. Mark Seymour had said publicly that the Charity Commission had not found any evidence of fraud or deliberate wrongdoing on anyone's part. He had confirmed that I was free to resume my charity work and expressed a hope that I would feel able to continue to associate with CLIC and give my support to the new body of trustees in their objectives. This was the closure I so longed for and which I felt I richly deserved.'

His thoughts—that at last he would have peace of mind and his pain, especially through the long nights, would be over—turned out to be short-lived.

44

The New Broom

The new chair of CLIC, Brigadier Hugh Pye, contacted Bob to discuss a new role for him: one with, perhaps, a lower profile.

'We discussed a position for me and agreed that life president would be most appropriate. I offered to take on a pastoral role, visiting supporters when they were ill and being in touch with families. Hugh said he would consider this.'

Meanwhile, the CLIC charities merged into one and its name reverted to the CLIC Trust with a single board of trustees. Ironically, this was the structure that Bob had always favoured during his leadership but was not adopted by the trustees.

At the inaugural meeting of the new board of trustees on 17 December 1996, the resignations of Bob, David Baum and Jim Carbines were accepted in the presence of a representative from the Charity Commission. The new trustees also agreed that Bob should be invited to become CLIC's life president. Statements were released to the media and on 19 December a press conference was held at the Merchants' Hall. Bob believed that there was fresh hope. Then, to his astonishment, he learnt that, along with Professor David Baum and Jim Carbines, he had been subjected to a new suspension order with effect for one year from 16 December 1996, fully three days before he had been publicly inaugurated in the position of life president.

Despite this extraordinary turn of events, discussions took place between Bob, Charlie and Mary Dobson, and Eddie O'Gorman, founder of the Children with Leukaemia charity, to explore the possibility of setting up a new charity called Child Health 2000 within the Institute of Child Health at the University of Bristol. The new charity was to focus on children with life threatening conditions other than cancer or leukaemia. As Bob was now CLIC life president, it was necessary to ensure that the initiative would not cause conflict or confusion with CLIC or any other existing charity and the university seemed satisfied that this was the case.

Bob was to be the chief executive on a three-year contract to start in April 1997, funded jointly by the Spandex Foundation and Children with Leukaemia. An office was allocated within the Institute of Child Health; telephone connections were installed, furniture was about to be moved in and Bristol University issued a press release on 19 April 1997 to

220

announce what was happening. They were ready to go.

Just three days later, Hugh Pye paid Bob a visit: he was unhappy with the arrangement. Soon after, Bob received a letter from the vice-chancellor putting Child Health 2000 on hold, citing the ongoing discord with HTV as the reason.

The dropping of Child Health 2000 was the latest in a series of disappointments and setbacks and it proved to be too much: on 1 June 1997 Bob wrote to Hugh Pye telling him that he could no longer be CLIC's life president and he wanted to disassociate himself from the charity. To this day, few people are aware of what prompted him to resign, and CLIC's subsequent press release made no mention of his reason for it.

'To have gone public would have risked causing serious damage to CLIC. Knowing of my deep passion for the charity, I have always felt that those who had gone to such lengths to discredit me had always been confident that they could rely on my silence.'

Over the previous eighteen months, Bob's health had suffered; he felt mentally, physically and spiritually drained and needed to wind down. In search of solitude he slipped away to Spain for a short 'crisis-break' of his own. Spain suited him: he thought it just a wonderful place to be. After a light breakfast, he was never happier than when he walked the beach from Marbella to Puerto Banus, rejoicing in the vista of the majestic mountains and the sparkling Mediterranean Sea. He spent this time in meditation, often praying aloud, but during these walks, he suffered some disturbing symptoms: his shoes became tight and his hands started to swell; the time had come to return home.

His doctor took a urine sample for analysis and referred him for tests. Just days later, a consultant nephrologist, Dr Charles Tomson at Southmead Hospital, diagnosed nephrotic syndrome: Bob's kidneys could be leaking. An overnight stay confirmed the diagnosis.

During a follow-up consultation three years later Bob was advised of a national study into nephrotic syndrome and was asked to participate in one of three courses of treatment. He and Judy were given a report on the procedures and the side effects associated with each treatment. It made grim reading, especially for Judy; she looked shocked and Bob told her not to read any further. The medication sounded all too familiar.

'Is this some sort of chemotherapy?' he asked bluntly.

He was told that anti-cancer medication could prove beneficial in the treatment of this problem but he refused to take the drugs until the results of that day's tests on his kidneys came through. The results were promised for the following afternoon.

'This was yet another worry for Judy. The next day, I tried to take her mind off things and took her to the shopping village north of Oxford. It was a lovely sunny day and we sat outside for tea.'

At just past four o'clock, Bob slipped away to call the hospital. Luckily, the news was good: much to the consultant's surprise there had been an improvement and further treatment was unnecessary ... for the time being at least. Three months on the results were even better; three months after that there was no sign of the condition. Nephrotic syndrome is something that Bob has learnt to live with and has shocked him into watching his weight and keeping an eye on his blood pressure and cholesterol levels.

On 17 July 1997 television reports linked two unrelated matters: Bob's resignation as life president and the Contributions Agency 'investigation'. 'A viewer could think that I'd agreed to leave CLIC quietly to try to avoid any further negative publicity,' he said. And although he continued to enjoy the support of many staunch allies, including David Baum and Sister Frances, some supporters and members of staff have admitted that their opinions of him changed because of the ceaseless flow of negative publicity and gossip.

The allegation that Bob was still the subject of a Contributions Agency investigation should have been laid to rest because the true facts had been acknowledged by CLIC's solicitors. In May 1997 the solicitors wrote to Bob's accountants stating that, with regard to the rumours that Bob was being investigated by the Contributions Agency, they could reassure the accountants that it was the charity, and not Bob, which was the subject of the Agency's investigation. The charity was fully aware of this and their solicitors were instructed that at no stage had their client suggested otherwise.

That same month the Contributions Agency wrote to Bob's accountants stating, '... the Agency is not investigating Mr Woodward personally regarding his National Insurance position ...'

Although it was a very unhappy time Bob received unflinching support from those closest to him. There were countless letters expressing regret that he was severing connections with a charity so dearly loved by so many and there were pleas for him to reconsider. He was especially touched when the Duchess of Kent sent him the prayer card *Someone Does Care* with her love, respect and admiration.

But rumours, insinuations and whispers continued unabated. 'Shortly before Child Health 2000 had been put on hold, I received reports from friends in the CLIC branches that defamatory remarks were being made about me and that my expenses were still under investigation,' Bob said.

These reports were all distressingly similar. He felt that there were those who were still intent on destroying any remaining popularity and respect that he had within CLIC. His solicitor was adamant that he should pursue a claim for slander but Bob simply did not have the resources to fight the onslaught. His son, James, reflected on what had gone so wrong:

'CLIC became a not particularly nice place to work. There were those who didn't want CLIC UK and CLIC SW united: money that was raised down in the South West had to stay down there, which I suppose was fair enough but these discussions went on for years ... CLIC had the personal touch because, for Dad, even the smallest detail was important. But when something becomes that big, it's not always possible. He needed a right-hand man, someone he could trust, and this was what I tried to be when I was his PA. I tried to relieve some of the stress but he was just non-stop. Mobile phones had just been invented and he was always on it. He couldn't even sit down for dinner without the phone going and him having to rush off and do something. He seemed to thrive on it, which is good but a bit mad really. He's double my age and he runs rings round me; he just doesn't stop. I don't know how he manages it. I guess he's focused. I sometimes wonder if he drinks Red Bull on the sly.

'He's a very thoughtful person. He still wanted to hand write letters to people, to thank them for the money they'd raised—especially little kids. A little kid gets sponsored for roller skating around the playground and sends CLIC £3, so Dad goes out to buy a special card to write a thank you, which was brilliant but he didn't really have the time to do it—he had mounds of paperwork everywhere. We said, "You're too busy to do that—we must have a set thank you letter." "No," he said, "no way. CLIC will never do that." Everything had to be personalised. At one fund-raising event, he asked volunteers to take the names and addresses of everyone who gave £5 or more and he hand wrote a thank you letter to every single one of them ... hand wrote to them all to thank them.'

The new broom swept away some of the most loyal and committed CLIC employees.

'I was finally made redundant in September 1996 but it had been rumbling on from about May,' said Gill Nickolls. 'When the administrators were brought in, it was obvious that the old school was out and the new boys were in ... watch your back, that kind of thing. You could see straightaway that they weren't interested in you as a person, or the fact that you'd been there for ten years, they were looking at the charity

224 Bob the Other Builder

as a whole. I don't say that the administrators didn't have CLIC's best interests at heart, but the whole thing changed—it became a business. I think there were about seven of us that went in the end ... In retrospect, I'm quite glad I was made redundant because the work ethos of CLIC changed completely and not for the better, I gather. In our day, the whole CLIC ethos tended to be more family oriented; we were treated more like friends than staff. Because of it, I think we worked harder; we had loyalty—without doubt, the families and the volunteers made the job. The fact that you were part and parcel of helping the process from A to Z was very rewarding.'

While Bob had been roundly blamed for the mass resignations of trustees in 1996, his absence led to more resignations from staff and supporters who had become disenchanted without him at the helm.

'I left CLIC after Bob left and had to sit back and watch this happening,' said John Nickolls. 'It was very painful for someone like me. Even former loyal friends, supporters and trustees did not stand by him; they just walked away. It was sad to see.'

'After Bob left CLIC, many changes happened,' said Ruth Cummins, who lost her son to cancer. 'I put the changes down to the fact there was no one at head office any more who knew exactly what it's like to lose a child. You haven't got to lose a child with cancer or leukaemia but you have to have empathy.'

The CLIC branch network slowly began to crumble and, over the next few years, almost halved in size. 'I don't think they were too worried about losing branches; right from the outset, there was no way they were going to have the amateurs telling the professionals how to run the organisation,' said Bob. 'They told me that letting CLIC be democratic was one of the mistakes I made.'

'The branch in Plymouth folded and I attended that meeting,' said Ruth Cummins. 'It was terribly sad to see ladies, who'd done all sorts of things for years supporting CLIC, crying in a meeting and saying they had to resign because of the changes. They just felt they weren't being appreciated.'

45

Follow the Trail of the Yellow Balloons

Quite unexpectedly, on 3 November 2000, Bob received a letter from Andrew Larpent, CLIC's chief executive officer, inviting him to become involved in CLIC's 25th anniversary year celebration. Although, in his heart, he would have loved to attend, Bob was wary. Rumours—that he had over-committed CLIC's finances by promising £1 million to the new children's hospital appeal, that he had received a salary while a trustee of CLIC and that he had double-booked his petrol expenses—were still circulating. He considered that two of these accusations could easily be countered. It was minuted that he did not propose or second the motion for the grant for the new children's hospital appeal. As far as his salary was concerned, the Needham Cooper Trust had indeed sponsored his work with Bristol University from 1990 to 1996 but it was permitted for a trustee to work for and receive a salary from another organisation provided there was no conflict of interest.

He felt that the rumours regarding his expenses were the most serious, not least because the phrase 'double booking of expenses' made it sound as if it had been going on for years. Digging a little deeper he heard from a former trustee that this appeared to have been based on a single incident: that Bob used a CLIC credit card in Cornwall when he claimed to be in Petersfield, Hampshire. Given this information, Bob was able to research the matter and he hunted through piles of CLIC papers for something that might shed light on the incident. It took hours and hours and cast a shadow over the family's Christmas but, piece by piece, he reconstructed the event.

On the morning of 23 April 1995 Bob's brother Alan had driven him to the Duke of Wellington in Bugle Street, Southampton, to attend a lunch with the Independent Order of Foresters who had raised more than £90,000 for CLIC that year. After spending some time with the Foresters and their partners, they left for Alan's home in Bournemouth. In the early evening they set off for Cornwall where they spent the night in a B&B in Newquay.

Next morning, they visited Christine and Freddie Palombo and their son Thomas in St Agnes. Daniel, their younger son, had died from neuroblastoma the previous week.

'We met Bob after Daniel was diagnosed,' said Freddie Palombo, 'and we were lucky enough to be able to stay at CLIC House. Without

CLIC's support, it would have been impossible to stay together as a family unit. Bob started Daniel on his collection of hats and would always bring Daniel a present whenever he went on one of his missions abroad. We were told that after meeting Mikhail Gorbachev, Bob looked for a new hat for Daniel. Whilst walking across Red Square, Bob saw the ideal hats; the problem was two military men were wearing them. That didn't deter him. He approached them and negotiated a deal.'

Bob had known Daniel for more than half of his young life and felt especially privileged to have had such a close friendship with him and his family. 'We went into the village of St Agnes and followed the instructions that Daniel had left for us. "Look out for the yellow balloons and follow the route." We followed the trail of balloons to the church, where we all assembled to say farewell to a tremendously courageous young man and we wept with the family at the graveside. Pressure of an evening engagement curtailed our time with them and other good friends, many from CLIC, who had joined us on that sad day.'

Bob and Alan left St Agnes, arriving at Petersfield Town Hall—a journey of some 230 miles and over five hours travelling—just minutes before the 7.30 p.m. start of the Hampshire CLIC AGM at which Bob was the guest speaker. Although drained by the emotional demands of the day, he told the gathering about the trail of yellow balloons leading to the church at Daniel's funeral to symbolise the challenge to achieve even greater goals in the continuing fight to save young lives.

Almost six years later, in his search for petrol receipts, Bob was able to ascertain that the amount in question was £37.78 (which had been reconciled by CLIC's finance department at the time). It was this paltry sum on this one occasion that led to years of 'double booking' innuendo, gossip and accusation: a most serious denigration of his integrity.

So, when Bob received CLIC's invitation to become involved in its 25th anniversary celebrations, he felt unable to accept it until they *publicly* acknowledged that his integrity had never been in question.

A meeting was arranged with CLIC at the Merchants' Hall where Bob, accompanied by Charlie Dobson, came straight to the point. 'Do you have or have you ever had any doubts about my integrity?' he asked. 'If you have no doubts, then why don't you say so in writing? I'm not asking for your trustees' comments or opinions. I am asking you.'

Hugh Pye said he did not and that he would put it in writing. Yet again, Bob was filled with the hope that his name would be cleared and his reputation restored. Finally, the war of words seemed to be over.

The letter duly arrived. Hugh Pye acknowledged that Bob's integrity had never been an issue and confirmed that neither he nor Andrew Larpent had any evidence, nor did they believe, that Bob's personal integrity was or had been an issue. They shared the view that without his outstanding and devoted personal commitment the charity would not have got going, nor would it would enjoy the position and reputation that it held within the voluntary sector.

This letter could have closed the lid on the preceding years of trumped up allegations of impropriety, it could have given Bob and his family the peace of mind they deserved; however, it did none of this because it requested that its contents be kept confidential. Nevertheless, because of his love for CLIC, Bob decided to accept the invitation to CLIC's 25th anniversary, at the Guild Hall, Winchester, after all.

'It was wonderful to meet so many old friends and to be introduced to new staff, supporters and trustees. It was a splendid day, which both Judy and I thoroughly enjoyed.'

46

Building Bridges to Nowhere

Bob wanted nothing more than to get on with what he felt was his life's work but, when a CLIC officer told him that some supporters felt that the problems of 1996 stemmed from the fact that Bob had been too popular and had become the public face of CLIC, it hurt him deeply. Later that evening, Bob stood in contemplation in the graveyard at the headstone of his two sons. How could anyone have construed his service to CLIC as merely an ego trip?

An estrangement had set in and Bob was not invited to further CLIC celebrations. His attempts at reconciliation—he held several meetings with Hugh Pye over this period—seemed promising but friends warned that, should he go back, he would be entering a minefield; nevertheless, Bob jumped at the chance at being involved again with his beloved CLIC. Hugh arranged for Bob's name to go on CLIC's circulation list to receive up-to-date information. There was talk again of a new role for him to play, and of using his name on CLIC's letterhead and printed material as, to all outward appearances, CLIC was without its founder. For Bob, there did not seem to be a 'them' and 'us' any more. But a friend thought differently: 'They crucified you once. If you go back, they will crucify you again.' Sister Frances was wary for him. As it turned out, apart from his name appearing on the annual report, little else happened, and his hopes of a possible new role within CLIC never materialised.

'What happened to Bob has happened to a surprising number of founders,' said Sister Frances. 'I know of a couple of people who set up really fabulous children's hospices and, as soon as they were ready to function—it's been horrendous—the founders were shown the door. It's an extraordinary phenomenon. All through the difficult years, I have tried to emphasise to Bob the importance of recognising that CLIC has changed the lives of countless people. I would just hate Bob to die thinking that all his life's work was spoiled by pettiness and jealousies.'

Although supporters had rallied in their droves, Bob never recovered from the experience of being suspended and 'publicly flogged' and so he continued his pursuit of a public apology from the Charity Commission. He felt it was owed not only to him and his family but, even more, to his supporters who had listened to his pleas and donated so generously to CLIC's cause: to his frustration, there seemed to be no one who wanted to deal properly with the situation.

'There is an arguable case that by the mid 90s CLIC had over-extended itself by trying to help too many people,' said Charlie Dobson, 'both in the UK and overseas. But I feel that this simply reflects Bob's compassion. If this was the case, as in any organisation, the person at the top has to carry the can, but those who orchestrated the campaign to oust him should be ashamed of themselves. They all but destroyed him and he will never get over it'.

Wounded by the events of the preceding years and the lack of redress, and helped and encouraged by David Baum, Bob felt compelled to write an account of what happened in order to clear his name and to right the wrongs that he passionately believed were perpetrated against him. But, while he was collating the facts, he got to the point where he began to doubt whether he was doing the right thing. Was he big enough to rise above these injustices? Was he able to shrug his shoulders and live with the situation the way it was.

'The trouble was—I couldn't live with it. It was a really deep, deep hurt because it was CLIC. CLIC—of all things. The other things, the mosaic, the building trade, whatever, nothing could ever compare with CLIC.'

His document, 'Events leading to the Charity Commission's enquiry in 1996, subsequent issues, and the founder's ongoing quest to secure a closure', was completed in October 2002; however, the stress he felt over its preparation became painfully evident, and the nightmares of 25 years ago returned to haunt him.

'I think Dad was very shocked and disappointed when the trouble in CLIC started and he got down, very down, about it at times, which was unusual for him because he's not that sort of person,' said Rachel. 'He's generally very positive. His faith has helped to keep him going and that's why, when he's down, it seems a bit strange. He felt let down by people. One of his failings is that he tends to be too trusting. The good thing is that it works with most people because most people are decent but at times it's got him into trouble; he's quite naive sometimes.'

Rachel made a telling point. Bob had always been quick to acknowl-edge the value of true friendship but the course of his life was also affected by those whose friendship waned, who absented themselves when needed, who did not stand up to be counted.

To protect CLIC Bob decided not to publish his document but it was distributed in early 2003 via Steve Webb MP to the Charity Commission and to Hugh Pye. Given the facts presented and the names it named, Bob expected the fall-out to be widespread. But if alarm bells rang, they were effectively muffled. If there was fall-out, it never came to light; it was met with an implacable indifference. To all intents and purposes the document's comments went unheeded.

Bob felt achingly sad—in despair but he knew to whom he could turn, and he spent several nights with his brother, who lives near the Devon–Cornwall border. 'Alan lives in the back of beyond,' said Bob. 'It's four miles to buy a morning paper. Whilst I was there, I witnessed a rush of traffic outside his house: ten cows, a farmer with his head stuck out of his van window and two sheep dogs. That was the big event of the day; it is so quiet there.'

'I think Bob comes down here to switch off and re-charge his batteries,' said Alan. 'We took the bikes on the Tarka trail; we cycled 38 miles all told. We were both absolutely shattered when we got back.'

The world stopped just long enough for Bob to get off ... and he did not want to get back on again. He speculated about selling up and moving elsewhere to shut life out but he knew in his heart that running away was not the answer.

Bob eventually received weighty support from the Association for Charities, which had been formed to present the cases of trustees who had been unfairly treated by the Charity Commission. They included him in their report, published in June 2004, entitled *Power Without Accountability. The Charity Commission as Regulator.*

Stephen Lloyd, chairman of the Charity Law Association, explained:

> *Power Without Accountability* catalogues a small but significant number of cases where the Charity Commission has failed in its duty. By and large, the Commission does a good job in dealing with the many cases in which it is involved. But the cases here, whilst they may be the exception, nonetheless have to be taken extremely seriously. They confirm the need for an independent tribunal to which people can appeal against decisions of the Commission in a straightforward, simple and cheap way. I hope the Charities Bill makes sure this happens. The Commission also needs to be obliged to act in accordance with the general principles of fairness and natural justice in accordance with prescribed and open procedures.

On Bob Woodward's case the report states:

> There is not much that needs saying here. Bob Woodward is one of the most outstanding servants of charity this country has seen,

but his life's work and his reputation were damaged by the unjust misbehaviour of the Commission. The story tells its own tale of the Charity Commission's style and performance. In its treatment of one of the most effective of this country's charity supporters, the Commission showed all of the following:

- Inconsistency in their advice over the resignation of suspended trustees
- Incompetence in the muddle of serving the second suspension order whilst taking part in appointing Bob Woodward a life president at CLIC
- Profligacy with the charity's funds towards the Receiver
- Bullying in their use of suspension orders
- Cowardice in their reaction to the threat of criticism on television
- Arrogance in their refusal to admit fault or apologise

In spring 2006 John Weth, chairman of the Association for Charities, challenged the Charity Commission to demonstrate that a new level of understanding had been achieved between former disgruntled trustees and the Charity Commission: he suggested, as a gesture of goodwill, that an informal review of some of the old cases be undertaken. The Charity Commission agreed but restricted the review to just two cases.

When Bob was invited to be considered, he warmed to the opportunity of having his case reappraised and agreed to be included. Then it was discovered that all of the files for his case had been destroyed on 6 June 2002 and there were doubts whether it would be possible to reconstruct a record of the Commission's actions for the purposes of a review. This news came as a surprise as correspondence exists stating that considerable research was still being made into these files in November 2002 and April 2003. Coincidentally, Bob heard that the files on the other case had also been destroyed.

47

'No, never alone, he promised never to leave me, never to leave me alone'

'I can remember when Judy talked about our retirement. She said, "Perhaps the day will come in this house when we will go 24 hours without saying the word cancer." For thirty years, I've been saying the word "cancer". I'm forever-lasting saying the word "cancer" and I've often wondered what it would be like if someone said, "*You've* got cancer." I thought it would be the ultimate—the absolute pits but it's nowhere near the worst it could be. The pits for me would be to hear that Judy or Rachel or James has it. I couldn't handle that.'

At his annual check-up at Southmead Hospital in the autumn of 2003 Bob expected a ticking-off from his nephrologist: he had let things slide a little, put on weight and his blood pressure was higher. His consultant did not seem best pleased: he would be writing to Bob's GP to arrange some tests and Bob would have to revert to six-monthly check-ups.

Bob resolved to do something about his weight before hearing from his doctor and bought an over-the-counter detox regime; within a month, he had lost a stone.

'You've proved that you are more than capable of getting your weight down but what a shame that you go through these peaks and troughs,' the doctor said. 'It would be much better for you if you kept your weight stable.'

Bob agreed, then, as an afterthought, he mentioned a new symptom: when he needed to pee, there was no time to think about it. His doctor referred to a large book. 'I've got a cure for that,' he smiled. 'This is a directory of every public loo in a twenty-mile radius.' Then, more seriously, added, 'Have I ever checked your prostate?'

Unfortunately, there was a problem, as Bob found out a few days later. 'You have a high PSA (prostate-specific antigen) reading,' said the doctor. 'We get a bit anxious if it's over four and, at eight, we get really worried. Yours is showing 22.'

Knowing that an enlarged prostate can sometimes 'gum up the works', Bob was unperturbed. He felt well and full of energy; most days he enjoyed a three- or four-mile walk; he was on the crest of a wave. That there could be something seriously wrong never crossed his mind.

A biopsy procedure left him unimpressed. 'Blimmin' pain in the rear,' he said.

David Gillatt, Southmead Hospital's consultant in prostate disorders, delivered the bad news by telephone the next day: 'You have cancer of the prostate,' he said. Bob felt so well he countered the pronouncement, 'Are you sure?' David Gillatt assured him he was.

The unwelcome news did not sink in until Bob put the phone down and crossed the hall into the sitting room to tell Judy; he knew by the look on her face that memories of Robert and everything he had gone through were sweeping over her.

Bob felt it was a blessing it was he who faced this new crisis; had it been Judy, it would have been too difficult for him to cope. 'We talked about it as best we could,' he said. 'It was a big step into the unknown. We had no idea what it really meant, no idea how life threatening it was. Did I have three months? Six months? Was this to be my last Christmas? Would I be here next year?'

As so many may have hoped in similar circumstances, Judy wondered whether Bob had been given another patient's results by accident. He checked: David Gillatt confirmed the diagnosis.

'I still didn't feel I had cancer. I didn't feel I had it. I didn't feel downcast; I didn't feel it was the end of the world. It was so odd ... but I knew that, in one way or another, I had to find a way to get rid of it. I knew that Judy was desperately worried about me but I tried to make light of it. It wasn't difficult, I didn't feel ill. When I thought back to what Robert went through for three and a half years, trying to stay alive, it would have been an insult to complain about my condition.'

First thing in the morning, Bob says a little prayer to thank the Lord for today and asks for help to make the most of it. He believes that his relationship with God is better now than it has been at any time of his life.

'My thoughts were of Robert telling me not to worry as long as I kept my promise to him that I would always be there for him. But I have a far better promise than Robert ever had from me; I have a promise from my heavenly Father, a promise that will never be broken. What have I got to fear? Absolutely nothing.'

God's promise notwithstanding, there was one aspect that Bob did find difficult: he dreaded telling his children. 'I think it's always awful — giving grim news over the telephone.'

Rachel had been working in Jerusalem when Bob phoned her; he tried to tone it down and, although he baulked at the thought of saying the word 'cancer', he knew he had to. He told her that, as far as he could tell, it did not seem to be life threatening. He played on the consultant's words that, even without treatment, he might be perfectly all right for one year, maybe five. He told her he was sure it could be contained.

'It was very difficult,' said Rachel, 'because he was at a distance. I worried about whether I should go home but if I did what could I do to be of any help. Dad said it was worse for us than it was for him. In a sense, we were all more worried than perhaps he was—although I'm sure he was worried too.'

The news hit Rachel hard but Bob was thankful that she had her husband, Rob, to support her. He was more worried about telling James who lived on his own. At the time, James was away snowboarding in a remote part of Argentina and was unreachable; Bob found that a blessing.

When James came home, Bob told him face to face. Again, he toned it down saying that it was not as bad as it sounded and was probably the type that is most receptive to treatment.

There were so many people to tell and Bob closed the office door to spare Judy hearing the same story over and again. He sent an e-mail to Professor Michael Baum, David's brother, who was taking a month's holiday in France. When Michael phoned, he told Bob it would be his privilege to help; while his field was breast cancer, he was also chairman of the British Medical Association committee which had been set up specifically to look at the treatment of prostate cancer. Bristol was one of the collaborative centres and, if Bob agreed, he would ask David Gillatt for a copy of Bob's medical notes. Michael offered to meet up at any time to discuss any other route that Bob might wish to take.

Bob took Michael up on his offer and they met in London for lunch to discuss the best possible way forward. 'What a bonus that was.' Bob and Michael meet up several times a year now.

Jim Hands, an alternative therapist based in Ottery St Mary, Devon, who had been of enormous help with Bob's nephrotic syndrome, advised against surgery. Bob trusted Jim's judgement and he felt this advice was right for him but he was concerned about telling the consultant that he was not prepared to undergo surgery.

At his next appointment, David Gillatt conveyed more bad news—the cancer had advanced, which might have led to secondary cancer in the bones. Scans followed: future treatment would depend on the results. If no secondary cancer was found, the consultant suggested hormone therapy, which consisted of one tablet a day; after three months there would be daily sessions of radiotherapy, 42 in all, and if necessary a follow-up of more hormone treatment. David Gillatt went on to say that he did not advise surgery. Bob felt relieved; at least that advice was a positive and he hoped that it would not be necessary to have intensive hormone treatment—injected in the stomach—that he had heard was tantamount to castration.

Suffering as he did from claustrophobia, Bob was already feeling anxious about the MRI scanner. It was not a problem; they would use a CT scanner instead.

'It was a slow procedure and took about 25 minutes to do head to toe. This huge machine almost touches the head and when it passes the neck and shoulders, you can turn your head if you want to. I can't think why but, at that moment, a little chorus from a hymn we used to sing in Young People's Fellowship came back to me—just a couple of lines that repeat themselves. "No, never alone, he promised never to leave me, never to leave me alone." When it came into my head, the fear left me and I just lay there with my eyes shut for the whole 25 minutes.'

The scan showed no further trouble but this welcome piece of news was tempered with: 'We must remember, of course, that if there are any microscopic bits, they would not have been picked up, so we cannot be 100 per cent sure.'

Bob and Judy paid another visit to Jim Hands in Ottery St Mary. They discussed every conceivable treatment at some length. 'Jim is convinced that the potent herb wormwood is the answer. Strangely enough, one of the places wormwood grows best is around Chernobyl. What could be the answer to many of those people's problems over there is growing alongside them but they're not aware of it. Jim sees a woman patient that medics gave up on. She's on wormwood—she suffered a double mastectomy and still has quality of life six years later. I take wormwood on and off and, on the advice of a herbalist in Bexhill-on-Sea, other supplements to boost my immune system.'

He followed a strict diet suggested by Jim Hands and the herbalist. 'If you're going to be serious about this, the first thing you have to do is to starve the cancer. Don't feed the cancer on the stuff it thrives on.'

'Mum felt she had a big role to fill in terms of Dad's diet,' said Rachel. 'She's very good about the kind of food she has in the house and keeping him on his diet.'

After taking wormwood for a fortnight, Bob suddenly felt much brighter. 'I felt I'd taken another huge step in the right direction. I went through this feeling of being super-well, which has been maintained.'

The doctors' reactions to his alternative medicine were positive and they admitted that a growing number of people believe that diet plays a significant part in personal well-being.

'I'm not saying for a moment that hormone treatment has not played its part but I don't believe it could have done it on its own. I don't know anyone in my position who has had quite such a dramatic turnaround;

going from a PSA reading of 22 to 1.4 in 30 days,' said Bob. But he cannot understand why, given that his father suffered from prostate problems, blood tests for his kidney condition were never checked for prostate cancer.

Since the diagnosis Bob has taken stock. 'It was divine guidance that I mentioned the urgency to pass water and I am thankful that the cancer was discovered when it was and that surgery is no longer an option.'

But even when life must have seemed unrelenting, Bob never let his family forget how fortunate they have been.

'Dad made us realise that there is so much more to life than money,' said James, 'but I didn't really realise it until I went to work in Texas, and had everything; a really nice apartment, swimming pool, sauna, Jacuzzi, gym and a Porsche to drive around in but I was miserable. All the people I loved were back in England, and I thought it just goes to show, money doesn't make you happy. Dad could have carried on building and been a multi-millionaire but it didn't interest him. He wanted to help people.'

'There was this story that I always liked as a child,' said Rachel. 'Dad's family had no money and he used to tell me that there were only two pairs of underpants between the four boys and the first two who got up in the morning got the underpants. I always thought that that was a good one.'

'I have never heard that one,' said James. 'He tells dreadful jokes that we've heard a hundred times before and they're not always that funny really.'

Part 3

Rebuilding

1996–2006

'Experience is not what happens to a man: it is what a man does with what happens to him.'
Aldous Huxley

48

Moving on

In the 1990s Bob became a patron of the University of Bristol's Campaign for Resource, set up to raise £100 million for a range of charity projects by the year 2000. Because of his contacts he was asked to be a 'Mr Fixer' and to help in a number of other ways. As patron Bob attracted over £10 million for specific schemes. 'I must say I feel quite chuffed about that really.'

The Campaign for Resource was brought to a successful conclusion at the end of 2002 having raised £89 million in philanthropic support. Bob also continued his work with the Institute of Child Health, which during the 1990s became involved with children's hospices and the setting-up of the Champions of Child Health charity with David Baum.

Around this time he became involved in another new charity. In search of a catchy name for it, he came up with the acronym ACT (the Association for Children with life-threatening or Terminal conditions and their families) and a logo of an umbrella with a child sheltering under it. ACT arose from research carried out under the direction of David Baum at the Institute of Child Health. It showed gaps in the provision for children and families so affected and a lack of recognition of what they needed. The research also highlighted the fact that there were at least 20,000 children in this category, four times as many as health officials had estimated. ACT acknowledged that all these children and their families have similar needs and should have access to the same services and quality of care, whatever their illness and wherever they live.

ACT remains very close to Bob's heart. 'It is a resource where anyone with a child suffering from any condition, however rare, can access information and help,' he said. 'It's very similar to BACUP and it works closely with them.'

The charity produced a directory of services, which Bob appositely titled ABC (taking the first letters from ACT, BACUP and CLIC). After several discussions with the Department of Health, the charity won government funding for a survey on the needs of children's hospices.

'ACT is the only UK organisation working to improve care and services for all children in the UK with life-threatening or terminal conditions and their families. It is a vibrant charity, which has done fantastic work,' said Bob proudly.

Without the focus of a single purpose in his professional life, Bob's activities inevitably became more diverse, as his exposure to helping other and different causes took over. In June 1997 Charlie and Mary Dobson offered Bob the role of chief executive of the Spandex Foundation. This offer of faith, given the obstacles that Bob still faced at CLIC, enabled him to continue with what he loved doing most and underpinned a new and successful second career within the charities sector. His work involved widening the scope of the trust, researching and prioritising the many applications for funds before reporting to Charlie and Mary. With Bob's experience, the foundation could offer a new dynamic to fund-raisers on all levels. 'I'm able to offer my services, sit down with the applicants and discuss ways to find additional funds or perhaps to take a completely different approach. I can almost second myself to them if necessary.'

While this was both challenging and absorbing, it required some adjustment: Bob had been just a teenager when he resolved to be his own boss and now, at the age of 63, he found himself an employee again.

'Bob is a figurehead for us because neither Charlie nor I like publicity,' said Mary.

'It's no good having a large sum of money in a charity and not doing anything with it,' said Charlie. 'We trusted him to find good causes; that's what Bob brought to us. It's a perfect marriage really. Ours is the easy option when you think that Bob has been to 300 funerals or more, hugging people, trying to do something ... his is the hard job—ours is easy, we just give the money away.'

In his new role with the Spandex Foundation Bob became involved with the Rhys Daniels Trust between 1997 and 1999. 'I knew Barry Daniels from when he first brought his son Rhys to Bristol in the early 90s for his first bone marrow transplant. Rhys had a rare and incurable neuro-degenerative disorder called "late-infantile Batten's disease."' The Daniels' daughter Charly had earlier been diagnosed with the same disorder and tragically both children died.

'Bob's help was fantastic,' said Barry. 'We had very few contacts in the charity world and it was a blessing to know him. I have a great respect for Bob; I've gained a lot of experience from discussing things with him over the years. He's a lovely man and we spent many hours together just talking.'

'Something that Barry and Carmen always wanted was to set up a Home from Home to benefit children with all kinds of disabilities and conditions,' said Bob. 'I was able to help: I knew of six new terraced houses in Kingsdown Parade in Bristol and the Rhys Daniels Trust bought two of them, next door to each other. A fund-raiser from another local appeal, the Jack and Jill Appeal, worked with me on the project and we wrote to fifty trusts in London; only one replied but it gave us half a million pounds, the figure we were looking for.

'Later on there was an opportunity to do something similar in Liverpool and they wanted me to be involved. I had to say no: I didn't want to start dashing all round the country. I set up the prototype so they could take it from there and that is exactly what they've done. They are going great guns and have set up more homes since then.'

'Bob's association with Bristol was as far as he could stretch himself,' said Barry, 'he wasn't a young man and he had other commitments. That was fine. I understood that. It was always such a welcoming sound to hear Bob's voice and I felt he gave me the strength to carry on. The beauty of Bob is that you always felt really relaxed talking to him and he just guided you comfortably and carefully. It's just a very warm feeling that he gives.'

'Barry and Carmen have two other children now who are absolutely free of the problem,' said Bob. 'Bliss and Hope ... great names, aren't they?'

49

The Starfish Trust

In 1998, when Charlie and Mary Dobson sold Spandex, they had to find a new name for their foundation and Bob and Mary, independently and remarkably, came up with the same suggestion: The Starfish Trust. They first heard the story of the starfish from David Baum, whose love for it prompted him to tell it on every possible occasion. David told the story in Moscow, in New York and just about everywhere else; he was renowned for using it most powerfully to allay concerns about fund-raising and he felt it epitomised the work of charities:

> As an old man walked the beach at dawn, he noticed a young girl picking up starfish and putting them into the sea. He asked her why she was doing this. Her answer was that the stranded starfish would die if left until the morning sun. 'But the beach goes on for miles and there are thousands of starfish,' countered the old man. 'How can your effort make any difference?' The young girl looked at the starfish in her hand and placed it safely into the waves. 'It makes a difference to this one,' she said.

This shortened version of the story appears on the Starfish Trust's stationery. 'I don't know its origin,' said Bob. 'It's so old, I'm not sure that anyone truly knows.'

The Starfish Trust benefits those with illnesses and disabilities living in the Bristol area and sometimes worthy causes can be found just on the doorstep. Bob's next-door neighbour's great-grandson George has cerebral palsy and his mother Claire, in spite of having no experience of fund-raising, took on the gigantic task of raising £140,000 for a high-tech hydrotherapy pool at Claremont School in Bristol. Bob guided Claire and she did really well. Then, when her fund faltered at £90,000, he spoke to Charlie and Mary Dobson, who finished the appeal with a donation of £50,000.

After that, Bob received an SOS from Brainwave, a charity based near Bridgwater that helps brain-injured children, requesting help in raising money for a similar type of pool. He helped at Brainwave's fund-raising meetings and the Starfish Trust topped up their appeal as well with another £50,000.

242

Charlie Dobson was all ears when Bob mentioned that Roger Cook, who lived close by, had written a song for CLIC.

'Roger Cook, the songwriter?' said Charlie. 'Do you know him?'

'Yes, of course I do.'

'I hadn't seen Cookie for 25 years,' said Charlie. 'I thought Bob was kidding, so I called his bluff. We were going over to see some friends who were staying in Thornbury Castle Hotel and I'd heard that to hear Cookie singing his songs on the ukulele was a real treat. So, I said to Bob, how about you and Roger joining us for coffee and, perhaps, he might be persuaded to sing a few songs?'

Bob felt a little anxious about arranging an unscheduled musical performance at such short notice and so he rushed straight round to Roger's house but could not find him in. He tried calling Roger from home: no answer. First thing next morning, he knocked on Roger's front door again. This time, his dishevelled friend, in old working clothes, opened the door: he was in the middle of re-plastering his dining room.

'Roger, I need a whopping favour from you,' said Bob. 'I'd like you to meet a very special friend of mine who has invited us to coffee this morning over at Thornbury Castle.'

'I promised Kitty that I'd finish plastering the dining room wall this morning,' said Roger. 'Are you serious?'

'Very,' said Bob, 'and bring your ukulele.'

When they walked into the lounge at Thornbury Castle, Charlie was confounded. After introductions and coffees all round, Roger sang to the group and delighted them all.

'What are you doing now, Roger?' asked Charlie.

'Over the last few years, I've been working on a new show based on the life of Zelda, the wife of Scott Fitzgerald,' he answered. 'I think it's got a really good chance of making it to the top.'

Roger was looking for an angel, a backer for his show and, opportunely, Charlie was looking for a new project.

'One thing led to another and we got involved with the musical that he'd written,' said Charlie. 'We just fell in love with the music and I persuaded Mary to use some of the family money on a flight of fancy. It turned out to be exactly that but we did have some fun along the way.' The musical, *Beautiful and Damned*, fully financed by the Dobsons, completed a sixteen-week run in the West End.

'Dear Pat Smith in Oldbury-on-Severn gave me a whole new lease of life when she introduced me to Charlie and Mary,' said Bob, 'and then I gave them a new lease of life by reintroducing them to Roger. He too has benefited, breathing new life into Zelda.'

Following the news of Bob's prostate cancer, some told him that he
should cut down on his workload.

'We were shocked about the cancer but there's no way that would
affect us keeping Bob with us,' said Charlie. 'I don't know what's going
to happen if anything happens to him, we'll probably wrap it up and say
to someone, here's a chunk of money. Someone's going to strike lucky
unless he manages to spend it all by then.'

Bob was still concerned. 'I said to Charlie that I would understand if
he and Mary felt they would rather have someone younger and fitter, and
not for one second would it cause any bad feeling between us.'

'But I told Bob, if you left, I don't know what we'd do but if you feel
you have to leave then it's up to you. As far as we are concerned, you
can stay as long as you like,' said Charlie.

It was exactly what Bob was hoping to hear. 'I don't think I will ever
stop until I'm carried out and then I shall have to be nailed down.'

'We're proud to have him.' said Mary.

The Jack and Jill Appeal, set up to raise funds for a new specialist
children's ward at Frenchay Hospital, limped along to the point where
it had raised half a million pounds. It needed to be sparked back into
life. A meeting took place between Bob, Charlie and Mary Dobson, the
appeal chairman, David Giles, the appeal fund-raiser, Diana Pomeroy,
and a neurosurgeon, Brian Cummins; they asked Bob if he would
become campaign director alongside his commitments with the Starfish
Trust. The Dobsons not only left it to Bob to decide but also donated £1
million to the appeal.

'So, I was their campaign director between 1998 and 2000. Although
I enjoyed it, there were aspects I didn't like. When there's something to
be done, I want to get on with it and get it done. I don't like hanging
around, waiting for someone else to make decisions. I can't be bogged
down with bureaucracy,' he said.

Ironically, to make room for this new children's unit, Ward 8 at
Frenchay Hospital (for which Bob fought so hard to keep open almost
10 years earlier) had to be bulldozed along with Ward 10.

'The peculiarity of it was that here was I, raising money to demolish
Ward 8. It was an all-brick building that had been put up for the
American war wounded and was way past its sell-by date but it was still
sad seeing it demolished, albeit for brand new facilities; it had given the
most wonderful care to thousands of children,' said Bob.

Tears were shed during the televised closing down party and local TV
reporter Sally Challoner asked Bob how he was feeling.

'I have mixed emotions,' he said. 'I feel desperately sad and I feel elated at the same time. Although I'm excited about the new unit, as I look around the ward today, every bed conjures up a hundred faces.'

Wards 8 and 10 were replaced by the Barbara Russell Children's Unit, which opened in June 2000. Although the appeal's early target was for £2 million, it closed having achieved almost double that amount. Bob was delighted with all but one aspect: there was a VAT bill to be paid out of the monies raised—nearly half a million pounds.

Sadly, according to press reports in early 2006, the Barbara Russell Children's Unit is to be closed. This follows the North Bristol NHS Trust's decision to downgrade Frenchay to a community hospital. During the £4 million fund-raising campaign the appeal statement said that the unit would 'serve children in the South West and beyond well into the next century.' Unsurprisingly, the local community, having raised so much money, and the Starfish Trust having donated £1 million, are extremely unhappy about this situation.

During the Chunnel Walk in 1994, Bob met Cliff O'Gorman whose father Eddie founded the Paul O'Gorman Foundation, later renamed Foundation for Children with Leukaemia. Eddie's loss was similar to the Woodwards, having experienced a double family tragedy when his son Paul and his daughter Jean succumbed to cancer.

Under the English Channel, Bob and Cliff had had time to discuss how the O'Gorman Trust was going and how it was supporting research in Great Ormond Street. Bob could see advantages should CLIC (Bob was still chairman of CLIC at that time) and the O'Gorman Trust work together at some stage and this brought Cliff and Eddie O'Gorman to Bristol to meet David Baum. 'I think they were absolutely mesmerised by him. They thought David was a wonderful guy, understandably so, and he became their number one medical adviser.'

The O'Gormans were convinced that Paul's illness had been caused by the proximity of an electrical substation in the garden and they wanted to set up a laboratory to research the effects of electro-magnetic fields generated by pylons, radio waves, mobile phones and substations.

Their wishes came to pass when, alongside Charlie and Mary Dobson, the O'Gormans donated a considerable sum for the Paul O'Gorman research centre to be set up within the Institute of Child Health. This centre, situated at the top of St Michael's Hill in Bristol, continues to supply information about this controversial subject, and of late on the effects of the use of mobile phones. The O'Gormans' commitment to the project, coupled with the interest of the Starfish Foundation, was the catalyst that brought their charity, Children with Leukaemia, into Bristol.

Later, Bristol University, in conjunction with North Bristol NHS

Trust, told Bob they needed a new facility for research into placenta and umbilical cord stem cells (an easier, safer alternative source of bone marrow for the treatment of cancers). The projected cost was £2.2 million and they asked Bob if he would organise the fund-raising.

He approached Children with Leukaemia for help with the funding and explained the new project to Eddie O'Gorman who, after visiting Bristol, agreed to support the new facility by underwriting any shortfall from fund-raising for what was to become the Paul O'Gorman Lifeline Centre laboratories. Detailed plans already existed to erect another floor on top of the medical school but, after waiting some months for planning permission, Bob found that the plans had never been submitted; the ensuing and frustrating catalogue of errors did nothing to improve his blood pressure.

No one had sought civil engineering advice to establish whether the structure would be strong enough to support another storey. As it turned out, the only way was to 'float' it over the original building supported on newly constructed pillars. An extra £2 million would have to be found.

Bob was upset and angry. The O'Gormans might feel that they had been misled or that he did not know his subject. With his reputation at stake, he confronted representatives of the North Bristol NHS Trust and told them how unimpressed he was. The trust had no option but to come up with an alternative and proposed three different sites for the new unit. One, an ideal choice, occupied a prominent position on the main road to Southmead Hospital—and Bob wanted it. He waited impatiently for several weeks for a decision: several weeks were wasted. This site had already been promised to another department.

'Why did you offer it to us then?' he asked.

Displeased at having lost his preferred option, Bob looked at site number 3. While it was not as good, it was acceptable. He waited two weeks before hearing that the authorities had overlooked a longer-term plan to house occupants of some Portakabins on the site, into a permanent building.

'Why did you offer it?' Bob flatly refused to look at the fourth site until they confirmed its availability. They double-checked. 'That site is to be used for car parking. Sorry.'

A fifth site offered: a fifth site considered; not suitable; more valuable time wasted. Site 6 also turned out to be unsuitable. Bob became concerned for his relationship with Eddie; he did not want him to lose faith in future university-backed projects and Bob felt it necessary to remind Bristol University of the extent of the O'Gormans' generosity.

Another site—the seventh—suddenly materialised and the site meeting agreed its suitability; but it transpired that under the path beneath their feet a concrete tunnel housed every public utility imaginable. A suggestion was made that these services might be re-routed.

'Hang on a minute, won't you have to shut the hospital down to do that?' asked Bob.

'You're right. We would have to shut the hospital down ... so we can't re-route.'

Eventually the architects came up with a design to straddle the service tunnel with access deep enough to crawl through. This further delay had several knock-on effects.

John Nickolls, CLIC's former trading manager, was forced to wait nearly two years before he could start work fronting the Lifeline Appeal. While John was not idle during this time, he was unhappy because he was unable to carry out what he had been employed to do.

'It was very frustrating for everyone because when momentum disappears, enthusiasm dampens. There was a team of eager volunteers and, one by one, they all left because there was nothing for them to do,' said Bob.

Finally, the new building was completed. It was magnificent, fully equipped to accommodate over a dozen staff, and was the envy of other research teams in the district. A year passed before Bob discovered that the team was to be disbanded and that the building was to be occupied by another team from the university doing unrelated work. This infuriated him. The project had been a long hard slog from the outset; it had been fraught with problems but he had forced himself to stay the course when he could so easily have walked away from it. He was greatly disturbed that the facility for research into placenta and umbilical cord stem cells was never fully utilised for its intended purpose and he considered it a great loss for the public who donated so generously for this specific project.

'The North Bristol NHS Trust sold it to the university for more than £4 million. At least they returned the charitable funds to the charity to reuse for the benefit of young leukaemia sufferers. Nevertheless, the funds were given in good faith for a specific use, and for the North Bristol NHS Trust almost immediately to sell the building for a handsome profit is outrageous.'

The relationship with the O'Gormans flourished: Bob introduced them to the vice-chancellor, who in turn invited them to patron dinners for the Campaign for Resource. After discussing plans for the new Bristol Children's Hospital, the O'Gormans gave £2 million and in 2000 the new hospital opened in the Paul O'Gorman Building. Several years later, at another patron dinner attended by Bob, Eddie O'Gorman and Michael Baum, Eddie jokingly said to Michael, 'You realise, don't you, that it was Bob who got us to come to Bristol … and so far it has cost us £6 million.'

50

'How often do you get a great big hug from a former world leader?'

Following the nuclear disaster at Chernobyl in April 1986 Raisa Gorbachev worked hard on behalf of the children who were contaminated during the accident and who subsequently developed leukaemia. She acted as a patron to Moscow Central Children's Hospital and became interested in modern techniques of treating childhood leukaemia in Russia.

It was in the summer of 1999 when Russia and the rest of the world heard how Raisa too was suffering with the same disease and was being treated by a world-renowned oncologist at Münster University Hospital in Germany. It seemed ironic that the couple who had been so widely despised in their home country suddenly received a flood of support; many letters and donations for the Gorbachev Foundation came from embittered elderly Russian citizens who had long resented Mikhail Gorbachev for the part he played in the disintegration of the Soviet Union.

When Bob heard how ill Raisa was, he tried, unsuccessfully, to send a message of support to the Gorbachevs but communication with Moscow and to the Gorbachev Foundation were always difficult. He discussed the problem with David Baum: the only way to show the Gorbachevs that they cared was to go to Münster and tell them so. Although David laughed at the presumptuousness, he knew Bob was serious.

Raisa's condition worsened: there was no time to waste and Bob headed straight for the city centre florists, The Christmas Rose, to buy a basket arrangement of flowers before going home to tell Judy of his plans.

'I'm just going to shoot away for the weekend to see Mr Gorbachev,' he said.

'Is it all arranged?' asked Judy.

'Yes, I'm going to fly to Frankfurt and then on to Münster. I've got the name of a hotel to stay in overnight.'

'Does Mr Gorbachev know you're coming?'

'No.'

'How do you know you'll get to see him?'

'I expect it'll work out.'

'Well it's up to you … if you've made up your mind,' said Judy.

During the flight the attendant commented on the beautiful flowers and asked, light-heartedly, whether she could have them. Bob astonished her by replying that they were for Mrs Gorbachev; her look of total disbelief told all.

He took a taxi from Münster airport to his hotel where the solidly built, female driver also expressed an interest in the floral arrangement. They were for Mrs Gorbachev, he reiterated.

'Are you going to see her?' she asked.

'No,' he told her, 'Mrs Gorbachev is in an isolation ward but I hope to see Mr Gorbachev.'

'Do you know Mr Gorbachev?' she asked.

Bob told her that they had met.

'What time is he expecting you?' she asked.

'He doesn't know I'm here,' said Bob.

It must have been the best joke she had ever heard and she laughed so heartily that Bob worried she might crash the car. When at last her laughter subsided, she told Bob that she could not grasp why he had come all the way from England to see a man who was not expecting him.

'What if you don't get to see him?' she asked.

'I shall see him,' said Bob.

At the hotel he asked if they knew the address of the clinic where Mrs Gorbachev was being treated; they did and he took a taxi straight there. He was unprepared for the barrage of people waiting outside the hospital but the arrangement of flowers turned out to be his passport through the crowd: security thought he was visiting someone else. At reception he advised them that the flowers were for Mrs Gorbachev and that he would like to see her husband: a request immediately denied. He produced a copy of *CLIC News* from his briefcase: the edition featured the Gorbachevs' visit to Bristol and showed a photograph of Bob and Mikhail in a bear-hug embrace. It was obvious they knew each other and so the receptionist rang Raisa's consultant.

Although he was more helpful the consultant told Bob that because of the risk of infection flowers were not allowed into the isolation unit; he went on to say that it was Mr Gorbachev's routine to arrive at around seven in the mornings and to leave between seven and nine at night. Feeling that it could be beneficial to build a rapport, Bob talked to the consultant about the medical work in Bristol. Then he mentioned that, as he was in Münster for only one night, it would be a lovely surprise for Mr Gorbachev to see him. The obliging consultant gave him the name of the hotel where Mikhail Gorbachev was staying and, it being mid-afternoon already, Bob left immediately.

The receptionist was decidedly frosty; however, Bob hung around until the staff changed shifts at 4.30 p.m. when he tried again. The second receptionist was more helpful; she accepted the flowers and promised to send them to Mr Gorbachev's room; she also paged Mr Gorbachev's interpreter but he could offer no further information. Displaying his well-practised unstoppable attitude, after spotting a good vantage point with an unrestricted view of both the reception and hotel entrance, Bob simply sat there for several hours waiting for the former president's return.

At quarter past nine, the doors flew open and Mr Gorbachev, accompanied by his bodyguard, marched in straight past the visitor from Bristol. Bob rushed after him, calling out, 'Mr Gorbachev, Mr Gorbachev.' Although he must have heard, Gorbachev continued on his way. Bob tried again; this time he called, 'Mikhail, Mikhail'. Gorbachev turned and looked back.

'I saw him as I had never seen him before,' said Bob. 'He looked drained and exhausted; normally he was so beautifully presented, always immaculate, and here he was with an open collar. When he saw me, he seemed to do a double take and then he beamed, his eyes widened and brightened and he came over and hugged me. I didn't think he was ever going to let go. I tried to explain how much we wanted him to know that we cared. We weren't there long together because he had to go … but it was a magic few minutes. It was worth the wait—the hustle and bustle, the bother of going over there. How often do you get a great big hug from a former world leader?'

Early next morning, when Bob took a short walk, he came across a beautiful church. He slipped inside and prayed for both Mikhail and Raisa.

Not long afterwards, on 20 September 1999, Raisa Gorbachev succumbed to her illness.

Mikhail Gorbachev struggled on through his grief to continue his work with the Gorbachev Foundation, which has always considered humanitarian and charitable projects but its main emphasis has been on childhood health protection. Overall it has channelled over $10 million to various programmes in Russia, particularly in the area of childhood leukaemia where, today, the survival rate among children is 70 per cent, compared to 10 per cent just a decade ago.

In sharp contrast to the respect shown to Gorbachev in the West, on his final visit to the Gorbachev Foundation, Bob observed a very different attitude in Russia. Mikhail told him that in the beginning he occupied the whole of the building (which was about twice the size of a grand sea-front hotel), then only one floor, then just three rooms. Then, they took his chauffeur away; then they took his car away and then they took his mobile phone away.

'They gradually degraded him; they did a real hatchet job on him,' said Bob.

Mikhail Gorbachev suffered the indignities of media coverage inferring that he had wealth and properties worldwide and suggesting that he lived off his Foundation. To answer the doubters, Gorbachev was compelled to state that all income from the Foundation and from his Nobel Peace Prize had been used for charitable purposes: none was ever used for his own or his family's benefit or comfort.

51

Below Us, the Sea of Galilee

To mark Bob's twenty-five years of fund-raising, Bristol University held a dinner, hosted by Sir John Kingman, at the splendid eighteenth-century Royal Fort House. Located next to the vice-chancellor's residence behind the Great Hall, the Royal Fort House is at the heart of the university.

After the dinner David Baum delivered the tribute; it was to be the last time that Bob would see David captivate an audience.

'He was, as ever, over generous in his comments,' Bob said.

That evening, David made it known that the Royal College of Paediatrics and Child Health intended to run a sponsored cycle ride in September for the devastated families of Bosnia and Kosovo and he joked about trying to find time to train for it. The ride was to start at Buckingham Palace and to finish at Sandringham in Norfolk where the participants were to be greeted by Princess Anne. Bob knew how unpractised David was at riding a bicycle and to undertake a 100-mile trip over two days seemed very ambitious.

David attempted to rally support for the sponsored cycle ride among members of the Royal College but the response was disappointing: only around 50 entrants from several thousand members. David's sense of responsibility determined that he should get on his bike and lead from the front but Bob remained concerned; he felt that David was completely unprepared for such a gruelling physical test of endurance. Before he left for the ride, David told his PA, Lorraine Cantle, that he was extremely worried about it and wished he did not have to do it

'If you feel like that, you shouldn't do it,' Lorraine told him.

'I can't let them down,' David replied.

The cycle ride went ahead on 5 September 1999, one of the hottest days of that summer. On the same day, Bob completed a ten-mile sponsored walk in the relentless heat; later, when he was running a relaxing bath, the telephone rang—a voice he had not heard for some time stopped him in his tracks. It was Martin Mott.

'Bob, have you heard the news of David Baum?'

'I don't follow you.'

Martin broke the tragic news: David had suffered a heart attack while riding his bicycle and had died at the side of the road. He was 59.

Please God, thought Bob, I am not hearing this; it just cannot be right. 'Are you absolutely sure?'

'Yes, the medics rang me.'

Bob went into the garden where Judy was working. 'I have the most dreadful news. David Baum is dead; he died at the side of the road.'

'It was Bob who phoned me,' said Sister Frances. 'He said, "The most terrible thing's happened. David is dead." It was just appalling, neither of us could take it in, it was awful.'

Professor David Baum's Child Health projects had taken him all over the world. His greatest compliment came from the Arab community when they approached him to set up a programme of child health in Gaza; though thrilled to accept, he felt the need to remind them that he was an Orthodox Jew. The response was that they knew David's calibre and he was the man they wanted.

'David used to describe himself as an unorthodox Orthodox Jew,' said Sister Frances.

Dispensation was obtained to take David's body to Israel and his funeral was arranged for the following Wednesday at Rosh Pina, north of the Sea of Galilee, where he had enjoyed many holidays with his wife Angela.

'The peace and tranquillity they found there led them to believe that it would be a favoured place to retire,' said Bob. 'Although David hailed from Birmingham he considered Israel his spiritual home and often said how much he would like to take me there. On the last occasion we were together he told me that, in one way or another, he would get me there: he had his son's wedding in mind. Within just a few weeks, I did go to Israel — but sadly for David's funeral.'

It was Rosh Hashana, the Jewish New Year; flights were scarce and Bob's attempts to buy tickets to Tel Aviv were unsuccessful. Both Sister Frances and Lorraine Cantle expressed a wish to be there but it looked as though their hopes would be dashed. Bob rang Charlie Dobson to tell him of David's death, of his wish to attend the funeral and of his difficulty in finding flights. When he looked in later at the Starfish offices to collect his mail, the Dobsons had already set wheels into motion: their travel agent could offer two first class tickets and one economy. The Dobsons personally covered the full cost of the tickets; they felt it an honour to have been instrumental in helping three of David's closest friends to attend his funeral. Coincidentally the travel agent knew Bob; his family lived in Frenchay and was one of Bob's regular ports of call as Father Christmas.

John Miles, the show business manager, also wanted to help and so arranged for his brother Tony Miles (Smiley Miley from the *Radio One Road Show*) to drive Bob and Lorraine to Heathrow where they met up with Sister Frances. After boarding the aircraft, Bob felt uncomfortable that he and Frances were enjoying first class luxury while Lorraine was travelling alone in economy. He approached the steward and asked whether the third member of their party could join them; soon after, all three were reunited. It was late evening when they arrived in Tel Aviv but there was little time to rest. They had an early morning flight to Rosh Pina and so it seemed prudent to request a 4 a.m. wake-up call.

The next morning they touched down in time for breakfast, which they enjoyed at a restaurant on the outskirts of the village, before fortuitously bumping into David's brothers who showed some surprise at seeing them in Rosh Pina. They immediately took them to where David's wife was staying with a family friend; when Angela opened the door, her expression told them that they were the last people in the world she expected to see.

'Angela was overwhelmed to see us,' said Bob. 'She had been through the most difficult period imaginable: trying to come to terms with the last few days, finding flights, getting special permission to delay the burial. When I last spoke to her and expressed our wishes to be there with them in Rosh Pina, she felt sure that as she'd had so much difficulty in finding flights, we just wouldn't be able to get there.'

Angela invited Bob, Frances and Lorraine to join them in the cortège. Everyone left the house together to follow David, who lay resting, wrapped in a traditional, simple white burial sheet, on the back of a truck, which made its way slowly through the village. The setting, the solemnity and the moment created a spiritual ambience that seemed to affect everyone and the procession swelled as others, some in their working clothes, joined them.

'There were about thirty of us when we started,' said Bob, 'but there must have been a hundred or so by the time we got to the end of the road. I was thrilled to bits—privileged—to be part of it although Frances was worried that we might be intruding, but nothing could have been further from the truth. It felt unreal. To me, it was as if I had taken someone else's place in the Jewish fraternity. Everything about this funeral was different from any I had been to before.'

The cortège slowly made its way up a stony hill to where David was to be buried.

'Just this crowd of us walking, walking, walking ...' said Sister Frances. 'It was all very stony and rocky on the hillside and below us was the Sea of Galilee. It was amazing. Jews aren't put in coffins; David was just in white linen. As Gentiles, Bob and I stood back a bit; I had never been to a Jewish funeral before.'

When they reached the cemetery on the side of the hill, David's four sons carried their father up a winding path until they reached his final resting place where they lowered him into the ground. Amidst the ritual wailing and renting of clothes, the boys dropped into the grave to fill it in with the sand surrounding the site.

'It was very moving,' said Bob. 'Those boys had seen their father only days before; they had thought he was going to live forever but now they were filling in his grave. It was so beautiful, so basic, yet so lovely, so natural and so simple.'

'I just remember the grief … and the four boys when they shovelled earth in, which the men do at a Jewish funeral,' said Sister Frances. 'I remember the four boys standing together, their arms around each other, tugging each other and rocking. Then Angela, who is tiny, said to them, "Can I come in too?" Then there were five of them, arms around each other, in a little circle by the graveside.'

Some mourners felt the need to speak. Bob was certainly tempted to say something about David and he wondered if Frances felt the same but being unfamiliar with the procedure of an Orthodox Jewish burial and mindful of causing offence by speaking out of turn, he resisted the impulse.

'We were saying farewell to a brilliant scholar, a man who had met the great and the mighty and had been respected by each and every one of them. It really was a wonderful experience—like being part of a biblical scene. That's the only way I can describe it. I was thrilled because it was so different and it needed to be different for someone like David.'

'Eventually, we all walked back to the house,' said Sister Frances. 'The family sat on the floor on cushions and everybody waited on them with food and drink. I just remember lots of crying and food … it went on all day. It was a huge privilege actually being there and being there with Bob as well because the three of us did get on so well. It was an experience that we will never forget and neither of us will ever get over David's death. There will never again be a David Baum.'

The following March the Chief Rabbi, Dr Jonathan Sacks, officiated at a memorial service for David in the Great Hall at Bristol University. There were no hymns and the readings were given in Hebrew before being translated into English.

'The Chief Rabbi had met David several times and had developed a tremendous regard for him. He spoke so beautifully about him; his voice was so compelling, so gracious and gentle,' said Bob.

Bob felt honoured to be numbered among those invited to speak. Although he almost always spoke in public unscripted, he felt this occasion warranted something different. He closed his address by conveying a message from Mr Gorbachev and his Foundation sending their love and sympathy to David's family.

A video collection of David—put together by his sons—brought the service to a fitting end. The first clip showed him in the Great Hall, resplendent in cap and gown, giving the oration at Mikhail Gorbachev's honorary degree ceremony. The images changed and the next clip showed him performing for the camera as Harpo Marx; he had always thought it great fun to be a look-alike and photographs of Harpo adorned his office. The film ended with David leading the dance, full of vitality. Seeing him moved many to tears.

'David was one of life's great enrichers,' said Bob.

At a ceremony at the Mansion House in Bristol in 2004, when Bob was honoured with the Lord Mayor's Medal for service to the community, he spoke of his friend again. He told his guests how, five years on, he misses David every day.

52

From John O'Groats to Land's End

Bob forged many lasting friendships with fellow founders, who, motivated by personal tragedy, established and ran their own charities. One such friend, Steve Dayman, lost his young son Spencer to meningitis at just fourteen months old.

Steve soon began to raise funds for meningitis and he became a founder member of the Stroud Meningitis Support Group in 1984. He then became founder and chairman of the Meningitis Trust in October 1986. The large number of friends he made from all over the country from when he ran a transport café at Alveston on the A38 readily supported his new charity. He went on to found the Meningitis Research Foundation in 1989; Steve and his wife Gloria have raised gigantic sums to investigate this appalling disease.

Like Bob, Steve too ran into problems with his foundation.

'When I left the Meningitis Research Foundation it was a difficult time for me,' said Steve. 'I remember Bob being very positive; we all get down at times and he's a real tonic; if I'm down in the dumps, he's the first person I ring and he soon puts me right.

'When I was a schoolboy in Wotton-under-Edge, I can remember the Woodward brothers building Parklands; they were quite prominent in those days. I remember when Bob set up CLIC, so when I set off wearing my meningitis hat 23 years ago, Bob was one of the first people I spoke to. Bob is my mentor. Over the years, we've become dear friends. He's such a lovely man and he's achieved so much.'

'Steve's been a very special friend and someone whom I have watched successfully found a charity from nothing and made it work,' said Bob. 'But then, later on, some of the things that happened to him were not dissimilar to what happened to me at CLIC. Steve went through the mill and decided to step out of the charity altogether. I could see what it was doing to him and there was no doubt at all that he was heading for a mega breakdown.'

Steve often talked with Bob about the work of the charity he was leaving. He had organised numerous epic fund-raising walks, many from Land's End to John o'Groats, and he felt a compulsion to walk one last time in memory of his son. He aimed to raise £100,000 in his final walk from John o'Groats to Land's End.

Bob joined Steve and his supporters in Cornwall for the last 22 miles.

'I learned an awful lot about meningitis that day. I heard the most horrifying things that I hadn't appreciated like developing septicaemia and the loss of limbs. Some of the cases were horrific.'

At Land's End, Steve's elation at finishing his swansong walk was tempered with doubt. 'I was thinking to myself, well, perhaps I've been a bit hasty. What am I going to do when I've finished this? Meningitis has been my life for the last 17 years.'

Although it had been hoped to raise £100,000, there was the likelihood of a deficit, and so Bob arranged a special surprise for Steve and Gloria, his wife.

During the speeches at the Land's End signpost, Bob presented them with a Starfish cheque for £25,000. They were overwhelmed.

'It was lovely to be able to do that, thanks to Charlie and Mary,' said Bob.

The money raised from Steve's last walk was to be used to build a laboratory for research into meningitis. It transpired, however, that neither of the meningitis charities could accept it for that specific purpose. While both could accept money for research work, salaries, equipment etc., the money could not be used to fund a building in which all these things could take place. Bob made a suggestion—why not set up a charity that develops laboratories?

They approached Bristol University who confirmed a desperate need for a suite of laboratories for meningitis research; to meet that need, the Spencer Dayman laboratories, dedicated to meningitis research, were set up.

'Steve's charity, Meningitis UK, is going like a forest fire,' said Bob, 'and it's rescued the guy—it's his life. Steve Dayman's walks have so far raised £1.3 million. He must have walked over 8,000 miles—it's mind-boggling.'

The Starfish Trust receives wide-ranging applications for funding. It may be that a newly disabled young person is finding it difficult living in a normal house, and it is Bob's job to meet the family to see how Starfish can help. Sometimes, he finds that good neighbours have already stepped in to raise funds for equipment to help the family overcome these difficulties. They may have a target of £10,000 and Bob thinks it is great to be able to tell them that when they have raised £5,000, Starfish will match it and give them the other £5,000.

'It's the old John James attitude,' said Bob of one of his heroes. 'John James was such a visionary and the biggest and best benefactor of Bristol ever. He came up with the fantastic idea of match funding: let's help people but let's not make it too easy. It is far better to give two people £5,000 each and help two causes than to give one person £10,000.'

Although Bob never met him, he remembers hearing a story about what happened when John James opened a new building at Frenchay Hospital. The press were there with their cameras trained on the centre of a smart new ribbon, which had been stretched tight across the front of the building. John took them by surprise when he walked to the corner of the building to cut the ribbon right at its end. 'There,' he said, 'now you will be able to use that ribbon again.'

'I think that's a lovely touch. One of my great disappointments is that I never actually met him ... I would have loved that,' said Bob.

One of the greatest compliments ever paid to Bob was his coming second to John James in a readers' poll promoted by the *Bristol Evening Post* to find the Bristolian of the century. 'John James won it by a mile.'

53

Would it Work?

In 2001 Bristol University asked Bob to become a vice-president of the David Baum Memorial Fund Appeal; other vice-presidents included eminent paediatricians from as far away as Japan, Tasmania and the United States. The aim was to raise £1.25 million of which almost half would be used to endow a university chair in David's memory. The balance would fund programmes in Kosovo and Israel, the latter involving Palestinian children.

In the autumn of 2002 Bob sponsored himself to visit the United States to raise funds for the appeal and at the same time to catch up with some of David's friends. In New York he met Dr Evgenia Lipkina, the Russian doctor whom he and David first met in Moscow, before going on to Boston to see Professor Jane Shaler, who was involved with paediatrics in Israel. From Boston he travelled to Newhaven to meet Professor Howard Pearson, medical professor of Paul Newman's Hole in the Wall Gang Camp. Howard was the most important as Bob wished to submit an application to the Newman Foundation to raise money for the appeal.

'There is no one I admire more than Paul Newman for his generosity to charity. I think he's given in the region of $175 million from Newman's Own foods; I don't know anyone who has given more,' said Bob. 'Howard was very helpful and it was well worthwhile as, later on, we received a cheque for $50,000 from the Newman Foundation. The trip also provided me with another wonderful opportunity to go back to the Hole in the Wall Gang Camp.'

When Bob arrived at the camp, he noticed something familiar about one of the camp leaders who smiled a million-dollar smile at him.

'You're Bob Woodward, aren't you?' said Bryony Daly, who, some years earlier, had presented Bob with his *Hearts of Gold* award.

Bryony travelled to America every summer to work as a camp leader in the Hole in the Wall Gang Camp. What made the coincidence even more special was that Bryony's parents were visiting that same day and Bob and the Daly family enjoyed an impromptu reunion.

Bob has great admiration for Pat Davis, the fund-raising manager for St Peter's Hospice in Bristol, whom he meets once or twice a year. During one of their meetings he told her that he would dearly love to see a children's hospice in Bristol. Pat agreed with him and, even though she was considering retiring, suggested they join forces to create it together. Although it was an excellent idea Bob had concerns over who would run it, as he had no desire to set up a new charity given his feelings for the Charity Commission.

A solution to this dilemma emerged when Bob and Judy attended a tree planting ceremony in memory of David Baum at Little Bridge House, the children's hospice in Barnstaple. David's family travelled down from London for the occasion and Bob and David's wife, Angela, relived memories of when he and David, as founder patrons, spent so much time there.

During the day the co-founder Jill Farwell told Bob that she and her husband Eddie would like to set up a children's hospice in Bristol. It was exactly what Bob needed to hear.

'Little Bridge House already had a board of trustees and they certainly had the track record; it was perfect,' he said.

They asked Bob to consider becoming the Babe Appeal honorary campaign adviser; he accepted, suggesting that those involved, including a firm of fund-raising consultants from Henley-on-Thames, could meet to discuss their business at a halfway house: his home.

Bob ventured a breakdown on the colossal £10 million appeal: £1 million for the purchase of the site, £3 million capital costs for the hospice, and a £6 million buffer to run it for the first three years. The trust already had £1 million for the site and its next task was to find £3 million for the capital costs. Bob suggested approaching three leading foundations in Bristol renowned for giving to Bristol projects: the Starfish Trust, the John James Foundation and the Harry Crook Foundation. All three foundations support projects where sick children are involved, though not exclusively so. Potentially, the three benefactors could be jointly responsible for the capital cost of the children's hospice.

'Would it work?'

'I have no idea,' Bob said. 'It might work with one of them; it could work with all of them. When a site for the hospice is found, I will approach all three.'

In the spring of 2003 the trustees found Charlton Farm, an idyllic site of 100 acres in Failand, part of the Wraxall estate. Bob's first approach was to Charlie and Mary Dobson; they paid a visit to Little Bridge House and, after admiring the excellent work there, pledged £1 million with an extra £150,000 for a Starfish pool.

Surprisingly, in spite of so many years in fund-raising, Bob had no previous dealings with the John James Foundation and he called John Nickolls for help.

'John was a great friend to me in CLIC,' said Bob. 'He almost single-handedly set up CLIC's trading arm, which brought in £1 million a year; I thought he was magic and his staff really adored him. John had already spoken to the John James Foundation on another matter, had got on fantastically well with them and was able to tell me the name of their administrator.'

With Charlie Dobson's birthday approaching, Bob thought a book on the life of John James, written by former Bristol Grammar School headmaster, John Avery, would make the perfect gift. 'I asked John Nickolls if he could get the book inscribed by James's daughter. He did and the inscription read, "From one benefactor to another."'

'I got another copy inscribed for Bob's birthday present,' said John. 'It came as a nice surprise,' said Bob.

The Harry Crook Foundation was Bob's next target for another £1 million. Harry Crook, the founder of KleenEze in Kingswood, left millions in trust for charitable uses in and around Bristol and, luckily, Bob had a contact: Richard West, a trustee of the foundation, had once gone out with his sister, Diane. Bob visited Richard in Plymouth to tell him about the plans for the new children's hospice, which he followed up in writing for their consideration. Bob's idea of approaching these three amazing benefactors was looking enormously promising. The Starfish Trust had already come on board—one down, two to go.

54

CLIC Sargent

On 2 November 2004 Hugh Pye called at Bob's home with some disquieting news.

'He told me that CLIC and the Sargent Cancer Trust were to merge and CLIC's name would disappear forever. The proposed name for the newly merged charity, 'Cancer Care for Children', would become a legal entity on 1 January 2005. Hugh was confident that CLIC supporters would soon recover from any initial sadness at the loss of the name,' said Bob.

Hugh Pye's visit left Bob in a state of despair.

In the days that followed, countless CLIC supporters rang Bob to express feelings of sadness at the loss of the charity's name; without exception, he was encouraged to take comfort from the living memorial that CLIC had become. For all time, CLIC would live on in the hearts of families who had benefited from its people and services. In reply to the question 'What is CLIC?' one mum had answered, 'It's the difference between coping and collapsing.'

Even though Bob was desperately upset at the loss of CLIC's identity, he made several statements to the press reiterating his support for any new initiative that provided further improvements in treatment and care for young cancer patients; however, many supporters and branch members determined to take action. Among them was Pat Dain, president of the Weston branch. 'I was furious and I wrote to Hugh Pye and told him so. If CLIC's name goes, I go.'

Several weeks of turmoil ensued, which resulted in an eventual U-turn. The CLIC name would remain after all and the newly merged charity would be called CLIC Sargent. Even then, Bob only learned about it from the local press.

There is no doubting the new regime's success: CLIC Sargent is now the leading children's cancer charity in the UK and is able 'to deliver more, for more children with cancer and their families.' Nevertheless, long-standing supporters of CLIC, whilst applauding the successes, lament the lack of warm personal engagement.

'Bob once said at a liaison meeting that we paid the highest price to belong to the CLIC family and we will always be part of it,' said Ruth Cummins. 'Come the end, I didn't feel part of any family.'

'If someone told Bob that there was something wrong with their child and they needed something in Scotland to help them, he'd be in the car and gone,' said John Woodward.

Gill Nickolls said, 'Bob had a tremendous rapport with parents, he would spend hours talking to them and talking is what they wanted.'

'He was an inspiration to us all,' said Liz Freeman, a long-standing branch member from Weston-super-Mare. 'To be honest, even now, I do it as much for Bob as for the children.'

'He's just a 100 per cent genuine person,' said Mary Dobson. 'When we are out and about and someone mentions a birthday or someone's not very well, with other people it would just go over their heads ... but next day there are flowers and a card. He is such a thoughtful person.'

'He must spend a bloody fortune on flowers,' laughed Charlie.

55

Budapest Revisited

On 10 September 2005, ten years after the mighty hullabaloo over the Hungarian Home from Home accommodation, Bob revisited Budapest in preparation for the handing over of the title deeds for the CLIC flats to Professor Deszo Schuler.

'It was a special joy for me to visit that wonderful city again and to renew my precious friendship with Dezso,' said Bob.

The Budapest children's unit had changed dramatically since Bob's last visit in 1994, when it had taken fourteen hectic days and four visits to Hungary to set up the desperately needed Home from Home. The immediate area around the clinic had been pedestrianised and, inside the hospital, artists had painted the walls floor to ceiling with vivid green trees and colourful, round-faced nursery rhyme characters; there was more evidence of their talent in the indoor play area where small children, unaware of the seriousness of their conditions, played happily. The long, white-tiled corridors displayed an occasional green plant and in the windows hung voile curtains patterned with golden teddy bears. The clinic was a world away from yesterday.

'It was difficult to recognise the unit, which I had last seen over ten years before,' said Bob. 'As I was escorted around the beautifully renovated facilities, my mind conjured up the faces of children and their parents waiting anxiously in the treatment areas. I wondered how they'd coped in the intervening years. I hope so much that the CLIC Home from Home accommodation helped.

'I saw the splendidly redecorated and equipped lecture theatre where I'd given a talk to a packed audience of mums and dads and where one of the dads presented me with a wonderful bronze sculpture he'd made of a young couple with their two children clinging to them, their mum clearly pregnant with their third child. The bronze was entitled "Expectation" with its promise of new life. It has taken pride of place above my desk at home ever since.'

The six CLIC flats, all with open balconies overlooking the street, are situated right next door to the hospital and are an equal delight to behold. They offer comfortable accommodation to families of sick children, some of whom live up to 155 miles from Budapest and who, most likely, would not be close to their children without them. Through the back door on the ground floor, landscapers have created a beautiful green space with a sandpit and climbing frame where the children play in safe surroundings. Bob was elated.

'Professor Schuler deserves the highest accolade for the magnificent job he has done with the upgrading of the unit and with the running of the CLIC flats, which he and I worked so hard to obtain for the benefit of families with children suffering from cancer,' said Bob. 'It was a very moving experience to tour the children's unit and to meet the young patients and their families. It was equally moving to tour the CLIC flats and to meet one family staying there and to hear of the "lifeline" that the excellent accommodation has provided for them and for so many families over the years.'

Professor Schuler told Bob that the flats were almost always full and have provided accommodation, respite and a safe haven to an average of 300 families each year. Bob met Professor Schuler's successor, Professor Gyorgy Fekete, along with Schuler's nephew, a doctor in the paediatric oncology unit, and Nellie, the housekeeper for the CLIC flats.

'I could feel the happy team spirit, which augurs well for the wellbeing of the families who rely so heavily on the expertise and dedication of the medical team,' said Bob.

Professor Gyorgy Fekete presented Bob with a splendid medal for bringing CLIC Home from Home accommodation to Budapest. 'Bob did fantastic work for that,' smiled Professor Schuler.

'I felt very honoured and I shall treasure the medal as a memento of the bond between us,' said Bob. 'And now, with Budapest being so easily accessible from Bristol, I hope to keep in more regular contact.'

In December 2005 Bob travelled to Budapest again to represent CLIC Sargent to give the Home from Home accommodation to Professor Schuler's foundation, which had been responsible for the successful running of the CLIC flats to date.

'It would be difficult to imagine how one could find safer and more caring hands in which to entrust the properties,' said Bob.

56

Epilogue

In 2004 Rachel gave birth to Laura, Bob and Judy's first grandchild.

'I suppose the greatest happiness that Bob has experienced since the CLIC crisis is the birth of his granddaughter and to have seen Bob holding this tiny, tiny baby, to me was just wonderful,' said Sister Frances.

Now in his seventies Bob is as energetic as ever and is still deeply involved in the world of charity. A hobbyhorse of his involves charity accountability and current accounting practice. He thinks that charity law should compel charities to disclose the exact percentage of their income that goes to the charitable aims of the cause. He believes that, all too often, when charities declare an amount spent on administration—to run the charity—they do not include other costs. It could be assumed, therefore, that the remainder goes to the charitable aims; however, when fund-raising and publicity are taken into account, this is far from the case.

'I think that the public should be made aware of the actual figures. The charity should come up front about any financial cushion it leans on as well: how much money it has in reserve. It's all very well to stand out in the rain rattling tins but if a charity is sitting on money in the bank, the public should know about it. Also, they should not be allowed to put that money in high risk investments.'

Bob's initiative to raise substantial sums for the Bristol Children's Hospice was rewarded when the John James Foundation donated £1 million to the fund. As a similar amount had already been pledged by the Starfish Trust (and a further sum for a starfish hydrotherapy pool) his idea has brought in over £2 million to date.

Bob is currently involved with the Vassall Centre Trust in the renovation and partial reconstruction of a building on a 3½-acre site in Fishponds. This trust was established to serve disabled people of all ages in Bristol and surrounding areas. He is also involved with the Hop Skip and Jump Play and Support Centre charity for children with special needs. He has just agreed to become a patron of Meningitis UK and to chair its newly formed fund-raising think-tank.

After years of being stowed away with its future hanging in the balance, the replica of the Great Orpheus pavement has at last found a home and is now a major visitor attraction at Prinknash, the Bendictine abbey in Gloucestershire, just a few miles north of the site of the original.

Abbot Francis Baird movingly observed:

> So many of the comments written in our visitors' book show just how much the mosaic is appreciated for its beauty and painstaking workmanship ... St Benedict himself grew up in the vicinity of Rome in the 5th century and would have been familiar with its culture. The Rule he wrote for his monks, based on the precepts of the Gospel and Holy Scripture, is both a book of wisdom and practical common sense. It has, like the Great Orpheus pavement, stood the test of time ... I am sure he would not only admire the great skill but also the patience of Bob and John, that must have been so sorely tried at times, as well as approving the present location for their fine work. We too are pleased to be able to exhibit such a wonderful treasure.

The replica of the Great Orpheus pavement is displayed in its own exhibition hall and features a galleried viewing platform on three sides. Visitors are able to enjoy a short video of the history of the original mosaic and the construction of Bob and John's replica. The video shows the two youthful brothers, as they were 30 years ago.

'I was in there recently, all on my own' said John. 'I stood on the side and thought, we did that. We built houses but it was nothing like building the mosaic. I'm very proud of it now.'

The Tabernacle and adjacent schoolroom in which the mosaic was constructed were sold to Jim Panes's firm. It trades today as Wotton Auction Rooms.

Even though Bob can no longer be Father Christmas at the CLIC Christmas party, '... a very precious experience for me,' every year his splendid suit is still put to good use in the season of goodwill when he visits Frenchay Church Sunday school party before doing the rounds of several houses in his neighbourhood. Attention to detail being every-thing, Bob removes his watch, wears false, bushy white eyebrows to match his beard and sprays his shiny, black boots with artificial snow piled so high that little bits fall off when he walks up the garden path to the front door.

On 14 January 2006 supporters and friends of CLIC from all over the country gathered in the Great Hall at Bristol Grammar School to mark the 30th anniversary of the signing of the CLIC Trust Deed. Bob related the story of CLIC's beginnings, and on behalf of CLIC Sargent, Brigadier Hugh Pye assured the assembly that the merged charity would continue the work that Bob had started. Afterwards, the Revd Derek Chedzey welcomed everyone to a service of thanksgiving at St John Baptist Church, Frenchay Common, where Helen Davies, a former CLIC trustee, led the service. Bruce Hockin introduced Margaret Edwards, one of CLIC's first supporters, who told of the work of the early fund-raisers. Parents Bob Thorndale, Gillian Smith and John Turner reflected on what CLIC meant to them through their dark days—and their good days too. The last to speak was Sister Frances Dominica, who delighted a full congregation with a special interpretation of the work of CLIC. Wide smiles and moist eyes were the order of the day; it had indeed been a celebration.

On 10 March 2006 the *Bristol Evening Post* reported that Bob was set to receive the highest civic accolade—the Freedom of the City.

> Too often we wait until people have gone before we recognise the contribution they have made to our city. Bob Woodward formed the charity CLIC to help children suffering from cancer and leukaemia. His drive ensured it achieved a worldwide reputation. President Gorbachev memorably came to visit Bob when he was in Britain and supported the charity's international arm. Bob later moved on to work with other charities but is known and admired throughout the city. The Freedom of Bristol is the very least we should give to him.

On 16 May 2006 Bristol City Council met to consider the proposal to confer the honour of the Freedom of the City on Bob.

'For three decades Bob Woodward has made a difference and, through CLIC, has saved many young lives,' said Peter Abraham, the Lord Mayor. 'He is a worthy recipient of the Freedom of the City of Bristol.'

'Dad has always said we should be thankful for how fortunate we are, and, as children, even when bad things were happening, he always said, we could be a lot worse off. He believes anything is possible,' said James. 'I am very proud of my father, and when I have kids, if I ever do, I shall tell them about their grandad—hopefully they'll get to meet him.'

Bob has often said, 'I shall never, never understand why Judy was interested in me. What she saw in me, I'll never know.'

'Bob was different even then,' said Judy. 'He was a committed Christian and I just knew everything would be fine. And it has been ... except, of course, for the tragedies. Our roots are in Christ Jesus, you see.'

Looking back on his life so far Bob reflected: 'I relate to the poem, *Footprints in the Sand*. No question, God carried us when Robert died. I thought, how on earth will we get through it? But here we are, thirty years on. We had the spire lit again on Frenchay common recently to mark the anniversary of Hugh's death; we do the same for Robert each year.

'Although I have followed a path that, in so many ways and for obvious reasons, I would not have chosen, I have been so privileged to meet such wonderful people along the way.

'It's not until I stop and think ... and then I'm really taken aback by how much I've packed into life. What a fantastic life. It's been quite an adventure. I can't believe I've been so fortunate and the more I look at it, the more I have to be thankful for. I feel as if I've lived a series of lives—and there might be a bit more to come. Some people say that I've had awful tragedies. Yes, I have; but to put things into perspective, it wouldn't take me long to tell you about the tragedies but if you'd like to hear about the blessings, I shall have to move in with you. The blessings keep coming—over seventy years of them.'